*Psycho*, *The Birds* and *Halloween*

ALSO BY RANDY RASMUSSEN
AND FROM McFARLAND

*Orson Welles: Six Films Analyzed,
Scene by Scene* (2006)

*Stanley Kubrick: Seven Films
Analyzed* (2001; paperback 2005)

*Children of the Night: The Six Archetypal Characters
of Classic Horror Films* (1998; paperback 2006)

# *Psycho*, *The Birds* and *Halloween*

## The Intimacy of Terror in Three Classic Films

RANDY RASMUSSEN

McFarland & Company, Inc., Publishers
*Jefferson, North Carolina, and London*

ACKNOWLEDGMENTS: My thanks to Kalan Davis, Colin Davis and Richard Suggs for technical assistance.

LIBRARY OF CONGRESS CATALOGUING-IN-PUBLICATION DATA

Rasmussen, Randy Loren, 1953–
    Psycho, The birds and Halloween : the intimacy of terror in three classic films / Randy Rasmussen.
    p.   cm.
    Includes bibliographical references and index.

    **ISBN 978-0-7864-7883-5**
    softcover : acid free paper ∞

    1. Horror films—History and criticism.  2. Terror in motion pictures.  3. Psycho (Motion picture : 1960)  4. Birds (Motion picture)  5. Halloween (Motion picture : 1978)  I. Title.

PN1995.9.H6R373 2014
791.43'6164—dc23                                       2013041471

BRITISH LIBRARY CATALOGUING DATA ARE AVAILABLE

© 2014 Randy Rasmussen. All rights reserved

*No part of this book may be reproduced or transmitted in any form or by any means, electronic or mechanical, including photocopying or recording, or by any information storage and retrieval system, without permission in writing from the publisher.*

On the cover: Tippi Hedren in *The Birds*, 1963 (Universal Pictures/Photofest); background film frame (iStockphoto/Thinkstock)

Manufactured in the United States of America

*McFarland & Company, Inc., Publishers*
  *Box 611, Jefferson, North Carolina 28640*
  *www.mcfarlandpub.com*

For the Movie Night Gang:
Kalan, Colin, Karlene and Terry

# Table of Contents

*Acknowledgments*   iv
*Preface*   1
*Introduction: Shadows and Sunlight*   3

1. Hitchcock's *Psycho*: Off the Main Highway   7
2. Hitchcock's *The Birds*: Hidden Talons   82
3. Carpenter's *Halloween*: Fear Itself   146

*Selected Bibliography*   209
*Index*   211

# Preface

If horror films are judged solely by their ability to scare the crap out of audiences, pure and simple, then the three examples discussed in this book are obsolete. Antiquated. Old-fashioned. Long since supplanted by more violent and gory fare. Unless, of course, their modern-day audiences possess a sense of historical perspective. An imaginative appreciation for the impact these movies had on audiences back in 1960, 1963 and 1978. Though I suspect even a new viewer of *Psycho*, if by some strange occurrence he or she had never heard about that movie's infamous shower scene, might be knocked back a bit by its two brief evocations of brutally violent murder.

Fear has many different faces, of which immediate shock is only one. And no other filmmaker explored fear in all its aspects more than Alfred Hitchcock. For example, *Psycho* is the most blatantly titled horror film of the modern era, yet unfolds as a carefully modulated, step-by-step dramatization of many different facets of fear. Starting with the fear of getting older, alone and unloved, stuck in a stale job. The combined fear and thrill of feeling tempted to commit a crime, and the fear of getting caught. The audience experiences so many "little" fears with heroine Marion Crane before she encounters Norman Bates, the Crown Prince of Fear, and the violence it can unleash when uncontrolled.

This project began as a study of Hitchcock's *The Birds*. I became fascinated by the brief yet complex relationship between two of its characters: Melanie Daniels and Annie Hayworth. Two rivals for the affections of the same man, they nevertheless become quite good friends and are able to discuss their differences with a good measure of frankness. They even form an alliance to save a group of schoolchildren from the film's "monster," a horde of attacking birds, before death removes one of them from the dramatic equation. How that relationship plays out in conjunction with other relationships in the story, and how they all relate to the bird attacks that are the principal horror element in *The Birds*, seemed a fascinating puzzle to me.

*Psycho*'s parlor conversation between Marion Crane and Norman Bates, followed by the violent shower scene in which Marion is killed, was an obvious complement to the Melanie Daniels/Annie Hayworth dynamic, which also ended in a death. By generating intimacy between two characters, then eliminating one of them, Hitchcock creates a powerful sense of loss. The waste of something worthwhile. *Vertigo* was to be the third and final anchor in that triangle, with Scottie and Madeleine/Judy the equivalent of Marion/Norman and Melanie/Annie. But *Vertigo*, though a highly suspenseful movie dealing with various aspects of fear, is not a "horror" film. *Psycho* and *The Birds* are, or at least contain elements common to, horror films.

A couple years ago a group of friends and I, who together make up the once-a-month Movie Night Gang, watched John Carpenter's *Halloween* to commemorate the holiday whose name that movie shares. Carpenter has frequently acknowledged the influence of *Psycho* on his work. But in addition, I was struck by the scenes in *Halloween* that take place *between* outbursts of violence. Scenes in which settings and characters engender a sense of something good being threatened by a lurking evil. A small town way of life. The friendships among three bickering yet affectionate high school girlfriends. Or between a trusting child and a devoted babysitter. Things presented by Carpenter in such an understated manner that they might almost go unnoticed, or unappreciated, except for the sheer amount of screen time he spends on them. *Halloween* seemed to me a good choice to both compare and contrast with Hitchcock's two forays into horror. All three films mix their terror with other, more congenial ingredients that render the terror far more intimate than is often the case in horror films.

# Introduction: Shadows and Sunlight

"There's something very beautiful about it," said Jamie Lee Curtis of *Halloween* in the 2012 documentary *Inside Story: Halloween*. "Beautiful" can mean any number of things when applied to a horror film. Often it refers to matters of movie technique: the meticulous construction of the shower scene in *Psycho*, the equally complex final bird attack on Melanie Daniels in *The Birds*, or the subjective traveling shot at the start of *Halloween*. Or from an earlier generation of horror films, the elaborate creation scenes in *Frankenstein* and *Bride of Frankenstein*. Sometimes "beautiful" is synonymous with "memorable." A film that makes a powerful first impression on audiences, then continues to do so, in some form or other, years and even decades later. An impression that builds and deepens over time.

I don't know precisely what Jamie Lee Curtis meant when she described *Halloween* as beautiful. How can stories about violence, terror and death be beautiful? That's a big question, encompassing artistic endeavors beyond the genre dealt with here. But I would argue that within the horror genre some of the best movies contain memorable elements of contrast that render their terror more terrifying because of what is threatened, lost or undercut. *Psycho* (1960), *The Birds* (1963) and *Halloween* (1978) are certainly not the only films to qualify in this regard. But they are, for me, three of the most interesting.

*Psycho* and *Halloween* feature two of the most famous and relentlessly grim music scores ever composed. Neither of them includes the usual happy interludes between moments of tension and fear. Yet both movies contain quiet scenes of intimacy, loyalty or simple pleasurable routine that render the terror all the worse for what it destroys. What would the justly famous shower scene in *Psycho* be without the back parlor supper conversation that precedes it? Just a spectacular murder instead of a shattering act of betrayal of the mostly friendly and therapeutic interlude that supper was for Marion Crane, and seemed to be for Norman Bates.

*Psycho* is by no means a hopeful movie. But it contains glimmers of what makes life enjoyable and worthwhile, despite the frustrations and disappointments of everyday living. And like the other two movies discussed in this book, it hammers away at our complacency and inattention to those good things. Among them Sam Loomis's tragically ill-timed letter of reconciliation to Marion, too late to save her from being a victim of her own frustration and the madness of a randomly encountered stranger. And then there is Lila Crane's fierce devotion to her missing sister.

In *The Birds* Hitchcock gives us a solitary big city heroine who, though privileged by wealth and beauty, is emotionally defensive and cut off from true intimacy with other people. During her weekend journey to a small town, Melanie Daniels catches fitful glimpses of understanding, friendship, affection and even love. Glimpses threatened and nearly overwhelmed by fear, jealousy and suspicion, arising from others and from within herself, as well as by a shockingly inexplicable and much bigger danger from Nature.

John Carpenter's *Halloween*, described by one film critic as "just fun" with no ambition beyond giving the kids "a good fright" (Newman, p. 66), contains a surprisingly subtle evocation of the pleasures of small town living and teenage friendship. Worthwhile things menaced by a blindness to anything beyond narrowly defined concerns and priorities, perhaps by subconscious jealousy and resentment, and by a mysterious boogeyman who comes from within the small town itself. From our own "home."

*Halloween*'s boogeyman, Michael Myers, is vaguely defined by Carpenter, in what seems a deliberate effort to render him a mythical metaphor for a wide variety of destructive elements that threaten our peace of mind and sometimes our very lives. Norman Bates, in *Psycho*, is a much more precisely defined and accessibly human character. Though the randomness of the heroine's fatal encounter with his madness renders him too, like Michael, a bigger representative of anything which might endanger us. And both monsters reflect troubled thoughts, emotions and, in the case of Marion Crane, actions of their films' more normal characters. Likewise the spasmodically attacking birds in Hitchcock's 1963 film. All of these memorable "monsters" embody forces both inside and outside ourselves that can suddenly, sometimes without warning, shatter the lives of ordinary people. Disease, accident, crime, war, jealousy, hate, resentment, paranoia, miscommunication, impulsiveness — the monsters of *Psycho*, *The Birds* and *Halloween* stand in for them all, and more. Writing about *Psycho*, critic Raymond Durgnat observed, "Complacency and paranoia... If the one doesn't get you, and if you weasel your way between them, that is more luck than judgment" (Durgnat, p. 167).

This book is obviously not a comprehensive assessment of the films of Alfred Hitchcock. Instead, it focuses on his two dark forays into a genre related though not identical to his favored "suspense" genre. A genre perhaps as embarrassing to Hollywood, at the time *Psycho* was made, as the word "bathroom" is to Norman Bates. A genre which Hitchcock helped raise to the level of art in the minds of sometimes reluctant, grudging film critics. John Carpenter's *Halloween* has proven, despite many sequels and imitations, to be a remarkably enduring and unique low-budget variation on Hitchcock's low-budget original. Attuned to the sensibilities of a different generation, it makes an interesting comparison/contrast with *Psycho* and *The Birds*. Marion Crane, Melanie Daniels and Laurie Strode, despite many differences of personality and social status, are equally linked, in various ways, to the nightmares (Norman Bates, rampaging birds and Michael Myers) that haunt their stories.

# 1

# Hitchcock's *Psycho*

## *Off the Main Highway*

Bernard Herrmann and Saul Bass kick off Alfred Hitchcock's 1960 horror film with an aural and visual assault on the audience. A quick plunge into the abnormal, in contrast to traditional movie credits, before gearing back down to normal in the first scene. Fast, aggressive music with a mechanical rhythm, like a train hurtling down the tracks. Out of control. But because the music is played by stringed instruments only, without metallic brass or pounding percussion, it evokes an unusually *intimate* sort of aggression, suggestive of compulsion.

Saul Bass's visual design for the opening credits complements Herrmann's manic music. Horizontal and vertical lines travel across the screen, side to side and up and down, of uneven length and trailing ragged edges. Titles and names, also traveling in mechanical fashion, arrive and depart from multiple directions, sometimes in fragments that unite to briefly suggest wholeness and then break apart again. Even the *manner* of fragmentation differs from credit to credit. "Anthony Perkins" arrives in two seemingly complete yet faded versions, one lagging behind the other, that combine to form a stronger impression, then split again. "Janet" and "Leigh" enter the screen separately from left and right, appear together in center screen, then depart as they came. Even the director's name breaks apart as though subjected to some unseen strain. The whole world of *Psycho* is cracking up, in one way and to one degree or another. Critic Raymond Durgnat says the credits in *Psycho* "presage its theme—disintegrating thought" (Durgnat, p. 21).

Hitchcock, Herrmann and Bass collaborated on two previous unconventional opening credits sequences, for *Vertigo* (1958) and *North by Northwest* (1959). The latter is a closer parallel to *Psycho* because both feature propulsive music and lines moving across the screen. But in *North by Northwest* Herrmann's orchestration is fuller, less intimate, more cosmopolitan. And the initially abstract lines forming on a plain green screen soon become the architectural outlines of a glass skyscraper reflecting busy vehicular traffic on the street below. This image segues to Hitchcock's montage portrait of the big city rat race: pedestrians moving as mechanically as automobiles, culminating in a battle between two women over a taxi both want to hire, and concluding with Hitchcock himself, in his obligatory cameo, rushing but failing to catch a bus.

Roger Thornhill (Cary Grant), initially a comic example of the rudeness and manic selfishness on display during the opening credits of *North by Northwest*, soon becomes the not so funny (but still a little funny) victim of much worse flaws in human nature. *Psycho*, for the most part, leaves behind the lighter side of those flaws. In stark black and white images, accompanied by Bernard Herrmann's stark "black and white" music (Sullivan, p. 254), we are plunged into a more ordinary, drab, workaday world than the one occupied by Roger Thornhill.

The last bit of animation during the opening credits features two vertical rows of uneven lines, expanding upward and downward from an imaginary horizontal line across the center of the screen. As the credits segue into the opening scene, those expanding lines reverse direction and converge back on their point of origin. As if the abnormal explosion of human emotion, suggested by both moving lines and music, were being suppressed. Or repressed.

*Psycho* thrives on sharp contrasts. Frenzied opening credits give way to a slow pan across downtown Phoenix, on what appears to be a pleasant day. Mostly sunny. A few wispy cirrus clouds overhead. Modest background noise of traffic on the street below. Nothing like the bustle of New York City. Two innocuously informative captions, "Phoenix, Arizona" and "Friday, December the Eleventh," enter the camera frame as separate pieces from left and right, continuing the mechanical pace and fragmentation of the opening credits, but now in jarring contrast to Hitchcock's leisurely camera movement and Herrmann's placid music. The latter consists of slowly descending, then rising chords. Nothing sinister, but not cheerful either. Languid, perhaps even lethargic, with just a touch of melancholy. As Robin Wood has commented, "*Psycho* begins with the normal and draws us steadily deeper and deeper into the abnormal" (Wood, pp. 142–143).

The camera moves slowly towards an open hotel window with its blinds pulled most of the way down. The caption "Two Forty-three PM" is very precise, emphasizing the fact that it is a *random* moment in the afternoon when we encounter our first two characters. Not "Two Thirty" or "Three." We read characters in between the lines in this film, catching them in off moments that have telling consequences. After an awkward jump cut (why not a quick dissolve, as already occurred twice during the pan shot?), the camera takes us closer to and then through the window and into the darkened hotel room. The room brightens, as though our intrusive eyes were becoming accustomed to the reduced light. The camera here functions the same way as

L. B. Jeffries' binoculars in *Rear Window* (1954), only more so, allowing us to intrude on a private rendezvous between two people who have taken precautions to keep their affair a secret.

The camera stops at the side of the bed. A woman lies on it, dressed only in a bra and slip, looking up at a man standing beside her, with an expression of sexual contentment on her face. The man is visible only from his chest to his knees. An indication of where the woman's primary interest lies? His chest is bare, but he has trousers on. The room they occupy is inexpensive, judging from its bare walls and plain furnishings. The man is Sam Loomis. The woman is Marion Crane. This is their afternoon tryst, hidden away in a dark room at a cheap hotel on a hot weekday in a sleepy metropolis.

Sam playfully points out that Marion never ate her lunch. Time is short. Their sexual need was urgent. And Marion has to get back to work if she wants to keep her job. Which is not Sam's priority. He sits down beside Marion, who is now sitting up, and pulls her back down on the bed, kissing and caressing her. He suggests they spend the rest of the afternoon there. Mutual stroking and kissing, more than is typical of Hollywood films of the period, continues until Marion expresses dissatisfaction with their secretive meetings. Sam disagrees. She sees their affair as slightly sordid. He sees it as exciting, pointing out that even married couples occasionally stay in a cheap hotel to spice up their relationship. She retorts, "When you're married you can do a lot of things deliberately," suggesting that her view of marriage is more idealistic than is his. The two lovers, though obviously compatible in bed, see the world differently.

Announcing that this is their last secret rendezvous, Marion gets out of bed and, facing away from Sam, starts to get dressed in front of a mirror. A mirror in which she takes a good, hard look at herself. Sam, by contrast, lingers in bed, lazing on his stomach, clutching a portion of the bedclothes in Marion's absence and sniffing her lingering scent on it. Because he wants to return the following week to continue their affair, he offers a compromise. Dinner with Marion, in public. Marion ups the ante, insisting on a respectable dinner with her sister helping to cook the meal and a picture of her mother on the mantle. She yearns for the *appearance* of propriety, whether or not that appearance has substance. And apparently the image of her late mother is linked in her mind with that propriety, or with the guilt that makes her yearn for it.

Sam gets out of bed, slouches in a chair in a corner of the room and drapes his shirt over his crotch. His bare feet and chest are modest tokens of the nudity he and Marion presumably shared minutes earlier. But they make the point. Sam knows he's good looking. Marion is equally so, but seems less conscious of it. Taking advantage of that attractiveness, and with a leering grin on his face, Sam "improves" on Marion's scenario. After dinner they'll send sister to the movies, turn mother's picture to the wall, and pick up where they left off in the hotel room. He has a way of cutting to the sexual chase. Is he indifferent to Marion's emotional need for more?

Marion is mildly shocked at Sam's revised scenario of respectability, pressuring Sam to further compromise. "All right," he concedes, spreading his arms in a gesture of defeat. He is *not* indifferent to her feelings. Marion turns to face him again. Background music returns. The same lethargic, slightly melancholy music heard during the scene's opening pan shot. Neither lover is completely satisfied with their new understanding. Sam gets up from his chair and puts on his shirt. Looking more "respectable" now, he approaches Marion and tells her, with evident sincerity, that he wants to continue seeing her under any circumstances. "Even respectability." Marion, amused but deep down not entirely so, turns away from him to resume straightening her clothes in front of the mirror, "You make respectability sound — disrespectful," she observes with a touch of sardonic humor. Yes, he does. Because for him respectability is little more than "hard work." But while embracing Marion from behind, he makes a further concession, saying he won't mind the burden of respectability if he can be just be with her.

This dialog occurs with the two characters shown in profile, against the confining backdrop of drawn blinds (more horizontal lines, like the ones in the credits). Contradicting his new commitment to Marion, if only indirectly, Sam turns away from *her* now and complains bitterly of two *other* burdens of respectability that have obviously soured him on the whole concept. He is "tired" (like the music) of "sweating for people who aren't there," paying off his late father's debts and paying alimony to his ex-wife. Two legal obligations that frustrate and confine him. "Sweating" was the same term he used moments earlier to describe the burden of maintaining the kind of respectability Marion desires. Raising the blinds over the open window with a jerk of his hand, Sam lets in some welcome sunlight and a little surge of traffic sounds from outside what now seems like a prison cell to him. Earlier in the scene the hotel room was an oasis of sensual escape from his frustrations.

This first scene tells a tale of ordinary, recognizable human passion and frustration. No international intrigue or conspiracy. Just the frustration of day-to-day, year-after-year living that confront many of us. Loneliness. Passion. Guilt. Debts. Resentments. Etc. But as Robin Wood points out, a theme is introduced here which pervades and darkens everything that follows. "The dominance of the past over the present" (Wood, p. 143). Whether it's Sam's years of paying off his deceased father's debts, an unhappy marriage followed by divorce and alimony, Marion's (as we soon discover) ten tedious years as a real estate office secretary and unfulfilling love life, or Norman Bates' unhappy and possibly horrific childhood. Everything preceding it takes a toll on and shapes the present. And for some characters, the past is a more dominating factor than it is for others.

Marion turns away from the mirror (self-scrutiny or self-absorption) and faces Sam again. "I pay too. They also pay who meet in hotel rooms," she tells him with humor, trying to lighten his mood. But in an offhand way, she reminds him that he is not the only person suffering under their present, unsatisfactory arrangement. Catching her drift while fiddling with the curtain drawstrings, Sam tries to be optimistic, speculating that in a couple years he'll have paid off his father's debts, and that if his wife re-marries the alimony stops. Marion, not satisfied, turns back to the mirror and away from Sam while gently chastising his delaying tactics, pointing out that she hasn't even been married once yet. Sam, putting a positive spin on that gloomy fact, predicts that when she does get married, "You'll swing!"

Apparently reconciled by that warm compliment, the two rush together and kiss passionately. Impulsively, impatiently, Marion pleads for them to get married. But Sam, who has experienced the worst of marriage, pours cold water on the idea. He paints a grim picture of their life together in the back of a hardware store in small town Fairvale, where she can lick the stamps on the alimony payments to his ex-wife. Earnestly she declares, "I'll lick the stamps." As someone who has never experienced marriage, perhaps she harbors as naïve a view of what it offers as Sam's, based on his one bad experience, is overly cynical. For Marion, love triumphs over poverty, bitterness and all other complications. Not so for Sam, who pulls away from her. Simultaneously the camera, and we, move *closer* to her. Marion appears alone in close-up, looking abandoned. The moment is beautifully underplayed by Janet Leigh, yet it plays a critical role in her later desperation to overcome the one obstacle that prevents her from being with Sam in the way she wants.

Sam returns to the open window, the way *out* of their pleasurable but in view of Marion's new demands somewhat stifling sanctuary. A quick leap to escape all his troubles? No. These two characters are not Madeline and Scottie from *Vertigo*. Their world is less colorful. More drab. Like the oppressive and relentless heat of Phoenix, it slowly, *grindingly* drains them of their hope, and better judgment.

Compassionately (or is he just trying to get out of her matrimonial trap?), Sam offers Marion a release from their flawed relationship. A chance to find a man more available. "I'm thinking of it," she replies half seriously, with her arms crossed, from across the room. Sam was bluffing. He doesn't want to get rid of her. Leaving the window of escape, he admonishes her rather sheepishly, "How could you even think a thing like that?" She smiles tolerantly in return, pleased a little to know he still wants her. They are back to square one. In a less than satisfactory relationship neither can abandon. Grabbing her respectable white purse that matches her respectable white dress, Marion heads for the exit. Sam takes her by the arms and tries to hold her back, hoping they can at least leave together, like a real couple. Perhaps fearing the disrespectability of being seen leaving a cheap hotel in the middle of the afternoon with a man to whom she is not married, she tells him no. But in an indirect way that masks her real reason. "I'm late and, uh, you have to put your shoes on." She leaves Sam alone, staring down at his naked feet. Raymond Durgnat sees Sam Loomis as childlike, "shirking responsibility, yet clinging to her [Marion]; she's like the disapproving mother" (Durgnat, p. 30). It does seem rather motherly of Marion to tell Sam to put his shoes on before he leaves the room. And he certainly *looks* rather boyish as he stares down at his feet.

The relationship between Marion Crane and Sam Loomis, established in only a single brief scene, is much more complex and interesting than that of casual lovers. Marion cares enough about Sam to eventually do something very *dis*respectable in order to be with him. And he eventually cares enough about her to ask her to marry him. Sort of. If only they could have reached an agreement about their future together in *this* scene, they might have avoided the horror to come.

In a shot from inside the offices of Lowry Real Estate, where Marion Crane is employed, we see Alfred Hitchcock standing on the sidewalk outside, making his obligatory cameo appearance. He wears a Stetson cowboy hat like the one soon to be worn by the unsavory Tom Cassidy. And he casts an interested glance in Marion's direction as she enters the office. None of us are immune to physical attraction and an occasional sexual thought about a stranger. But Hitchcock does not *act* like the unromantic cad Cassidy proves to be by propositioning Marion. At least not within the confines of the movie. The famous director's behavior towards at least one of his other leading ladies, Tippi Hedren, suggests he was not always so well-behaved.

Marion rushes in, looking worried, and asks her co-worker, Caroline, if their boss has returned yet. No, he's still at lunch with a wealthy client. The coast is clear. But above Marion's desk, and occasionally aligned with her head in this scene, is a large framed picture of the desert. A reflection of her feelings of emptiness about life in general and her relationship with Sam in particular. Caroline, sensing something wrong, asks Marion if she still has a headache. Marion avoids answering the question directly, commenting, "Headaches are like resolutions. You forget them as soon as they stop hurting." Is she thinking about Sam's resolution to see her from now on under "respectable" conditions?

The pictures on the wall over Caroline's desk are smaller but less bleak than the desert scene over Marion's. Caroline offers her colleague some tranquilizers given to Caroline on her wedding day by her mother. Husband Teddy was "furious" when he found out about them. The implication being that dear old mother interfered in their sex lives on their wedding night. Furthermore, when Marion inquires if there were any phone calls while she was out, Caroline reveals that Teddy called her, then her mother called to see if Teddy called. More intrusion by an apparently domineering mother. All very amusing, but one of the loose thematic threads, like Marion's association of her deceased mother's picture with respectability, that eventually culminates in Mrs. Bates. Caroline's relationships with her mother and husband are domestic dramas not pursued in depth in *Psycho*. But the mere fact that writer Joseph Stefano and director Hitchcock raise them should make the audience keenly aware that *every* character in the film, no matter how briefly he or she appears on screen, has a complicated private life that involves frustrations, joys and motivations analogous to those of the major characters. In fact, Norman Bates starts out as one of those minor characters, whose passing acquaintance with major character Marion Crane turns into something far from trivial when *his* private life intrudes on and displaces hers.

Seated at her desk, Marion puts on a new coat of lipstick, repairing the damage done earlier during her close encounter with Sam. Restoring the respectable look of a secretary in a real estate office. But undercutting that appearance of propriety, at least in retrospect, is Caroline's disclosure that Marion's sister, Lila, phoned to say she'd be out of town on business for the weekend. Which, of course, leaves Marion alone to brood about her unhappy situation with Sam and ponder a not so respectable solution to it.

Real estate business owner George Lowry enters with client Tom Cassidy, who wears his Stetson hat like a crown of swaggering authority. Noting how hot it is in the outer office, Cassidy advises the secretaries to petition their boss for air conditioning. We discover a short time later that Lowry's private, inner office *is* air conditioned. One more little reminder of the differences between Marion's world and that of the financially well off.

Sitting rather too familiarly on the edge of Marion's desk, Cassidy refers to "my sweet little girl." Marion, thinking he is addressing her in an inappropriate manner, looks at him quizzically. He immediately corrects himself. He was referring not to Marion but to his eighteen-year-old daughter, who is getting married soon. For Marion, perhaps a depressing reminder of her own single status, and at an age much older than the engaged girl's.

"She never had an unhappy day in any one of those years," Cassidy boasts of his daughter. Really? Eighteen is young for marriage. Is it possible Cassidy's "baby" is getting married in order to get away from her boozy, domineering, loutish father? If Mrs. Bates is later revealed to be, at least in Norman's memory, the essence of bad mothering, Cassidy provides a sketchy glimpse of dubious parenting by a father. The gift of a new house for his daughter and son-in-law will place them in *his* debt. Eventually, perhaps, they may resent that indebtedness, since he seems like the kind of man who would take advantage of it in order to control their lives.

Without uttering a word (it wouldn't do for a mere employee to antagonize a wealthy if rude client), Marion listens to Cassidy's blather and looks appreciatively at a photo of the bride-to-be. For one camera shot, Cassidy is aligned with a large framed picture on the wall depicting a lush lake scene, contrasting the dry desert still visible above Marion. In terms of money and power, he possesses what she lacks. And soon so will his daughter. At least that may be how Marion sees it. I'm guessing the daughter might see things differently.

Tipsy and flirtatious, Cassidy brags about his ability to buy off unhappiness with his considerable fortune. He inquires if Marion is unhappy. She replies noncommittally, "Not inordinately." Which is not a definitive "No." But even if she were unhappy, she wouldn't tell a jerk like Cassidy. Viewed from over Marion's shoulder, Cassidy appears higher and dominant, with his eyes riveted on the pretty secretary and his face blatantly betraying his sexual interest in her. From over Cassidy's shoulder, Marion appears smaller and lower in the frame. But she studies him with cool detachment as he crudely waves forty thousand dollars in cash, the amount he will pay to Lowry for the house he's buying his daughter as a wedding present, in front of her face.

Lowry is apprehensive about the reckless way in which his client handles so large a sum of cash. Caroline is astonished at the mere sight of it. "I declare!" she gasps. "I don't! That's how I get to keep it!" Cassidy crows, obviously trying to impress Marion with his financial clout. If air conditioning is a mild display of the difference in social status between Marion and her boss, money marks an even greater distance between Marion and Cassidy. And the fact that Cassidy cheats the government out of taxes in order to increase his fortune makes the discrepancy sharper.

More concerned about the cash Cassidy flaunts than his client defrauding the IRS, Lowry suggests putting it in the safe until Monday morning "when you're feeling good." This is Lowry's euphemistic way of saying, "When you're not drunk." But Cassidy is in a boorish, not a discreet mood. He inquires about the bottle of booze Lowry told him was in his desk, then covers his mouth in an exaggerated fashion for his deliberate indiscretion. Caroline smiles. Lowry doesn't. He's embarrassed. Compared to the personal secrets of Norman Bates, Lowry's fondness for booze in the office, Cassidy's cheating on his taxes, Caroline's mother/husband issues and Marion's secretive affair with Sam are mild examples of the little lies we live behind our facades of respectability. But they are nonetheless dramatically important steps leading up to the shocking revelations to come. And who's to say we've plumbed the depths of Cassidy's misdeeds as a parent and a taxpayer, or Caroline's problems with her mother and husband? Our acquaintance with those characters is brief and fleeting, as it will be later with the highway patrolman and the used car salesman. Critic David Thomson has said that in this scene, "the nastiness can be felt like sandpaper" (Thomson, p. 22). So it can, even though much of that nastiness remains hidden beneath the deceptively ordinary surface of things.

## 1. Hitchcock's *Psycho*

Thomson further claims that "the central killing grows out of the grim unkindness of the world we have seen, not from the lurid casebook of the Bates family" (Thomson, p. 22). I disagree. The two are linked. Norman Bates possesses a façade of American charm: shy, awkward, compassionate, unwittingly appealing, but with fear, resentment, desire and violence lurking in his heart. The twisted mother/son relationship that manifests itself in him makes all that generalized cultural nastiness more specific. Its consequences more real. Such explosive violence may be extremely rare in the daily lives of most of us. But the haunting possibility of it exists nonetheless. Most of us occupy the middle regions of the broad spectrum of human feelings, thoughts and behavior. But what occurs out on the edges occasionally intrudes on that middle. Sometimes a Marion Crane encounters a Norman Bates, with devastating consequences, and in purely dramatic terms throwing her comparatively minor troubles into stark perspective.

Before retiring to Lowry's air conditioned office to complete their transaction, Cassidy turns back once more to Marion and assures her, in a conspiratorial tone of voice, that he *can* be discreet about some things. She is not flattered by his less than subtle proposition. Yet she cannot verbally reject it without endangering her boss's business deal with Cassidy, and possibly even her job.

Prudent yet discreet as always, except for the secret bottle in his desk, Lowry quietly instructs Marion to deposit the $40,000 in the bank after Cassidy passes out of earshot. Caroline walks over to Marion's desk and fondles the money in her hands while commenting, "He was flirting with you. I guess he must have noticed my wedding ring." We're all capable of deluding ourselves. Clearly Tom Cassidy had no sexual interest in Caroline. But it pleases her to think he *would* have if not for his respect for her marital status. If he had found her attractive, would that really have stopped him? Marion now acts respectably by taking the money away from Caroline, who seems embarrassed at her own little indiscretion (fondling the cash and speculating on its owner's possible sexual interest in her) and annoyed at Marion's exposure of that indiscretion. Marion places the money in a discreet white envelope, and then into her discreet white purse before proceeding to the bank to discreetly deposit the naked cash into an account.

Delivering some real estate papers to Lowry in his private office, Marion tells him she has a slight headache and would like to go right home after stopping at the bank. Cassidy, leering at Marion again, usurps Lowry's authority by giving her permission to do so. Apparently still hoping to charm her into bed, he indiscreetly offers her the livelier alternative of a weekend in Las Vegas. All but ignoring him, Marion turns to her boss and announces her contrary intention to spend the weekend in bed. Meaning her *own* bed, not Cassidy's.

On her way out of the reception area, Marion is again offered the better-intentioned (than Cassidy's) headache cure of Caroline's tranquilizers. "Can't buy off unhappiness with pills," Marion jokes. But Caroline was talking about curing a simple headache, not unhappiness. Marion's choice of words reveals that she has more on her mind than just an immediate pain in her head. She's thinking of her longer term troubles with Sam. And her use of the phrase "buy off" in conjunction with "unhappiness" suggests that what Tom Cassidy told her earlier about buying off unhappiness with money lingers in her thoughts. Maybe pills can't buy off unhappiness, but Marion did not say money couldn't. As she leaves the building she walks past the refreshing lake picture that earlier in the scene was visually linked with Cassidy. While bragging about his money, Cassidy indiscreetly revealed, "I never carry more than I can afford to lose." For someone sitting on the fence of moral ambiguity, that statement plus Cassidy's admission that he cheats on his taxes (the forty thousand dollars doesn't officially, legally exist) amounts to an open invitation to theft.

Alfred Hitchcock and Janet Leigh enjoy a laugh on the set of Marion Crane's modest bedroom, in *Psycho*. According to Leigh, games, practical jokes and risqué stories were part of the fun of making the movie (Leigh, p. 46). Perhaps the creepy nature of the story they were filming contributed, by way of grim contrast, to that spirit of fun.

# 1. Hitchcock's *Psycho*

At home, in her modest bedroom, Marion is dressed now in a black slip and bra that symbolically reflect her shifting moral perspective. Standing by an open closet door, she stares pensively at something on the bed and below the camera frame. When her attention switches to the closet, the camera tilts down and closes in to the previous object of her interest. Tom Cassidy's $40,000, partially concealed in an envelope. Clearly she has not deposited that money in the bank, as she promised her boss she would. Herrmann's brooding, insidious music conveys Marion's unspoken temptation to steal that money. Half of that music feels like the calm, slow, rhythmical in-and-out breathing of sleep. But the other half is more agitated, less regular. Troubled. It's almost as if Marion were asleep and *dreaming* about stealing the money. Most of us, of course, wouldn't actually do it. But how many times over the years have you heard of an outwardly respectable individual, man or woman, stealing substantial sums of money from the church council, charitable organization, or small business of which he or she was a member, treasurer or employee? It happens. And when it does, it's a very big deal in the lives of those who commit the crime. What motives, what frustrations and weaknesses, led up to the decision to steal? Each example would have its own background story to tell. With Marion, "we lose all power of rational control, and discover how easily a 'normal' person can lapse into a condition usually associated with neurosis" (Wood, p. 145). And how dramatically interesting it is that perhaps the most famous *horror* film of all time begins with a crime much less extreme, or irreversible, than what its title suggests and what it ultimately delivers. Twice. Hitchcock draws his audience into a broad *spectrum* of human misbehavior and motivation, encouraging us to be simultaneously aware of the different levels, their similarities and differences. Marion's theft of $40,000 may be motivated by similar frustrations, but it also differs in vital ways from the subsequent crime that will end her life. She's stepped onto a slippery slope, but she has not yet plunged irretrievably to her doom.

The camera pans left to show us, also lying on the bed, an open suitcase full of clothes. So much for Marion's announced plan to spend the weekend in bed. As she retrieves more clothes from the closet, we notice on the wall a framed photo of a little girl dressed in white. Marion as a child? Innocence juxtaposed with at least the potential for guilt. Marion slips on a dress and sweater, both dark in shade but not quite black. Then she glances furtively at the money again. She adds more items to the suitcase. She may have doubts about what she's doing, but her criminal plan is already in progress when this scene begins.

Looking at herself in a mirror, ostensibly to adjust her clothes, Marion wears a silent expression of remorse. Then she looks *away* from the mirror, in effect turning her back on herself (we see both Marion and her reflection) and her moral self-scrutiny, and again glances towards the money. The envelope full of promise is like an illicit lover luring her back, always to the bed. She packs a few more items into her suitcase and some personal papers into her now *black* purse. The symbolism of color is such an arbitrary thing. Closing the suitcase, she casts one more long look at the money. A final struggle with her conscience. Then the struggle ends. She sits down on the bed beside the source of temptation. Visible on the wall behind her is the framed photo of an older couple. Her dead parents? They seem to be looking over her shoulder as she contemplates committing theft.

But if they *are* Marion's parents, their influence, rooted in the past, is not sufficient to stop her now. She puts the envelope into her purse, quickly retrieves her suitcase and a coat from the closet, and departs. In the course of this brief, wordless scene, Marion makes a fateful decision that radically changes the course of her life. What we don't realize yet is that the change results only indirectly from her decision to steal Cassidy's money. The cruel fate awaiting Marion Crane is not some cosmic punishment for her crime, but instead the random consequence of a chance encounter with a far more seriously troubled stranger during her flight from the law and to her lover.

Frontal shots of Marion driving through downtown Phoenix and occasional subjective shots of what she sees through the front windshield. Visual simplicity that is cheap to shoot but also sharply focuses audience attention on Marion's facial expressions and on what she reacts to. And part of what she reacts to is her anticipation of a reunion with Sam, which we hear in voiceover as she imagines it. The results are ambiguous, partly but not entirely reassuring. He's surprised, but "glad to see you. I always am." That sounds nice. But Sam's reaction to Marion's theft on their behalf is less so. "What is it, Marion?" he asks in a concerned, perhaps wary tone of voice. Marion pursues this line of speculation no further. Instead, she places her left hand against her temple. Has her tension headache returned? Or never gone away? Whichever the case, her briefly fantasized reunion with Sam hasn't alleviated it.

Aggressively, mechanically mobile music from the opening credits returns in this scene. Marion's abnormal, criminal act of desperation has caught up with what the music promised at the start of the film, though in a slightly less frantic version. Another car follows closely behind Marion's. Normal traffic in a busy city. But in the context of Marion's fear of getting caught, its headlights seem tokens of unwanted scrutiny and menace. Her emotional state transforms an ordinary automobile into a stalker. The encroaching vehicle seems to gain on hers.

Marion stops, obediently, at a traffic light. She's not *completely* oblivious to the rules and regulations of society, and not particularly confident in her violation of one. From Marion's point of view, we watch pedestrians routinely cross the street in front of us, secure in their assumption no lawless vehicular driver will mow them down. We assume so much predictability and security in our lives, often with justification, occasionally without. Marion bites her finger impatiently. Any delay in her flight from Lowry, Cassidy the police and her own troubled conscience is cause for frustration. But not as bad as seeing her boss cross the street in front of her car. Lowry smiles at her in recognition, and she at him, nervously and deceptively. Then he realizes she should be home, resting from her headache. He turns back again towards her, this time with a frown on his face. Marion's phony smile turns into an expression of consternation, as it might for any of us caught cheating on sick leave. Which is all Lowry can suspect of her, so far. But Marion's crime is far more serious than taking sick time under false pretenses. Just as Norman's emotional troubles are far more serious than our, and Marion's, initial impression of them.

Out on the highway, day turns to night. The headlights of oncoming cars beam harshly in Marion's eyes, which also droop with fatigue. She closes them. The screen fades to black as the camera follows her lead. The next morning, in an extreme long shot that removes us from our previously close proximity to the protagonist, we see Marion's car parked by the side of the road, next to a looming black telephone pole that dwarfs her vehicle, and in front of a treeless hill in the background that dwarfs both. At foreground left is a clump of sagebrush. Marion has found a piece of landscape only slightly less dry and desolate than what appeared in the framed picture over her desk at the office. If she's looking for the oasis, or its financial/emotional equivalent, shown in the *other* picture in the office (the one linked to Cassidy), she obviously hasn't found it yet. There isn't even any bleak background music to enliven her rest stop. Perhaps she parked next to the telephone pole because it is at least *something* to keep her company in this empty landscape and on her lonely journey. She is not by nature solitary. And perhaps it is for the same reason that she later accepts Norman's invitation to supper and conversation in the back parlor at the Bates Motel.

Things get worse. A highway patrol car cruises past Marion's vehicle, stops, backs up and parks behind her. Normal behavior for an officer of the law investigating an apparently abandoned vehicle. Nevertheless, the choreography of the two vehicles, one parked and the other moving, makes it feel vaguely like a predatory intrusion. And, of course, from Marion's guilty perspective, it is. The patrol car is a stark combination of black and white. Or, in the context of the car switch Marion will make in the next scene, of guilt and innocence. As an enforcer of the law, the patrolman is just doing his job in this and the next scene. By and large, that job is good. Ferreting out and putting a stop to crime. But from Marion's current perspective, the patrolman is an agent of fear and potential punishment. And as is clearly evident in an earlier Hitchcock film, *The Wrong Man* (1957), the policeman's role can be one of intimidation and *in*justice, if motives are bad or mistakes are made.

In other words, lurking within the patrolman and his black and white vehicle is a potential (however rare) link with the very worst that lurks within the puritanical, mother side of Norman Bates' personality.

From a camera position near the driver's side door of Marion's car (we are back in close proximity to her now), we watch the patrolmen get out of his vehicle and approach hers. Peering in through the window, he sees a very vulnerable looking Marion lying across the front seat, asleep. The patrolman is briefly visible as a double image, his reflection appearing in the window. Like so many other characters in this movie, he is, at least potentially, a person of many personality traits, some of them perhaps contradicting others. And some of them possibly concealed.

The patrolman knocks on the window. Marion wakes up, sees him and bolts upright. In big back-to-back close-ups we see Marion's startled, fearful face and the poker-faced patrolman, his eyes and intent concealed behind a pair of dark sunglasses. It's an intimidating sight, especially for someone who has committed a crime and is fleeing capture. From her point of view, the patrolman truly is a frightening monster lurking just outside her personal space. Even though he *behaves* professionally, courteously and, ostensibly, with Marion's safety in mind throughout this scene. He is in every way the law enforcement figure she could use by her side when she arrives at the Bates Motel. But she's not there yet. She's in a neutral, bleak but not immediately threatening world where anonymity is a good thing and the patrolman is a menacing intrusion.

Marion switches on her car's engine in at attempt to make a quick getaway, until the officer tells her, understandably, "Hold it there!" Her behavior arouses his suspicion. She's an inexperienced criminal and it shows. In a series of alternating big close-ups conveying unwelcome scrutiny and unintentional intimidation, Marion tries to explain why she spent the night by the side of the road. It is, of course, ironic that the patrolman's concern for her safety is also the cause of her anxiety. Pushing back too hard, Marion tries a little intimidation herself. "I'm in a hurry and you're taking up my time." Once again she starts the car. And again the patrolman stops her, a bit more forcefully this time. The stakes are higher now as he demands to see her driver's license.

From the vehicle's passenger seat (we are her companion on this journey) we watch Marion turn her back on the patrolman, so as to partly conceal what she's doing, and retrieve her license from her purse. Removing the envelope containing the stolen money from on top, she tucks it between her purse and the back of the car seat before digging for the license. And just as Marion takes advantage of her turned back, the patrolman does so too, using the opportunity to glance through the window at the car's back seat. Looking for anything incriminating. It's an unsettling image, with the patrolman looking almost predatory from our point of view inside the vehicle.

The patrolman takes Marion's license, walks around to the front of her car and glances at her Arizona license plate. Seeing nothing suspicious, he returns the license to Marion and then returns to his own vehicle, not exchanging another word with Marion. A strange, disquieting conclusion to a mildly antagonistic encounter. Much remains unsaid but implied between these two characters.

Marion re-packs her purse, starts her car and leaves. The travel music, now *escape* music, resumes, but more fiercely this time, as she resumes her flight from the law. Frontal shots of Marion mix with subjective shots of the road ahead and of the rear view mirror in which we see the patrolman's car ominously following (maybe trailing, maybe not) hers. Marion turns right onto a highway leading to Bakersfield. The patrolman follows her, until veering right onto the Gorman exit. Marion is relieved.

Lap dissolve to a subjective shot, from Marion's point of view, of downtown Bakersfield, California. Herrmann's music of terrified flight stops as Marion drives into a used car sales lot, plotting her next evasive maneuver. Replacing it is the same lethargic, slightly weary music heard during the downtown Phoenix pan shot. A return to a sense of normalcy, however unfulfilling it might be. While waiting for a salesman to come, Marion glances at a few cars for sale bearing California license plates, then at her own Arizona plates, which she knows the patrolman looked at a few miles back.

Spotting a newspaper dispenser nearby, she pays for a copy of a Los Angeles paper and anxiously peruses it for any news about the money she stole. Spotting Marion while driving by, the patrolman makes an *illegal* u-turn (the prerogative of power, I guess), parks on the opposite side of the street, gets out of his car and stands there watching her. Preoccupied with her own investigation, she does not immediately notice him. Good news (which means *no* news) in the newspaper diverts her from bad news across the street. She doesn't even notice the car salesman's approach, until he speaks to her.

"I'm in no mood for trouble," the salesman announces jokingly, beginning his obviously well-rehearsed sales pitch. Which Marion interrupts with a question that catches him by surprise, since he's more accustomed to dealing with reluctant, wary and even hostile customers. "Can I trade my car in and take another?" Like a fish jumping into a fisherman's net. The salesman is momentarily befuddled, but quick to recover, clarifying and reinforcing Marion's lame excuse for wanting to trade vehicles. "I know. Sick of the sight of it." No, Marion is not sick of the sight of her car. She has other reasons for trading it in on a different one. But she *is* sick of her job, her static romantic life, perhaps her lonely and unfulfilling life in general. Just as Sam is sick of toiling away for the benefit of his ex-wife and the creditors of his late father, and Tom Cassidy's eighteen year old daughter is perhaps sick of her father's domineering ways and seeks escape by getting married, and Caroline's husband is sick of his mother-in-law's meddling in *his* life. The salesman's sales pitch unwittingly touches on a much broader, commonplace complaint. And all of these variations on emotional sickness are beautifully evoked by the background music.

The salesman is happy to expedite Marion's request, shooting her car into the garage for a quick inspection by the mechanic, telling her to look around the lot for something new she might like, and offering her a cup of coffee. But she is in a hurry and doesn't want any coffee. Unaccustomed to being hurried by the customer (usually it's the other way around), the salesman advises her not to rush things. Maybe he isn't a complete jerk trying to take advantage of a customer. Nevertheless, he accommodates Marion's haste. No reason not to. Yet.

While the salesman drives her car into the garage, Marion spots the patrolman watching her from across the street. We see him from her vantage point, leaning back against his patrol car, slouching a bit, with his hands resting against the doors. He looks almost arrogant, and vaguely sinister, as though he were scrutinizing *us*, regardless of Marion's crime. We all feel guilty about *something*. An automobile zooms past the patrolman at what appears to be, and sounds like, an excessive rate of speed. He ignores it, fixated instead on Marion/us. Giving her another reason to be in a hurry. She tries to make a good show of casually looking around while awaiting the salesman's return.

The salesman returns, finding Marion apparently perusing one of the used cars for sale. "That's the one I'd have picked for you myself," he declares. More than likely he would say the same about *any* vehicle in which she showed an interest, because it helps promote a sale. He doesn't care which car she buys, as long as she pays for it. But again his slick salesmanship is overtaken by the customer's haste. When he suggests she take the car for a test drive, Marion insists, "It looks fine," and asks about the price. She doesn't even want "the usual day and a half" to think about it. Taken aback, the salesman jokes, "Somebody chasin' ya?" He has no clue that is, or soon will be, the case. Marion insists not. "First time the customer ever high-pressured the salesman," he concludes, slightly befuddled. What sales person ever knows the true motives or background of his or her customers?

When Marion balks at the price he quotes for the newer vehicle, the salesman is momentarily reassured. Her reaction is what he would normally expect from a prospective customer. But Marion's subsequent, all-too-quick agreement to meet his price arouses his suspicion again, so he asks to see her proof of ownership. A prudent hedge against simple trust in one's fellow man, or woman. As they walk towards the garage, Marion glances back nervously in the direction of the patrolman, while the salesman glances at Marion glancing at the patrolman. More reason not to trust her completely.

Seeking privacy to conceal her ill-gotten gains, Marion retreats to a restroom in order to retrieve the necessary seven hundred dollars from the envelope in her purse. The restroom itself is a very plain facility, again evoking Marion's humble social and economic status, and the more general world *Psycho* depicts. No rich and famous here, with the minor exception of Cassidy. Hitchcock shoots her from a high, oblique angle, giving us a double image of Marion and her reflection in a mirror over the sink, as she removes the money and ownership papers from her purse. Herrmann's temptation motif returns as the heroine yet again gives in to her need to escape unhappiness at an illegal cost. And she is always *alone* when she succumbs to such temptations.

The salesman waits for Marion outside, with her new car. He tries one last time to persuade her to take the vehicle out for a test drive. But it isn't the customer's satisfaction alone that motivates him to do so. "Don't want any bad word of mouth about California Charlie." In other words, Marion's unconventional method of purchasing a used car might potentially damage the salesman's future business. Tired of his delays and refusal to take her at her word, Marion challenges him directly. "Do you think I've stolen my car?" she asks bluntly? The salesman backs down. No need to insult the customer and spoil the deal.

While Marion and the salesman head for the office, the patrolman gets in his car and drives it onto the used car lot. When Marion exits the office, she spots the patrolman, now out of his car, and quickly gets into her new vehicle, which is of a much lighter shade than her old one. A mask of innocence that cannot hide her suspiciously nervous behavior throughout this scene. Driving out of the lot, Marion is stopped short by a shout of "Hey!" from behind. She forgot to retrieve her luggage from her old car. An oversight that betrays her preoccupation with other, secret matters. From near her point of view, the camera looks back at the puzzled salesman, at the mechanic who transfers her neglected bags to her new vehicle, and the patrolman, who scrutinizes the suspiciously hasty transaction. With her old baggage (literal and figurative) aboard her new car, Marion drives quickly out of the lot and out of the camera frame. The salesman, the mechanic and the patrolman form a trio of suspicion as they stand watching her depart. Only when Marion encounters Mrs. Bates will she have cause for greater fear.

On the road again, we observe Marion in frontal close-up as she imagines, in voiceover, the conversation the salesman and the patrolman must be having about her. She looks worried as the patrolman asks to see her ownership papers for the car she left behind. How quickly the law can trace her back to Phoenix and the crime she committed there. Day turns to dusk as Marion's flight from the law continues. Images of the road ahead mix with more frontal shots of Marion. Still feeling the pressure of suspicion among the three men she left at the used car dealership, she worries about the discovery of her crime on Monday morning. In voiceover, she imagines Caroline and Lowry slowly reasoning their way to the truth. It is not a comforting thought, since their discovery will mark the end of her power to undo what she has done.

But as dusk turns to the darkness of night, fitfully illuminated by the headlights of heavy traffic on the road, Marion's thoughts become less constrained by ethical considerations, or even self-preservation. She imagines, again in voiceover, Cassidy's anger at learning that the woman he propositioned so flagrantly, and with no intent of lasting commitment, made off with $40,000 of his undeclared (to the IRS) and therefore illegal money. In her mind, he falsely accuses Marion of flirting with him (a self-delusion, because the opposite is true) and vows to get all the money back or "replace it with her fine, soft flesh!" From what *we* saw and heard of him back at the real estate office, Cassidy is a selfish, manipulative liar. But he becomes even more so in Marion's re-creation of him now. A re-creation perhaps subconsciously designed to justify her criminal act. In extreme close up we see the trace of a wicked smile of satisfaction cross Marion's face. She cheated the cheater, and got away with it. His accusation that she "planned" the heist further flatters her ego. There is little prior evidence to suggest the crime occurred to her before she left Lowry's office. But if she's going to be a thief, why not cast herself as a *good* one. It's a boost to her confidence to think so, and soothes her troubled conscience to think a creep like Cassidy *deserved* to be robbed.

Marion's striking, wide-open eyes are focused more on the happily larcenous thoughts within her mind than on any external reality. Until the combination of rain-drenched windshield and headlight glare from oncoming traffic intrudes on her private fantasy. Foreshadowing a much more brutal intrusion yet to come. She turns on the windshield wipers, squints, averts and even briefly closes her eyes to avoid the harsh light (of moral scrutiny, as well as physical discomfort?). Herrmann's traveling music is more frenzied than ever. Until the oncoming traffic diminishes and then disappears altogether, and the music along with it. Marion is left alone on a deserted highway, accompanied only by the sounds of falling rain striking her car and the metronomic windshield wipers trying to clear the rain away.

It should be a comforting situation. Escaping under cover of darkness and rain with $40,000 (minus $700) of someone else's money, observed now by no one. Yet somehow it isn't. In the short period of relative quiet, aural and visual, between the disappearing glare of approaching headlights and the distant, vaguely defined appearance of "Bates Motel — Vacancy," Marion seems a very lonely and vulnerable figure. Trapped in the claustrophobic shelter of her car, traversing an immense, indifferent, if not outright hostile world outside. The darkness and anonymity that comforted her earlier, and allowed her to contemplate, through fantasy, her triumph over the boorish, rich and larcenous Mr. Cassidy, now closes in around her like a shroud. The illuminated Bates Motel sign standing alongside the deserted highway seems like a beacon of welcome, warmth and security compared to the open road.

Marion pulls in to the motel lot. The beaming neon sign looms above us through the windshield, from her point of view. Then the motel, with its well-lit office at one end. One empty, lonely-looking chair sits outside the motel, on the sloped lawn. In retrospect, that chair is a forlorn symbol of the absent Norman Bates. Everything we see through Marion's windshield is partially obscured by rain. Nothing is exactly as it seems.

Hesitating for a moment, Marion gets out of her car, dashes through the rain and enters the motel office, where she finds no one. Light from a lamp in the outer office made her and us assume the place was inhabited. The parlor behind the front counter is dark, unoccupied. Vaguely sinister. One of the few objects visible to us as we peer through the office door is an ornate, Victorian style inkwell sitting on the counter. An almost ludicrously detailed approximation of female breasts, right up to the nipples on top. If Hitchcock intended the object as a symbolic signal of Norman's repressed sexuality, it is laughably blatant. Much more dramatically potent is the fact that the ink container *belongs* to Norman Bates. Presumably he chose it for the front counter of his motel office. One of several erotically charged objects in his possession, it is much more a *symptom* than a symbol of his obsessive, repressed sexuality. Not inherently perverse. But only by association with *his* perversity. Returning outside, Marion searches for the proprietor. She walks to the end of the boardwalk, peers around the corner and sees an old, Victorian style house up the hill, behind the motel. We didn't even suspect it was there. The house looms large, domineering and ominous from Marion's point of view. Light emanates from two second story windows, as it did from the office windows in the motel. But this time the light signals the presence, not the absence, of someone. Appropriate for a character with a double personality, one of which increasingly dominates the other. The silhouette of a tall woman passes across one of the lit windows.

Marion returns to her car and honks its horn several times, trying to signal the woman in the house through the loudly pouring rain. Instead a *man* steps out of the house and, holding tight to the collar of his jacket, runs down a series of steps and through the rain to the motel below. Norman Bates rounds the corner and encounters Marion Crane. In a soft, youthful and cordial voice, he apologizes to Marion for not hearing her drive up, then ushers her into the office.

Inside the office, from a position at one end of the counter, the camera points towards a mirror on the wall at the other end. We see a double image of Marion as she enters. A reflection of her now double life as ordinary traveler and felon on the run. Of Norman's reflection we catch only a fleeting glimpse as he walks behind her. We don't see the *real* Norman at all in this shot. In a sense, the *real* Norman is increasingly displaced by his reflection — the false personality he invents to compensate for his tragic loss.

Norman describes conditions outside as a "dirty night." Not really. The rain is a cleansing agent, and in the form of a shower will later serve Marion in that capacity, both physically and emotionally. "Dirty" more accurately describes the extreme mix of sexual obsession and puritanical repression that duels in Norman's mind. But for now, our and Marion's initial impression of Norman Bates is one of boyish good looks and easy charm. A younger version of Marion's lover, Sam Loomis. But, as we soon learn, without Sam's sexual confidence. Explaining why the motel has so few customers since the main highway was rerouted, Norman concludes, "There's no sense dwelling on our losses. We just keep lighting the lights and following the formalities." Marion might assume the "we" refers to Norman and a wife. She later learns it refers to Norman and his mother. But there is no real "we," only the fiction of it in his mind. A fiction he created precisely because he *does* "dwell on his losses." The loss of his mother years earlier.

Norman opens one of the breast-shaped inkwells and hands Marion a fountain pen so she can sign the motel register. Only for him is this a kind of sexual act. She suspects nothing. But at the same time, she deceives Norman by entering a false name in the register. "Marie Samuels" (the last name derived from the name of her lover, whom she hopes to marry one day) instead of Marion Crane. Viewed in close-up while Norman's back is turned, Marion draws inspiration from the Los Angeles newspaper sticking out of her purse. She write "Los Angeles" in the register as her place of residence, and says it out loud to make sure Norman gets the point, in case he is questioned later by the police while they search for her. In the very next shot, a matching close-up, Norman performs his own act of deception. He reaches tentatively for room keys to Cabin #2 or #3, then instead pulls key #1 off its hook. He justifies his choice by explaining that Cabin #1 is closer to the office in case she needs anything. But he has an ulterior and much stronger motive for selecting it. A motive rooted in emotional compulsion, like Marion's theft of forty thousand dollars. The two characters deceive each other simultaneously, during what otherwise seems like a routine guest/manager transaction. The fact that both of them hesitate for a moment before perpetrating their deceptions suggests they feel some reservation about the act. But not sufficient to stop them.

In response to Norman's promise of close proximity should she need anything, Marion declares the only thing she needs is sleep, and food. Norman, not knowing that Fairvale is Marion's destination, tells her there is a diner just outside the town, only a few miles up the road. Marion asks if she's *that* close to Fairvale, as though reconsidering her stay at the Bates Motel.

After all, a quick drive and she could be with Sam. Norman, as though anxious not to give Marion a chance to change her mind, leaves the office to retrieve her bags from the car.

A single porch light illuminates the door to Cabin #1. The light looks small and vulnerable against the gloomy backdrop of the cabin. Norman courteously waits for Marion to enter the cabin first. He switches on the light and comments on the room's stuffiness. A comment that could as easily refer to the fetid, claustrophobic atmosphere of his own life. He opens windows to let in fresh air. For Norman, *Marion* is the breath of fresh air.

In his charmingly self-deprecating way, Norman makes fun of the cabin's humble amenities. The soft mattress, hangers in the closet, and Bates Motel stationary to make friends back home envious. He knows the place has little to offer a stranger, just as he is convinced that he *himself* has little to offer. He switches on a blinding white light in the white bathroom to show Marion where it is, but cannot bring himself to say the word "bathroom" in front of her. It's a very odd reticence, linked to his extreme repression about anything having to do with bodily functions. But Marion is amused rather than alarmed by his reticence, and speaks the word *for* him. Norman acknowledges with a perfunctory "Yeah," looks down sheepishly, then quickly wraps up the tour by telling Marion, in his stuttering voice, to tap on the wall next to the office if she needs anything. Which makes that wall seem a comforting agent of social contact. Instead, it will become a lethal agent of intrusion.

Norman's reluctance to say "bathroom" aloud is also an amusing comment by screenwriter Joseph Stefano and Hitchcock on Hollywood's reluctance to show a toilet, much less a functional one, in its movies. Norman's hang-up is America's broader, cultural hang-up of the time.

As Norman heads for the exit, we catch another fleeting glimpse of his reflection as he passes yet another mirror. Marion we see again as a double image: the real Marion and her reflected image. On the one hand, a beautiful, intelligent, charming woman. On the other, fleeing criminal with a phony identity and a new car. Her duplicity is already known to us. Norman's is not.

Marion thanks "Mr. Bates" for his courtesy to her as they stand facing each other near the exit. Then, in an intimate close-up, he corrects her. "*Norman* Bates," he gently insists, asserting the dominance of his first rather than his familial name. Only with hindsight do we see the distinction as, possibly, evidence of Norman's inner struggle with the memory of his dead mother. A struggle for control over his life. For the time being, we see and hear Norman at his most nearly sane. At times endearingly so. He smiles warmly, reducing the formality between Marion and himself. But in a similar close-up profile of Marion, with her reflection visible in the background and the burden of her crime no doubt on her mind, she fails to reciprocate. No "Marie," and certainly no "Marion." She cannot afford such intimacy, under the circumstances. The smile on *her* face, unlike Norman's, fades rather than broadens.

Taking another stab (sorry about that) at increased intimacy in their budding acquaintance, Norman invites Marion up to the house to have supper with him. Nothing "fancy," but "awful homey." His charm works. Somewhat hesitant, Marion accepts. Hunger plus Norman's disarming kindness trumps her fear of discovery. A lonely fugitive from the law, she could use a little friendly companionship. Handing Marion the key to her cabin, Norman suggests she remove her wet shoes. The first step in undressing her? Or merely a kindly precaution to keep her from catching cold. At this early moment in their acquaintance, probably the latter. He promises to return shortly "with my trusty umbrella." Like a knight protecting a lady with his sword. A quaint notion, in keeping with the Victorian décor in the Bates house up the hill and the parlor behind the office (both yet to be seen). But just because something is old-fashioned doesn't mean it has no bite left. Many horror films are rooted in the premise of a past that haunts the present. Norman's promise is made in his usual humble, self-mocking manner. He departs on his mission of gallantry. Or so it appears. But there is more to that mission than meets the eye.

While shown in profile conversing with Norman, Marion appears as a double image: herself and a reflection in a mirror. Visually suggestive of the secret, second, criminal identity she harbors. Norman casts no reflection from this camera angle. But the number "1" appears on the open cabin door behind him (a "1" curiously shaped like the long-necked head of a bird). There is another side to his personality. Someone whose acquaintance, unlike Marion's double, both we and the heroine have yet to make. Someone who is an even bigger secret than Marion the thief. Someone who, unlike the thief persona of Marion, will prove dominant in a struggle to the death. The superficial warmth and lightheartedness of the present conversation between Norman and Marion masks the separate, private dramas going on in each of their lives. Separate dramas that have yet to thoroughly merge and produce a third.

From the moment Norman departs, the oppressive atmosphere of Marion's criminal burden returns, along with Herrmann's music of temptation. She starts to unpack her suitcase, then gets distracted by the envelope full of guilt and promise in her purse. The white envelope containing and concealing the stolen money crinkles at an exaggerated volume as she handles it, perhaps in her fearful state of mind calling attention to itself, threatening to expose her crime to the outside world. Marion searches for a place to hide the incriminating evidence. Perhaps a drawer in the dresser near the door leading outside. She opens it, then casts a wary eye at that door. If someone enters the cabin while she is having supper with Norman up at the house, it's probably the first place they'd look. She turns next to a different drawer in a different dresser, at the back of the room. Rejecting that one too, she moves to the nightstand by her bed and opens a third drawer. Still no good. She has no clue that an invasion of her privacy in this anonymous little cabin will take her *life*, not merely her money and freedom.

Marion returns to the suitcase on the bed, still searching for a good place to conceal the money. Then, for the second time, she draws inspiration from the Los Angeles newspaper sticking out of her purse. She opens the newspaper, places the two bundles of cash between the folds, then neatly re-folds it. She places the simply concealed stolen loot on the nightstand beside her bed, in plain sight. Next to it stands a lamp, its shade imprinted with a picture of a sailing ship. A symbol of travel, sometimes of escape from the past. Linked now with the barely concealed money that Marion hopes will facilitate *her* escape from an unhappy past, it will soon be re-defined, in effect *stolen*, as a symbol of *Norman's* fantasies of escape from the motel, the house on the hill, the memory of his mother, and himself.

In the midst of her most recent act of deception, Marion is interrupted by the *sound* of Norman apparently arguing with his mother about inviting Marion up to the house for supper. She opens the window wider to eavesdrop on the argument and get a better view of the house from which it emanates. The rain has stopped. Just a few drops dripping off the motel roof. The old Victorian house stands black and menacing up the hill, silhouetted by storm clouds racing across the sky. The clouds visually echo the animated disagreement coming from inside the house. In the wake of the storm, the atmosphere seems supercharged. Sounds carry further than they normally would.

The voice of Norman's mother sounds crude and intolerant as she refuses to let her son bring Marion up to the house for supper. "By candlelight, I suppose, in the cheap erotic fashion of young men with cheap erotic minds." In this short burst of dialog, we get a sharp and sinister impression of sexual repression, puritanical intolerance and parental tyranny. Norman's soft voice tries to reason with her, unsuccessfully. To his mother, or as we discover, the imaginative re-creation of Mrs. Bates in his mind, Norman remains forever just a "boy." A dirty-minded "boy" who must be controlled. Who must obey his mother. And yet she also *taunts* him for lacking the "guts" to tell Marion she cannot come up to the house to indulge her "ugly appetite" for sex and food. Whether meek or defiant, Norman cannot win this debate. So he runs away from it, shouting at his mother, "Shut up! Shut up!" Which sounds uncharacteristically defiant of him, were it not for the fact that he shouts it while retreating from *her* house.

Raymond Durgnat argues that the question "You have the *guts*, boy?" sounds less like a mother and more like taunts a boy might receive from other boys on a school playground. If Mrs. Bates truly exists in *Psycho*, she is "a thing of shreds and patches, a crazy quilt of fantasy, memory and quotes from disorganized readings" (Durgnat, p. 99). How much of what Norman preserves or makes of her in his haunted memories accurately portrays the real Mrs. Bates? We'll never know. Though it seems wildly unlikely he invented a domineering, puritanical, abusive parent out of nothing at least resembling it.

The self-taunting of Norman, whether or not proceeding from maternal taunts during his childhood, will be eerily echoed in a next generation horror film. John Carpenter's 1978 *Halloween*, in which we witness the taunting of a young boy by his schoolmates. They threaten him with future attacks by the mythical boogeyman, leaving him in fear and questioning his own courage. He, in turn, passes on the same taunt to a young girl his own age. Nothing excessively mean or damaging. But suggestive of our human tendency to pass on to others what we ourselves have endured. Going from powerless to powerful by exerting power over others. Mrs. Bates, judging from her tone of voice and the content of her speech, is a classic example of extreme Victorian repression and oppression. Quite similar to the character Rebecca Femm (with rapist Morgan and murderous madman Saul lurking in the wings) in another classic horror film that preceded Hitchcock's *Psycho* by nearly thirty years. James Whales' *The Old Dark House* (1932). The older film too features an old gothic house haunted more by emotional than by supernatural ghosts. But Mrs. Bates' accent and verbal crudity are distinctly *American*.

Marion eavesdrops uncomfortably on the argument between Norman and his mother. She is L. B. Jeffries spying on his neighbors in Hitchcock's *Rear Window*. But her exposure to the lethal private drama of a stranger, unlike the exposure of Jeffries, does not proceed from her deliberate intrusion on the stranger's privacy. Marion's crime has no connection to Norman. Nevertheless, she will pay the ultimate price for stumbling across *his* secret. Already burdened by the shame of her criminal secret, she cannot feel any better about herself after hearing Mrs. Bates describe her as a slut in all but name. She spots Norman leaving the house that visually dwarfs him, carrying a tray of food in his hands. Herrmann's music of weariness, previously linked to the frustration and hopelessness exhibited by Sam Loomis and Marion, now adds Norman to the roster of *Psycho's* profoundly unhappy characters.

Marion, apparently not fazed much by the rather quaint-sounding Puritanism of an old woman, puts on her wet shoes and goes outside to meet Norman. That she doesn't hold him responsible for his mother's unflattering remarks is a measure of her compassion for the young man who has been so courteous to her thus far. And who at least *tried* to defend her against his mother's ranting.

We wait with Marion for Norman on the boardwalk outside her cabin, under a lone porch light. Norman appears from around the corner of the motel, pausing under *his* singular porch light, outside the office. As individuals, they seem far apart. Lonely ships passing in the night. He approaches

Norman Bates (Anthony Perkins) and Marion Crane (Janet Leigh) establish friendly relations outside her cabin at the Bates Motel, in *Psycho*. But both characters hide criminal secrets from each other. Note Norman's reflected double in the window behind him. And Marion uses an alias, Marie Samuels, to conceal her real identity.

her with his guilt offering in hand. For a moment they stand together under Marion's porch light. The camera pivots to show them in profile as they face each other. Norman's reflection is clearly visible in the shaded window behind him. At least on a symbolic level, his duality is becoming more obvious.

Marion apologizes for the trouble she has caused Norman. Stumbling for the right words, then stuttering when he finds them, Norman dismisses his mother's rude outburst with a euphemism. A very *self-conscious* euphemism. "My mother, what *is* the phrase, she isn't quite herself today." On the contrary, she is very much *herself* today, and everyday. Marion tries to let him off the hook by telling him she isn't really very hungry. But he is a bright young man who recognizes a pity lie when he hears it. He apologizes. Then apologizes for his apology. "I wish you could apologize for other people." Marion, with equal perceptiveness and compassion, suggests they eat supper inside her cabin, backing up a couple steps to let Norman enter through the open door. We see the edge of her bed and her open suitcase on it. Marion's kindly, nonsexual invitation carries the hint, the *threat*, in Norman's mind, of a sexual overture. He takes a step towards the doorway, then backs up and looks down, avoiding Marion's gaze. Lighting from the porch light above casts black shadows over his eyes. If eyes are the windows to the soul, then for a moment Norman's soul is completely hidden from us. The visual effect is a chilling hint of the monster within.

But that ghoulish impression quickly brightens when Norman raises his eyes, looks at Marion and cheerfully invites her to have supper with him in his office, where it's "nicer and warmer." "Nicer" for *him*, in the sense of being untainted by forbidden sexual desire. With a few shy backward glances, Norman retreats to the motel office and beckons Marion to follow. With an amused though compassionate (and, as it turns out, dangerously naïve) smile of understanding, she closes her cabin door and follows Norman into the office.

Inside the office, Norman ups the ante on intimacy by inviting Marion into the parlor behind the counter. Said the spider to the fly, except the spider isn't fully aware of what he's doing. The parlor is Norman's home away from home, not his place of business, especially since Mrs. Bates apparently rules over the house up the hill. Standing in the doorway behind the counter, next to a window with a shade halfway pulled down (*partial* concealment), Marion peruses the parlor's unusual décor while Norman sets out food and drink for her. She seems a trifle confounded, momentarily concerned at what she sees. Stuffed birds on perches line the walls and tops of furniture. The most prominent is an owl with its wings spread, as though swooping down in attack from the ceiling. A black crow and its shadow double perch near an oval, old-fashioned, framed painting of angels. Norman's head is briefly visible beneath that double portrait that suggests a duality of animal predation and religious fervor. In the next shot Norman appears surrounded by his stuffed birds, an ornate old lamp, a row of books and, on the wall behind him, a reproduction of an old painting, "Susanna and the Elders," depicting the rape of an innocent woman by two lying, manipulative men. What an odd piece of art to be displayed by the sexually repressed son of a puritanical, domineering mother. Unless it's merely the nudity of the painted woman that interests him, not the story behind the painting. Even more curious, the artistic mix of angels and predation/rape is echoed by a brief image of Norman, standing up after setting out Marion's meal, with angel-like wings sprouting from his shoulders. The wings are supplied by the attacking owl mounted on the wall behind him. Norman Bates will shortly become a sort of avenging angel, expunging his own sexuality by exterminating the object of his arousal.

Amidst all the passive symbolism surrounding him in the parlor, Norman smiles his winning smile and invites Marion to sit down and eat. She gratefully accepts. She *is* hungry, despite her earlier, kindly intended fib. Until she stands up again to leave the parlor, most wide shots of Marion surround her with ornate Victorian décor. Wooden stand, doily, curtains, lamp, angel painting, pitcher, etc. The parlor, despite being Norman's private sanctuary, tucked away in back of the motel office, is an oppressive extension of the big old house on the hill. A cut-rate version of his mother's elaborately Victorian bedroom, which we'll see much later. The rest of the motel, by contrast, is very plain. Shabbily modern.

Background music fades out as conversation commences. Strangely, Norman doesn't eat with Marion. His initial invitation implied he would. Instead, he sits down in a chair on the opposite side of the room and watches her eat. He desires intimacy, yet cannot easily or fully indulge in it. He can only *observe*. And comment from afar. "You eat like a bird," he remarks. Glancing around at his collection of stuffed birds, Marion replies, "You'd know, of course." Norman denies any scientific knowledge of birds, in his typically self-deprecating way, but then contradicts himself by demonstrating that he knows quite a lot. He describes the appetite of birds as ravenous, contradicting his initial comparison to Marion's delicate eating habits. A comparison he knew to be false even as he made it. But because he wanted to flatter Marion, he employed the conventionally accepted lie. He struggles to say the word "falsity." Talking to Marion makes him nervous. Nevertheless, he opens their conversation by admitting his initial, harmless lie. A good start to building intimacy between them.

Reversing himself yet again, he once more demeans his own intelligence, claiming to know nothing about birds. His real interest is in stuffing them — taxidermy. A more practical hobby than we or Marion yet realize. He refuses to stuff other animals, which he refers to as "beasts," because they don't look right in that condition. Birds do because they are inherently passive. That's not the impression *we* get from the attacking owl mounted near the ceiling. Or will get from the birds in Hitchcock's next movie, *The Birds* (1963).

Marion tries to feign interest in Norman's hobby, tactfully describing it as "curious" and "strange." Norman chooses to interpret her description as complimentary rather than disparaging. "Uncommon too," he echoes Marion, trying to make himself sound special. Assuming, probably incorrectly, that Marion is sincerely interested in his hobby, Norman supplies further details. Marion's response is patronizing. "A man *should* have a hobby." She's just making polite conversation out of gratitude for the meal Norman brought her. But he takes her remark seriously, and uses it as an invitation to spill his guts, so to speak, about his sad plight. Leaning back in his chair and reaching up to fondle one of his stuffed, lifeless companions, he confesses, "It's more than a hobby. A hobby's supposed to *pass* the time, not *fill* it." It's remarkable how insightful Norman is about his own pathetic life, and yet how powerless he is to change it for the better.

The entire conversation between Marion and Norman is shown in separate, alternating shots of the two characters as they occupy opposite corners of the parlor. The growing sense of intimacy suggested by their dialog is undercut by their divided images, which reminds us they are very far from attaining a comprehensive understanding of each other.

Sincerely interested in Norman now, as she was not about his hobby, Marion asks if his time is really so empty as his remark about hobbies implied. Norman backs away from his own remark, and from the increased intimacy Marion offers. His eyes shift nervously back and forth until he thinks of a suitable refutation. His life at the motel is quite full, Norman insists. He runs the office, tends the grounds and cabins, and does errands for his mother. But then he sabotages his own defense by adding, "the ones she allows I might be capable of doing," tacking on a little smile at the end of the line to diminish the significance of his painful admission. But for at least a moment, he allows himself to complain to Marion about his mother. The growing trust between he and his guest seems to have a therapeutic potential for him.

Logically, Marion follows up Norman's confession by turning their attention to a happier alternative, asking him if he goes out with friends. She hits a raw nerve. Withdrawing his hand from the stuffed bird, which may be a surrogate for Marion, whom he could not even bring himself to sit near much less touch, he tucks it defensively with the other one between his legs. After a long, awkward pause, during which he searches for a satisfactory reply, he finally comes up with, "Well, a boy's best friend is his mother." It's a pathetic attempt to defend his pathetic lifestyle to an attractive, intelligent, articulate woman to whom he is already attracted. In retrospect, it's also howlingly ironic. But in the context of Norman's state of mind, it's a chilling admission that he has no friends, and a defensive denial of his previous accusation of maternal cruelty. This is one of those quietly shocking moments when Norman behaves like a dangerously trapped animal.

Marion, sensing the young man's emotional vulnerability with regard to his mother, awkwardly refrains from revealing her true thoughts on the matter.

Norman recognizes her discomfort and concludes, incorrectly, that she's "never had an empty moment in your entire life." The grass is always greener, and so forth. For Norman, any woman as beautiful and articulate as Marie Samuels *must* lead an exciting life, compared to his own. The excitement that presumption brings to his existence is revealed by his agitated hands, which fidget between the safe confinement of his legs.

After a moment's hesitation (openness is difficult for *both* characters, since both have much to hide), Marion cautiously admits, "Only my share." Norman is immediately intrigued, and inquires where she's headed. Marion's lack of reply draws an apology from him for prying into private matters. *This Norman Bates is almost invariably sensitive to and considerate of others.* Without disclosing her crime, Marion reveals the truth of her situation in safer, veiled terms. She's searching for a "private island." The paradise she hopes to build with Sam Loomis and $40,000.

Even more intrigued now, and stuttering because of it, Norman leans forward in his chair to lessen the distance between them and insightfully asks what Marion is fleeing from. Suspicious and defensive now herself, Marion inquires why he would ask such a question. Norman's response is to shake his head and quietly remark, "No." As caught up in the machinations of his own life as Marion is in hers, he adds, "People never run away from anything." Is he on the verge of a major revelation to Marion about his sad existence? She looks away from him without replying. He looks away from her, breaking their intimacy, and makes a trivial comment about the rain not lasting long. But Norman is in a sharing mood, and quickly returns to the topic they left off. He makes the grim observation, "We're all in our private traps. Clamped in them. And none of us can ever get out. We scratch and claw, but only at the air. Only at each other. And for all of it, we never budge an inch." The rain outside may have been of short duration, but inside Norman it never stops.

What a powerful expression of Norman's fatalism. And imbedded within that philosophical generality is a frightening, if metaphorically disguised, warning of the danger he poses to Marion. "We scratch and claw, but only at the air. *Only at each other.*" *Other* people must occasionally pay the price for *our* despair, frustration and anger.

Marion responds empathetically to Norman's fatalism, but in terms drawn from her own experience. "Sometimes we deliberately step into those traps." As she did by stealing Cassidy's money. Norman, still wrapped up in the contemplation of his own private trap, replies, "I was born in mine. I don't mind it anymore." Marion tries to bridge the gap between them, entering Norman's struggle to escape. She tells him he *should* mind. And once again with acute insight into himself and into the human inclination to conceal the truth even from one's self, he admits he *does* mind, even when he claims he doesn't. And he laughs at himself again, as though not taking himself too seriously.

Building on her new intimacy with and compassion for Norman, Marion brings up the topic of Mrs. Bates' recent rude behavior towards him. Suddenly we see Norman from a new camera angle — a low angle profile in which the predatory stuffed owl and the rape painting are visible behind him. His smile turns into a frown. Marion has again touched a sensitive emotional nerve. He *wants* to respond favorably to Marion's suggestion of a way out of his private trap. He wants to curse, defy and leave his mother. Visually, in two-dimension, his head overlaps the swooping owl. Is he defying the mother that owl represents to him? Or has he *merged* with the owl? Become one with it? The paintings depicting rape are mounted on the wall *below* the predatory owl. In the hierarchy of Norman's disturbed mind, respect for his mother's puritanical views dominates his own repressed sexuality. The more he gives in to the latter, the stronger the reaction of the former.

Leaning back in his chair again, this time in a posture of resignation, Norman admits he cannot defy his mother. But all defeats must find a palatable excuse. Norman insists his mother is ill, and needs him to take care of her. Marion questions that excuse. "She sounded strong." But Norman maneuvers around her. "No, I mean ... *ill*," euphemistically referring to a *mental* illness. In his world, admitting mental illness is as shameful as discussing bathrooms with a stranger. And he expands his excuse for passivity by telling the story of his mother's widowhood, maternal sacrifice on his behalf, exploitation by a man who preyed on her for her money, and finally grief beyond the breaking point when she lost that man in some gruesome, unspecified manner. If true, Norman paints the story of a woman burdened in different ways by *three* males, and in her acute distress learning to distrust and hate *all* men. Even, perhaps, her son. Is it possible Mrs. Bates was a "normal" person driven to abnormality by others, as she apparently drove her son to the same? A tragedy within a tragedy?

Pausing in his tale, and proving that he is still sensitive to the needs of his guest, Norman smiles warmly and apologizes for intruding such a gruesome topic of conversation on her meal. But he *needs* to explain and justify his passivity to his new and only friend. Mrs. Bates was overwhelmed by her losses and had nothing left to cling to for support. Marion draws the obvious conclusion to the story. "Except you." Norman, excusing his mother again, adds grimly, "A son is a poor substitute for a lover." That line suggests an unsavory mix of parental and sexual roles. What exactly *was* the relationship between Mrs. Bates and her son, especially when he was a child? There is as much left unsaid as there is revealed in Norman's story.

Marion, intending to be helpful, suggests that Norman leave his mother and go away. "To a private island, like you?" Norman replies, gently mocking her own flight from unhappiness. Their private stories are merging, becoming analogies to each other, as the two characters grow closer. "No, not like me," Marion shrugs, mindful of what she now realizes is the biggest mistake of her life.

Though talking about the same general topic, namely escaping from private traps, the two characters rely on their own, personal experiences as grist for their comments. They do not fully understand each other. Marion advised Norman not to flee to a private island to escape his problems, like she is trying to do. Yet Norman reacts as though she *had* recommended doing so. He has an emotional need to stay with his mother. A need he justifies to Marion by re-casting it as a son's *responsibility* to care for his sick mother. "Her fire would go out. Be cold and damp like a grave." This unusually grim and vivid simile for his mother's fate should he desert her hints at something obsessive in their relationship. "If you love someone, you don't do that to them even if you hate them." Love and hate for the same person. It's an astonishing admission by a character who was not long ago so reluctant to vent his deep resentment of his mother. So bold, in fact, that Norman backs away from it a moment later, explaining that he doesn't *hate* his mother, only her *illness*.

Marion, riveted now by Norman's tale, tentatively offers yet another possible way out of his private trap, since he refuses to leave his mother alone in her house. Why not put her "away ... someplace," which would leave Norman free to pursue his own life unencumbered. By "someplace," Marion clearly means but doesn't want to say "asylum." While giving this well-intended advice, Marion nervously rubs her upper arm with the fingers of her other hand. She knows she is skirting the edge of polite conversation between relative strangers.

The last several camera shots of Marion listening to Norman's story about his mother have been closer than those preceding it, reflecting her increased interest. She is no longer faking that interest, as she did while he expounded on his taxidermy hobby. Now the camera cuts closer to Norman too, as he reacts with atypical passion and bluntness to Marion's advice. He leans forward in his chair, his head, neck and shoulders filling much of the screen. But this is *not* the same Norman who leaned forward earlier, expressing interest in *Marion's* story of escaping from a private trap. There is a glint of fanaticism in Norman's widely staring eyes as he de-euphemizes Marion's vague "someplace," calling it "institution," then "madhouse." Unusual and hypocritical behavior for Norman, who earlier couldn't say the word "bathroom" in Marion's presence and twice employed euphemisms to cover up for his mother.

Bernard Herrmann's three-note "madhouse" theme creeps onto the soundtrack and insinuates itself into the conversation as Norman, his head still jutting aggressively forward, savagely mocks Marion's euphemistically disguised advice. His voice is still quiet, but his tone and meaning are passionate. For the moment he perceives Marion as just like all the other people in the world who hide their cruelty behind a façade of politeness. She tries to apologize, but he undercuts her by questioning her capacity for compassion. And goes on to describe the horrors of being confined to a madhouse. His imagination (we have no reason to believe Norman was ever confined to an institution himself) supplies the horrors that help justify his determination to stay with his mother.

"She's as harmless as one of those stuffed birds," Norman insists, by way of invalidating any need for her confinement. Marion, still defensive in the wake of his adverse reaction to her advice, apologizes again for overstepping her bounds. She tries to justify her actions by claiming she only wanted to spare Norman the pain it seems his mother is inflicting on him. "I meant well," she pleads feebly. Still in his belligerent posture, Norman mocks her again, even more viciously, and curiously using the same bird analogy he previously used to describe his mother as harmless. But this time the bird is cruel, not harmless, clucking its thick tongue, shaking its head and "suggest[ing] so very delicately..." The hypocrisies and lies and viciousness of all humankind seem to be Norman's target at this moment. And the entire burden of that guilt is placed on the shoulders of poor Marion.

Regaining composure, Norman leans back in his chair and admits, with remarkable frankness, he has had the same thought Marion expressed earlier. "But I hate to even think about it." One of his stuffed birds, perched atop a nearby dresser, seems to be keeping watch over him. As does that part of his mother's personality that he keeps alive in his mind. "She needs me," he pleads in defense of his mother. Leaning forward again, but this time seeking Marion's understanding rather than assaulting her credibility, Norman asserts that his mother is *not* "a maniac — a raving thing. She just goes a little mad sometimes." Or, as in his previous characterization of her, "She's not quite herself today."

Marion's unspoken facial reaction to Norman's assertion is one of skepticism. Leaning back again, Norman churlishly insists, "We all go a little mad sometimes." Then the "mad" glint in his eyes disappears, replaced by a warm, friendly smile as he offers Marion an olive branch of sorts. "Haven't you?" Relaxing a bit after their tense confrontation, she accepts it. "Yes. Sometimes just one time can be enough," she adds ruefully, referring obliquely to her own mad attempt to escape from unhappiness.

The battle is over. Marion offers Norman a sincere "Thank you." Presumably his tale of madness and woe has helped clarify and resolve hers. Norman, seeking to increase the intimacy of this moment, and for the second time (the first was in her cabin) gently insisting on the dominance of his first name, corrects her. "Thank you, *Norman*." Marion complies. But then she stands up to leave, pleading exhaustion and a long ride back to Phoenix in the morning. Norman responds, "Really?," his tone of voice concealing more than it reveals. Marion speaks in general terms of escaping a private trap she stepped into back in Phoenix, "before it's too late for me too." "Too" implies, perhaps unintentionally, that for Norman, whose predicament he just explained to Marion, it *is* too late for escape. But Marion doesn't know the half of Norman's story, which is buried too deep in hellish memory to be exposed, much less expunged, in a single supper conversation. The black silhouette of a crow mounted on the wall, its beak pointed at her neck, symbolically menaces the unsuspecting Marion. What she doesn't know *can* kill her.

When she stands, Marion is shown from a low camera angle while Norman, still seated, is viewed from a high angle. Marion appears to occupy the dominant position. Norman gently pleads for a continuation of their talk. But when she just as gently declines, he politely concedes, then generously offers to get up early to prepare breakfast for her before she leaves the next morning. With her guard down, perhaps because of her new resolution to face the consequences of her crime, Marion lets slip that her last name is Crane. "Crane, that's it," Norman repeats softly, knowing full well it wasn't the name she wrote in the motel register. He doesn't ask for an explanation of the discrepancy. So much for the spirit of honesty between them. Instead, he *feeds* on her unwittingly revealed deception to fuel his erotic fantasies.

As Marion's smiling image exits the camera frame, Norman's head rises into the same frame, staring after her with new, concealed interest. Mysterious music rises on the soundtrack. Marion disappears out the office door. The camera films that departure from behind her, which is to say from Norman's point of view. To a curious effect. It almost seems as if Marion were deserting him. *Betraying* him with her departure. Walking out on him forever, to be gone early the next morning. Of course, she's *not* betraying Norman. She's just returning to her cabin to wash up, get some sleep, and in the morning return to Phoenix to free herself from a self-inflicted trap.

From Norman's perspective we hear the sound of Marion's cabin door open and close. He is alone again, with himself. His own worst enemy. No longer obliged or inclined to tailor his actions to Marion's sensibilities. He retrieves a piece of candy from his pocket and slips it into his mouth. As we discover later, it's a habit, a sort of pacifier.

Norman walks to the front desk and looks down, apparently at the outrageously suggestive inkstand. Surely not to fondle the twin, breast-like containers. No, he's reaching for the motel register, on which he reads the alias "Marie Samuels" and the phony hometown Marion gave him. A slight smile flickers across his face. Not the open, boyish smile we saw earlier, but instead a smirk. Marion's twin lies titillate Norman, making the crude inkstand metaphor no longer so amusing. Herrmann's music speaks of Norman's sexual temptation, as it did many scenes ago, in a somewhat different form, of Marion's temptation to steal. Visible behind Norman, a stuffed crow throws up a much larger shadow silhouette of itself on the back wall of the parlor. In anticipation of the much larger impact Norman's shadow self will have on Marion's life. Is it a crow, or a raven? Son of Edgar Allan Poe's infamous bird, emblematic of another fictional character's unhealthy obsession with a woman.

Norman returns to the parlor and shuts the door. And just as Marion did back in her Phoenix apartment, he hesitates before yielding to temptation. Moving closer to the wall that separates the parlor from Cabin #1, he first violates Marion's privacy by eavesdropping on sounds coming from her room. A comparatively modest crime, perhaps, but one particularly egregious for someone in the business of providing shelter and security to strangers. As he stands silently in the shadows, listening intently to her activities in the adjoining room, Norman is pictured between two stuffed birds: a game bird passively sitting on top of the dresser, and the predatory owl mounted on the wall above, frozen in the act of diving on its hapless prey. With which bird will Norman most identify? The division within his mind is further echoed by his reflected image in what appears to be a glass display case on the dresser. But he can't have it both ways. His head is much closer to the predatory owl, with its wings outspread in a posture of attack. It seems more likely his repressed sexuality will express itself somehow *through* rather than in defiance of his mother's puritanical disapproval. But that critical moment of decision, or compulsion, hasn't arrived yet.

Unable to stop himself, Norman quietly removes one of the rape paintings from the wall, uncovering a large hole in the plaster and a smaller hole in the wood behind it. Light from Marion's room enters through the latter. Lighting from below and off to one side accentuates the jagged edges of the larger hole Norman has dug into the plaster, suggestive of an act of violence. We watch Norman in profile as he watches Marion through the smaller hole. Will he discover her criminal secret and call the police, in the manner of L. B. Jeffries in *Rear Window*? From Norman's point of view we watch Marion undress. Framed pictures of non-threatening birds hang on the wall behind her. The metaphor is everywhere, but is multidimensional. Sometimes associated with aggression. Other times with victimization. In 1960 the words "bird" and "chick" were considered by many acceptable slang referring to a woman.

An extreme close-up profile of Norman's eye peering intently through the pencil-sized hole, which now appears much larger and as jaggedly cut as the plaster hole surrounding it, draws us deeper into his crime. Seeing his eye at such close range, and detached from the rest of his face, reduces Norman to a clinical case. A body part. Even as he reduces Marion to the sum of her sexual attributes. Another subjective shot of Marion shows her donning a bathrobe. Norman has obviously seen her naked. High-pitched strings take over from lower strings as temptation yields to indulgence. They echo Norman's sexual arousal, and in equal measure scream in protest on behalf of his unsuspecting victim.

Returning the rape painting to the wall, and covering up his illicit peephole, Norman seems uncertain. The claws of a bird of prey are prominently visible between him and the painting/hole/Marion. The shame of living down to the stereotype of "young men with cheap, erotic minds," offered up earlier by his mother, battles with his desire for Marion.

Norman casts a defiant glance in the direction of his mother's house, directly opposite Marion's cabin, and walks confidently out of the parlor. Exiting the office, he pauses once more to throw another angry look towards the old Victorian house. The camera half circles round his face to give us a close look at his expression. Then it and we backtrack with Norman as he strides purposefully around the corner of his motel to do battle with his domineering, contemptuous mother in her lair (perch?). But in the very next shot we see his comparatively small figure ascending steps to the much larger, looming edifice on top of the hill, all sinister black outlines pierced by light from the windows of mother's second story bedroom. Suddenly Norman looks like a fragile, overmatched Don Quixote.

Like Norman himself, the camera fluctuates nervously in its perspective, emphasizing first his determination and then his vulnerability. From a slightly low angle that emphasizes the intimidating height of the windows and door inside the entryway of the Bates house, we watch Norman enter and without hesitation head for the stairway leading to his mother's room. But a reverse angle shot reverses that impression. He stops. The staircase in front of him appears large and intimidating. He rests his left hand on an ornately carved post at the bottom of the banister. Taller than Norman, it looks like something from a church altar. Norman's reverence for the memory of his mother is too strong. His body visibly sags, along with his will to fight. His head lowers and his hand drops away from the banister post that visually embodies the superior strength of his mother. Norman all but slinks from the field of battle, slouching slowly down the hallway instead of advancing confidently up the stairs. His hands passively tucked into his pockets. A fleeting, forlorn glance up in the direction of his mother's room is all the protest he can muster.

Hands still in his pockets, Norman wearily saunters into the kitchen and sits down at the table. His long legs, bent awkwardly, look too big for his chair. He looks like an overgrown child. But the stationary camera, from whose point of view Norman appeared very large as he approached the kitchen, now depicts him as a small human figure hemmed in by the kitchen's narrow, coffin-like doorway, by windows so tall they stretch beyond the top of the camera frame, and by the ornate décor of the hallway visible at left and right foreground. Norman doesn't stand a chance against the ghosts haunting *this* old dark house.

Norman fiddles uselessly with the sugar bowl on the kitchen table where he once hoped to enjoy an intimate supper with Marie Samuels. Juxtaposed with that image of futility is a contrasting one of Marion Crane seated at a modest-sized desk in her motel room, working to free herself from her own private trap. Calculating on a notepad the math of her theft and expenses since fleeing Phoenix. She tears up the incriminating paperwork and glances around the room for a safe place to dispose of the evidence. She heads for the bathroom, dumps the evidence in the toilet, closes the lid and flushes it. On her way to the bathroom she passes by a mirror that supplies yet another double image of her. A criminal double from whom Marion is determined to free herself.

The bathroom of Cabin #1 is blindingly white. And as Herrmann's music fades out, it proves to be an environment of amplified sound, as was the adjacent bedroom when Marion removed her stolen forty-thousand dollars from a concealing white envelope and hid it in a newspaper. In *that* instance, the exaggerated sound betrayed the character's enhanced sense of guilt and fear of discovery. In the bathroom it speaks to her resolution to come clean and make amends for her crime.

The sound of a flushing toilet draws attention to itself. Marion is disposing of a reminder of her crime. Then she closes the bathroom door for privacy. From whom? There is no one else in the cabin and she doesn't know about Norman's peephole. Still, it's something many of us do, maybe for an added sense of security. Disrobing, she steps into the bathtub and pulls the shower curtain shut behind her. It makes a loud, ripping sound. The camera brings us inside the tub with her. The tub, the tile above it and the shower curtain are all very white. A reflection of the moral state to which Marion wishes to return. Having discarded the black bra and panties she put on in Phoenix when she decided to steal Cassidy's money, she is naked now. The crackle of the paper wrapper she tears off the soap that will figuratively wash away her sins (on a literal level, clean off the grime of two days travel since she fled Phoenix) is almost shattering.

Marion turns on the water, clearly enjoying its warm, cleansing effect. A subjective shot from her point of view shows us the shower head emitting those healing streams. Marion smiles as she washes herself. The sound of the water is loud, even exaggerated, like everything else in the bathroom. Marion's self-healing reverie so absorbs her attention that she is oblivious to the silent entry of a tall shadowy figure through the bathroom door. Until Hitchcock gives us a camera angle from inside the shower that allows us to see the world *outside*, albeit through a curtain that partially obscures it, we were encouraged to share in Marion's pleasant experience of privacy, security and rejuvenation.

## 1. Hitchcock's *Psycho*  43

The obscure shape approaching Marion from behind brings menacing shadow into her intensely white world of re-captured innocence. It is not, by any objective measure, a ruthless moral avenger imposing harsh retribution on a sinner. Marion has already signaled her intention to return to Phoenix and make amends for her crime. The sinister figure invading her privacy is a randomly encountered nightmare come true. Marion Crane has simply crossed paths with a character whose emotional problems and private traps far exceed and are about to overwhelm her own. Despite her best intentions, the world at large is not a mere extension of her private journey. A journey which Hitchcock, Joseph Stefano and Janet Leigh have done so much to emotionally involve us in for the past forty-five minutes. A journey about to be ripped from our minds. Inside a *bathroom*! The place where we are often most private, solitary, self-absorbed and least aware of the outside world.

As the sinister shadow approaches, the fearful yet fascinated camera (*us*) slides away from an oblivious Marion, whose shower we share, and concentrates wholly on the approaching intruder. We don't know precisely who the figure is, or what it brings, but the mere fact that it violates Marion's privacy at a moment of extreme distraction and vulnerability implies something bad. Very bad. We're no longer in *Rear Window* territory, observing unsuspecting people with casual curiosity and amusement. We are the *observed*. And the observer is neither curious nor amused.

The intruder rips open the shower curtains. Backed by bright light and therefore visible largely in silhouette, it vaguely appears to be a tall woman with crazed eyes and a kitchen knife in her uplifted right hand. An ordinary *kitchen* knife! Perhaps even the same knife with which Norman cut the sandwich he kindly prepared for Marion a short time ago. Music intrudes, slashing and screaming at the same time. Marion turns to see the intruder, and screams. The camera cuts closer and then closer to her screaming mouth. Back and forth we jump rapidly between images of the killer, images of the victim, and overhead images of both, all from a chaotic variety of camera angles. Marion's cries are loud, piercing, terrible. Filled with shock, panic and pain. We also hear the sickening penetration of knife into flesh as the killer, in staggered camera shots, invades further and further into Marion's privacy. She takes a stab to the chest. Then, in one fleeting shot, we see the knife plunge into her belly. Simultaneously the metaphorical fulfillment of Norman's sexual desire for Marion, and his mother's ultimate thwarting of that desire.

Marion's blood mixes with water at the bottom of the bathtub. Enough is enough. Marion *must* be fatally wounded by now. But the blows keep coming. She turns away from her assailant, and receives a vicious stab in the back. At long last the killer leaves, her abrupt exit through the bathroom door looking oddly like Marion's departure from the motel office after conversing with Norman in the parlor. Visible through the open door is the wall containing

Norman's peephole. How trivial his illicit spying on Marion now seems in the wake of what we've just witnessed.

Slashing, screaming, high-pitched strings are displaced by jabbing downbeats played on low strings as the horrible final moments of Marion's life play out. An extreme close-up of her left hand, fingers splayed out, grasping in vain at the white ceramic tiles for support, sliding inevitably downward, downward, as Marion's strength ebbs and gravity takes control. The last few gasps for air. Marion turns to face the camera, her eyes staring but not seeing, her mouth open but uttering no more screams of protest, her head and neck tucked into the lower right corner of the camera frame, looking small and frail, almost incidental, against the indifferent squares of white tile. As Norman looked small and vulnerable against the backdrop of his mother's old house on the hill. The camera follows Marion as she slowly slumps down along the white tiles, accompanied by heavy musical downbeats that descend viscerally with her. Strands of her wet hair cling to the tile, as if vainly trying to hold her up.

More heavy breathing as Marion reaches out her right hand in search of something, anything, any*one* to help her. In extreme close-up that hand slowly, reflexively grips the shower curtain. But that curtain fails her now, just as it failed to shield her from the knife assault. A quick overhead shot of naked Marion, all but anonymous beneath a sheet of water, crouching on the floor of the bathtub, clutching the shower curtain for support. Herrmann's music grinds to a halt and fades away, along with the last vestiges of life in Marion's body. A close-up of the shower curtain snapping loose from *its* metal supports informs of us Marion's death, once removed, before we see her lifeless head and arm falling over the edge of the tub and striking the floor. Anyone who watches and hears this scene and doesn't feel a gut-wrenching identification with Marion is someone I would not want to encounter.

Water continues to stream from the shower head — a curiously lonely sound now that it no longer serves Marion's purpose. Water that moments earlier contributed to her physical and moral sense of renewal now merely washes away the bloody evidence of a much greater crime committed against *her*. Blood-stained water flows past her lifeless, helpless bare feet and down the bathtub drain, into a black hole of nothingness. The camera closes in on that dark, mysterious oblivion.

Lap dissolve from an extreme close-up of the drain to a similar shot of Marion's wide-open eye, its sightless black pupil mocking us with a phony expression of shock. The camera rotates slowly as it pulls away from that dead eye, continuing the "drain" analogy as Marion and all that we knew of and felt for her drains away. Ironically, the same act of distancing ourselves from her corpse restores to us Marion's eyelashes, an eyebrow, strands of blond hair, a nose, mouth and chin, pressed uncomfortably into the bathroom floor tile. The *whole* face of Marion Crane finally comes into view, restoring her visual identity, if nothing else. The lifeless drone of running water continues unabated. But Marion herself, her fears and hopes, her terrors and her pleasures, has been removed from the equation. Only the slight movement of Janet Leigh's neck muscles betray the fictional illusion of this shot. And in a way, that's a relief. After all, it's *only* a movie.

Few if any depictions of violent death on screen rival *Psycho*'s famous shower scene for its unusual combination of visceral shock and the emotional shock of the sheer outrage done to a human being. Marion Crane is not some anonymous victim hacked apart by a madman. She is the flawed but warm, compassionate (towards Norman) and (yes, we have to admit this is part of her appeal) beautiful woman we have come to know and care about. The savagery of her murder and the aching, ironically mechanical (her movements are automatic, not willed) pathos of her final moments of life bring *to* life Hitchcock's larger point about the utter fragility and unpredictability of the human condition. Nowhere else in his work is that point hammered home with such shattering impact.

Leaving Marion Crane to her fate, the camera slides away from her, past the turned down bed where she hoped to get some rest, and to the tattered newspaper concealing the stolen money she planned to return. Hopes and plans now irrelevant. "Late News Flashes" declares one of the smaller headlines in the newspaper. Something the sad ending of Marion Crane's life will soon become. At the used car dealership, she had perused the same newspaper in hopes of *not* finding her name in it. Now she'll be there, but won't care about it. After pausing on the newspaper, the camera continues on to the open window to show us the old house up the hill. Now only *we* eavesdrop on Norman's voice, coming from that house, calling out in horror to his mother about the blood stains on her hands, dress, wherever.

Norman emerges from the house and races down towards the camera (we are waiting for him), the motel and Cabin #1. Frantic music erupts subjectively with him, then stops abruptly when *he* stops in the bathroom doorway, stunned by what he sees inside. The camera shows him from behind. The back of his head and shoulders convey his reaction. Seen from this angle, Norman cuts a figure curiously reminiscent of James Whale's introductory shot of the Monster in *Frankenstein* (1931) as he backs into his creator's laboratory. Both characters are pictured from the rear, then turn to face the camera, albeit in a different manner. Could this analogy, if intended, be Hitchcock's sly hint that Norman *is* the monster in *Psycho*? Nowadays, of course, nearly everybody knows.

Horrified, Norman quickly backs out of the bathroom and turns to face the camera, covering his mouth with his hand as if about to be sick. He accidentally knocks one of the framed bird pictures off the wall. The picture of an inoffensive bird in a non-predatory pose. A bird symbolically linked to Marion and the saner side of Norman himself. One has been knocked off her perch forever. The other is about to be. After a few moments Norman regains control over himself and closes the cabin window, beginning the process of dutifully covering up his mother's crime. But his composure returns fitfully, suggesting that he is sincerely shocked and appalled at the crime he believes his mother committed.

Norman sits on the bed, again struggling to get his emotional bearings. His agitated eyes, mouth and jaw betray his internal struggle. He is sitting on *Marion's* bed, yet no trace remains of the sexual arousal he felt while spying on her through the peephole. Back in action again, he closes the cabin door and switches off the light, to conceal the crime and his cover-up from the outside world. Passersby are rare at the Bates Motel, but one cannot count on *anything*. Light from the bathroom illuminates the newspaper on the nightstand across the room. The newspaper still conceals *Marion's* crime, even as Norman acts to conceals the much more serious crime against her. Even in death, Marion keeps her secret.

Norman exits the cabin and closes the door behind him. Will he flee the motel, the house, the murder and his mother? His reflection in the cabin window reminds us, if only in retrospect, of his duality. He is tied to the murder and to his mother in ways we don't yet understand.

Another moment of uncertainty and paralysis grips Norman. He grabs a post supporting the motel roof overhang, then wipes one of his hands on his shirt. Wiping away evidence that doesn't even exist yet, because he hasn't touched the body. After a glance or two back at the cabin door, Norman becomes decisive again. He switches off the lights in the office, to discourage unlikely customers, and emerges with a mop and bucket in hand.

Herrmann's cover-up music consists largely of repeated pulses. Three short ones to build tension, followed by an elongated fourth to release it. The point is, we the audience are being encouraged to identify with and participate in Norman's effort to cover up the murder of Marion Crane. A murder *he* committed, as we eventually learn, but which he believes was committed by his mother. In a bizarre way, Norman's is an unselfish act, even if also an act of self-preservation.

Background music turns darker and heavier, under the weight of Marion's violent death, when Norman returns to the cabin with his instruments of concealment in hand. He hesitates, again, in the bathroom doorway, on the threshold of facing the horror and becoming truly complicit in his mother's crime. His tall, thin, black silhouette illuminated by bright light from the bathroom, Norman is for the second time a monstrous figure shown from behind. Perhaps this time more reminiscent of Cesare, the thin, black-attired, homicidal, somnambulist puppet of Dr. Caligari in *The Cabinet of Dr. Caligari*

(1919). As things turn out, Norman Bates too is not always pulling his own strings. At least not his *conscious* mind.

Norman hesitantly enters the bathroom, clutching his collar around his neck for self-protection, as he did while running through the rain to assist Marion upon her arrival at the motel. Shutting off the now infernally irritating shower, Norman pauses again, then acts. Watching from just outside the bathroom door, we see Norman pull the shower curtain away from the side of the bathtub. Marion is present in this shot only as a lifeless arm, a trickle of blood down the side of the tub, and a larger pool of blood staining the floor.

Composed and methodical now, Norman lays the detached shower curtain on the carpet just outside the bathroom door, then drags Marion's limp body onto it. Particularly noticeable in this shot are the clear-cut, even enhanced sounds of Norman's footsteps and Marion's body as it is being dragged. Those sounds, added to the backtracking camera that accompanies him, help pull us emotionally into Norman's world. Just as we were lured into Marion's world of renewed hope and cleanliness just before she was killed. We look at his/our bloody hands. He does exactly what most of us would do, wash them off in the sink and then wash out the sink itself. More evidence of guilt down the drain. Background music pauses so we can clearly hear that water drain away, taking its gruesomely precious cargo with it. Then Herrmann's music switches to a more conspiratorial tone as we watch Norman, more confident and determined now, wash out the inside and then the outside of the blood-stained bathtub. As her blood disappears, only Marion's slippers remain to "speak" for the victim.

Running the water again in the tub, now to a *purpose* (if an illegal one) instead of reminding us of Marion's *extinguished* purpose, Norman quickly washes down the tiled walls above the tub, then the tiled floor. As he does so we see Marion's robe sitting on the toilet seat, where she left it. The robe replaces Marion's slippers as a forlorn token of her rapidly disappearing presence. Norman moves carefully around the body, which is carefully kept off screen most of the time. Is there a trace of remorse in him? Or is it just a little squeamishmess? Are they the same thing? Slipping outside the cabin, Norman backs Marion's car up to the entrance, moving now in a ruthlessly efficient manner.

Norman returns to the cabin to fetch the body, wrapping it first in the shower curtain before picking it up. Again Herrmann's music pauses to let us hear the prominent crinkling of the curtain as Norman wraps and hoists Marion's body. We are encouraged to be acutely aware of every detail, visual and aural, as we uncomfortably participate in Norman's cover-up while still reflecting on our loss of Marion. The awkward deadweight of her body, with its bare legs and feet sticking out beneath the concealing curtain, adds greatly to the unsavory atmosphere of this scene. By lingering on the inanimate remains of a woman who just a short time ago was so vibrant, articulate, compassionate (to Norman) and near the end hopeful, Hitchcock reminds us of the shocking reality of her loss. Dramatically, it's an amazing balancing act of identification with victim and killer. The latter because even though most of us would never commit so terrible a crime, we are all capable of acting selfishly, callously and even ruthlessly when motivated by fear or driven by compulsion.

Norman deposits the body, with neither care nor cruelty, into the trunk of Marion's car. Then he returns to the cabin, along with Herrmann's three-note madhouse theme. Again we see a double image of him, thanks to the same mirror that reflected Marion's duality earlier. The number "1" is also again prominent, first on the door of the cabin and then on the key ring Norman picks up off the floor. "1" complements the mirror reflection, both hinting at the presence of the *other* Norman. The one capable of such savagery.

Norman packs Marion's clothes and belongings, scattered around the cabin, into her suitcase. He checks various drawers and the medicine cabinet in the bathroom. And he returns the framed bird picture to the wall from which it came. The old order is being restored, and Norman is quite thorough about it. But the camera, stepping outside his efforts for a moment, reminds us of the neglected newspaper on the nightstand.

Carrying Marion's suitcase and his own mop and bucket outside, Norman is briefly startled by the headlights of a passing car. He drops the incriminating evidence and freezes, like a deer caught in the headlights. His confidence, which had increased as the clean-up progressed, momentarily evaporates. It was paper thin all along. But the headlights pass on by (there are advantages as well as disadvantages to being left behind by the march of progress) and the danger of discovery along with them. Returning to the cabin for a final look around, Norman spots the newspaper, grabs it and, moving efficiently again, tosses it into the trunk. He has no idea the newspaper conceals nearly $40,000—a sum that could considerably ease the financial troubles of his failing motel. If he knew about it, would he care? Would he use it? Or would the money have ended up in the same place it does anyway? Norman switches off the bathroom light, closes the cabin door and slams the car trunk shut. Mission accomplished. Or so it seems.

Marion's car glistens with droplets of rainwater, as her body once did with remnants of her shower. Phony though it is, with its misleading California license plates, that car is now the only remaining tangible evidence of her life, her frustration and mistakes, her renewal and hopes, and her violent, wholly unjustified death. And Norman now treats it with the same callousness his mother displayed towards Marion herself, pushing it into a swampy bog somewhere out back of the motel. Presumably far from prying eyes. All is concealment, except for a few brief, exhilarating moments of openness, in *Psycho*.

# 1. Hitchcock's *Psycho*

Herrmann's music pauses so we can hear the rustle of reeds and the gurgle of the swamp (like the gurgle of the flushing toilet and the bathtub and sink drains — previous acts of concealment) as Marion, her car and the evidence of her crime disappear into oblivion. Shots of black muck swallowing the white car alternate with full frontal close-ups of Norman watching the process anxiously, his hands clasped together as though in silent prayer. The leafless branches of a dead tree hover over his right shoulder (screen left) like something out of a classic old horror film. A metaphorical perch for his dead but not quite departed mother. And while he watches, Norman munches on candy. Something we'll see him do again and again. It's a childish habit that, without proper parental guidance, he now indulges to the point of compulsion.

Mission not *quite* accomplished. A breathless moment of suspense as Marion's car gets stuck in the muck. The gurgling (repulsive or encouraging, depending on your point of view) stops. Norman glances around in panic. Can anyone see him? Or the car? He chews his pacifying candy furiously. Then the gurgling resumes, the white car disappears, and the gurgling stops again. Norman smiles. There is no remorse for Marion in that smile. His private fears, compulsions and needs overwhelm his otherwise pronounced capacity to sympathize with other people. All is buried in blackness, including, *especially*, the terrifying truth he hides from himself.

Marion's disappearance into the swamp is juxtaposed, after a fade to black that separates Part One of *Psycho* from Part Two, with a close-up of a letter Sam is writing to her. The gist of that letter is Sam's admission that Marion was right, and what appears to be his proposal of marriage. Eight days late and $40,000 short, tragically. A poignant demonstration that sometimes in life timing is everything. If Sam had come to his senses in the hotel room he shared with Marion, she might still be alive. Though a closer look at the letter casts some doubt on the credibility of Sam's proposal. "So what if we're poor and cramped and miserable, at least we'd be happy!" is a contradiction in terms. "Miserable" and "Happy" under the same circumstances? Does Sam even believe in the *possibility* of domestic bliss anymore? But at least he's finally making the effort.

Cutting to a shot from behind Sam, who is seated at his desk in the storeroom behind his hardware store (the same room of which he spoke so contemptuously to Marion in the movie's first scene), the camera slowly withdraws, giving us a new perspective. The room is as "cramped and miserable" as Sam described. The equivalent of Norman's private little parlor in back of the Bates Motel office. Norman is a slave to his memory of Mother. Sam is a slave to his debts. By the time we've backed up into the store proper, the doorway to the storeroom, through which we can see Sam's coat hung up, appears as narrow and confining as the kitchen doorway through which we saw Norman as he struggled in vain against the domination of Mother.

It's a typical small town American hardware store, neat but crowded with a variety of merchandise, including quite a number of knives and other bladed instruments intended for ordinary domestic chores. A tidy row of metal rakes stands guard just outside Sam's office, as though shielding his privacy from intruders. As we leave the storeroom, the soundtrack replaces our interest in Sam's letter to Marion with an unseen customer pondering aloud whether or not the insecticide she is considering purchasing causes pain to the creatures it is designed to exterminate. As she comes into view, the customer declares, "Death should always be painless." There is a typically Hitchcockian touch of ghoulish humor to her fastidious moral code about the act of killing. Were any of the Nazi bigshots concerned about the suffering of the people they so blithely exterminated? On the other hand, Marion's killer was not the least bothered by the terror and pain caused to her. Perhaps even enjoyed it. Maybe the fastidious customer is not so ghoulish after all.

While the customer drones on and on, the camera passes her by and cuts to a reverse angle to show us Lila Crane, Marion's sister, emerge from a black taxi and enter the store. She wears black gloves and carries a black purse and a black suitcase with white trim. Her dress is gray tweed. Appropriate for someone who clearly does not come in peace, as her facial expression and body language telegraph.

Walking briskly to the checkout counter, she addresses the cashier as "Sam?" The cashier summons the real Sam from the back room. Sam greets Lila pleasantly, with no trace of flirtation even though he doesn't know she is Marion's sister. When she says as much, he becomes even friendlier, in a respectful manner. Lila comes right to her point, inquiring if Marion is in Fairvale. A camera shot from behind Lila crowns her head with the tines of a rake. Not exactly equivalent to Norman's knife, but sufficient to accentuate her hostility.

After the insecticide customer leaves the store, Lila divulges the reason for her visit. Marion's mysterious disappearance from Phoenix a week ago. Just as it interrupted Sam's letter to follow the customer's lecture on insecticide, then left the customer to bring us Lila entering the store, the camera now cuts away from Lila's expression of concern about her sister to introduce a new player to the scene. A private detective named Arbogast. Our first image of him is a big, intimidating frontal close-up as he spies on Sam and Lila through a window in the store's entryway. He appears as sinister as did the patrolman spying on a sleeping Marion through the window in her car. Though maybe not quite as chilling as Norman peeking through a hole in the parlor wall to spy on Marion in her cabin. All three examples are morally related, if situated at different points on a sliding scale of right and wrong.

Arbogast's black hat, black eyes, mostly black tie and the black shadow on his right (screen left) shoulder all contribute to his menacing presence.

Even the black metal ring and chain, and their black shadow, hanging from the inside of the door seem a bit ominous in the context of his arrival. But like the black tie with the white spots, the black ring and chain are counterbalanced by a white window shade pull string on the opposite side of the camera frame. The two objects visually bracket the detective. Every character in *Psycho* exudes some form of dual personality, metaphorically echoed in one way or another by Hitchcock.

Increasingly anxious, Lila reveals her suspicion that both Sam and Marion are involved in the theft that Marion in fact committed alone. Not yet aware of Arbogast's presence, Sam tries to shield his potentially incriminating conversation with Lila from prying eyes and ears, telling his employee Bob to leave for lunch. Even though Sam has nothing to hide, his girlfriend *might*. And he is protective of her. Bob, however, like most of us, is nosey. He wants to hear more of Lila's story, so he tells Sam that he brought his lunch to work. With a trace of wit and more than a little irritation (is there pre-existing tension between employer and employee?), Sam tells him to "Run out and eat it!" Reluctantly, Bob obeys.

While we watch a grim-faced Arbogast silently enter the store and move into a huge close-up even more imposing than before, we eavesdrop, from the detective's auditory perspective, on Sam practically whisper a question to Lila, "Now what *thing* could we be in together?," and Lila apologize for crying. Sam inquires if Marion is in trouble. Arbogast chooses that particular, tactical moment to intrude himself into the conversation. "Let's *all* talk about Marion, shall we?" And he does *not* whisper.

Arbogast joins Sam and Lila at the center of the store. His black hat and dark suit contrast with Lila's gray dress and even more with Sam's white shirt. But various sharp implements, like Norman's kitchen knife intended for innocuous domestic use but with the potential for misuse, are visible above and around all three of them. There are no guiltless characters in this film, at least in the sense of their potential for *some* kind of violence. Even if it's just the violence of intimidation.

Sam addresses the intrusive stranger sarcastically as "friend." Arbogast, identifying himself as a private investigator, responds in kind. He and Lila immediately butt heads when he demands to know Marion's whereabouts. Lila refuses to answer. She doesn't even know who he is. And Sam wants to know what business it is of his. Arbogast, in a deceptively casual manner meant to impress the taller, younger and stronger man, leans back against the checkout counter, physically separating himself from the other two, and explains about the $40,000. When he claims that Marion stole the money, Sam and Lila are pictured by themselves, as though now allied against the detective. Sam asks her for more details, but the abrasive manner in which she provides them makes it obvious they are *not* allies. After failing to bank the money for her boss, Marion left Phoenix, and "no one has seen her since." She looks directly and accusingly at Sam as she says this. Clearly she suspects him of manipulating her sister into committing the theft.

"Someone always sees a girl with $40,000," Arbogast responds. It's a Sam Spade/Humphrey Bogart sort of line, full of wise cynicism about dames and stolen money. But in fact, no one has "seen" Marion for the reasons Arbogast suggests. Not even he suspects the shocking, random, brutal truth of Marion's disappearance. *Psycho* is no latter day ode to film noir. It is Hitchcock's darkest portrayal of unpredictable people in an unpredictable world. Like Arbogast, Lila too suspects that Marion has contacted Sam. She tells him, with less hostility now and more pleading in her voice, that no one wants to prosecute Marion. They just want the money back. Sam insists Marion has not contacted him.

Relations between Arbogast and Lila soften a bit when he asks her if she came to Fairvale on a hunch or something more. Lila, betraying vulnerability and shown in close-up, replies that it wasn't even a hunch, "just hope." Still leaning casually on the counter, Arbogast makes a tactical mistake by not cultivating Lila's confidence. Instead he callously remarks that with a little investigative work he might come to believe her. Lila, still in close-up, turns on him, looks him straight in the eye and tells him she doesn't care whether he believes her or not. Arbogast's interest in Marion is strictly professional. Lila's is deeply personal. So is Sam's. Unlike Arbogast, they both earn close-ups during this part of the three-way conversation.

Sam offers alternate, morally more comforting explanations for Marion's disappearance. Perhaps she was the victim of an accident, or a hold-up. Better dead than a thief? Arbogast shoots them down, pointing out that Marion's employer saw her leaving Phoenix. Sam responds, "I can't believe it." Arbogast now approaches the other two, slightly increasing the intimacy between himself and them, and remarks, "We're always quickest to doubt people who have a reputation for being honest." Is he defending Lowry's statement about seeing Marion leaving Phoenix in her car? Sam's expression of doubt was not so much aimed at Lowry as at the notion that his lover would commit such a crime. And besides, we know very little about Lowry. His statement about seeing Marion leave town is accurate. But he keeps his own little secrets, including the bottle of booze hidden in the desk in his office (to alleviate his own, private frustrations?), and the truth about one of his prominent clients, Cassidy, cheating on his taxes. So Arbogast's broad comment about people being quick to doubt those with a reputation for being honest is disputable.

At any rate, the detective remains convinced that Marion is hiding in Fairvale, probably with Sam's help. With a quiet vow to find her, he departs. Sam and Lila watch him go, each reacting differently. Lila's face expresses hope that Arbogast will find her sister. That possibility softens her hostility towards the detective. Sam, by contrast, resents the detective's dual accusations that Marion is a thief and that Sam knows it.

Before the scene ends, background music anticipates the next scene, Arbogast's hunt for Marion, with a lighter variation on the intense travel music that accompanied the opening credits and Marion's flight from Phoenix. The detective makes the rounds of local motels, hotels and boarding houses, to no avail. But at one stop he interviews a proprietor who, viewed from behind and from a low angle, appears considerably taller than Arbogast and has hair that, in retrospect, resembles that of Mrs. Bates. A darkly humorous bit of foreshadowing by Hitchcock, and maybe a hint that this anonymous, briefly seen character too has something to hide in her private life. Something neither we nor Arbogast will ever discover.

Wearing a black sweater, Norman sits comfortably outside the motel office, reading a magazine and compulsively eating candy. No indication in his demeanor of remorse over what happened to Marion. The camera lingers on Norman and his reaction as we hear Arbogast's car approach. He seems calm and collected, treating the detective like an ordinary customer in search of a room. Minus the extra charm and nervousness he expended on the attractive Marion Crane. He mentions that he neglected to switch on the motel sign, repeating the same self-deprecating line he used on Marion about "twelve cabins, twelve vacancies." Why bother with the sign? But the sign *was* switched on the night Marion arrived. Perhaps Norman, in the wake of the murder, is now discouraging other guests from stopping. Arbogast picks up on that thread, if only casually at first, by remarking that of all the motels and hotels he's visited in the past two days, "this is the first place that looks like it's hiding from the world." Perceptive man. He's already marked Norman as a possible recluse. But Norman has his standard excuse ready, about the main highway being re-routed away from his business establishment.

Norman invites Arbogast into the office to register, but the detective only wants to ask a few questions. Still confident and composed, Norman explains that even though he gets few guests these days, he still maintains the routine of changing linen in the cabins once a week. Because he finds the smell of dampness "creepy." Apart from his mother, he is a rather fastidious young man. He was embarrassed by the smell of dampness in Marion's room too, and could not say the word "bathroom" in her presence.

Like boxers, but throwing words instead of punches, the two men spend the next few minutes sizing up each other. Even as he himself is being scrutinized and evaluated, Norman probes for information about the stranger. Speculating hopefully, or rather *pretending* to be hopeful, that Arbogast is looking to purchase a motel (Norman is emotionally incapable of leaving the place), Norman betrays his first hint of nervousness in the scene when he realizes the detective is after something else. After all, Norman has much to hide.

Private detective Arbogast (Martin Balsam) and Norman Bates (Anthony Perkins), despite their friendly demeanor, maneuver for tactical advantage as they discuss the missing Marion Crane inside the office of the Bates Motel, in *Psycho*.

Inside the office, Arbogast is visible as himself and as a reflected image in a mirror at the far end of the registration desk. The same mirror that doubled Marion as she deceived Norman about her true identity and place of residence. The detective explains that he's looking for a missing woman from Phoenix whose family wants to forgive her in some private matter. "She's not in any trouble," he lies, hoping that will encourage the motel-keeper's cooperation. But Marion *is* in trouble. And Norman, pre-armed with knowledge that Marion was running away from *something*, challenges Arbogast by asserting that the police seldom look for people who aren't in trouble. The detective insists he's not a cop. Maybe not, but he represents the injured party in a criminal investigation of Marion. Round to Norman. But half-visible through the doorway leading to the back parlor is the oval Victorian angel painting that hung above Marion while she conversed with Norman on that evening that now seems so long ago. The past will not be permanently suppressed.

Norman claims to have had no guests for the past two weeks and pretends not to recognize a photo of Marion the detective shows him, Two outright lies, one of which no one can prove. But the other one rests on quicksand. Arbogast points out that Marion could have registered under a false name and asks to see the register. Norman defensively claims to have dropped the formality of having guests sign in. Funny, he already invited Arbogast into the office to do exactly that. And he has *not* discontinued the formality of changing sheets. Nervous now, and forgetful of what he said just moments earlier, Norman switches on the motel sign, commenting that just a week ago a couple almost passed by the place until they saw it. So much for having no guests in the past *two* weeks, and for not bothering to switch on the sign anymore.

Smooth as silk in his phony, nonchalant manner, Arbogast pounces on Norman's mistake by asking to see the register. Norman can hardly deny him without looking like he has something to hide. While Hitchcock gives us a huge, low angle close-up of Norman's jaw working furiously as he munches on his pacifying candy, we hear the detective's calm voice effortlessly solve the riddle of Marie Samuels with foreknowledge of her boyfriend's name, Sam Loomis, and a sample of her handwriting. The shot of Norman's jaw is as mercilessly revealing in an emotional sense as Norman's peephole spying on Marion was in an erotic sense. Hitchcock may want us to empathize with the young man caught in a trap, but he intends to expose the young man's secrets as well.

Arbogast gives Norman a second chance to identify the photo of Marion. Retreating from his earlier lie, and trying to cover it up with a few lame excuses that don't convince, Norman supplies a few cursory details about Marion's stay at the motel, some of them false. But his stuttering and candy chewing betray him as a liar, so the detective bores in for the kill. "Did you spend the night with her?" No. Then how can he be sure Marion made no phone calls?

Backed into a corner, Norman stalls for time, babbling about making a mental picture of events in his mind so he can remember more about Marion's visit. But each time he re-invents his story, he adds more detail that provides Arbogast with new openings for probing questions. By this method the detective learns that Marion had a meal with Norman in the back parlor. So much for her going straight to bed. Viewed by the camera with his face half in light and half in darkness, Arbogast looks as intimidating as Norman finds him to be. Norman tries to end the conversation at this arbitrary point, but the detective presses onward, claiming the young man's story doesn't quite make sense.

"She isn't still here, is she?," like "Did you spend the night with her?," is intended to disorient Norman and perhaps draw more information out of him. But this gambit plays to Norman's strength instead of his weakness. Marion is gone and buried. Having no fear of her being discovered on the premises, Norman smiles broadly and invites the detective, sans legal warrant, to search the cabins for himself. "You can help me change beds," he jokes. Arbogast, replying "No thanks," seems ready to concede. But Norman, as we witnessed so vividly during the parlor scene with Marion, is *always* skating on thin ice when it comes to his self-confidence.

The two characters leave the office, Arbogast heading in one direction and Norman in the other. Game over? Not quite. Disturbing music creeps back onto the soundtrack. *Psycho* screenwriter Joseph Stefano once remarked about Herrmann's score, "He had just taken everybody's guts and used them for music" (*The Making of Psycho*, a documentary accompanying the film on DVD). The detective, turning back, watches Norman skittishly avoid entering Cabin #1 and move on towards #2. Then he spots the house up the hill behind the motel. The silhouette of a woman is clearly visible in one of the upstairs windows.

When Norman notices Arbogast looking in the direction of the house, he tries to distract the detective with the business of changing linen in the cabins. He remarks on his own trustworthy face, which people can't seem to help believe. False bravado, meant to curry favor with the inquisitive stranger. Refusing to be distracted, and proving the truth, at least as regards himself, about people always doubting those who seem most honest, Arbogast asks if anyone else is at home. Norman reflexively responds, "No," but again gets trapped in his lie. Arbogast points out a person visible in the window. So again Norman tries to backpeddle and re-define the truth to fit his lie. Living with an invilid mother is "practically like living alone."

Having exposed another of Norman's deceptions, Arbogast turns aggressive again. He asks point blank if Norman is hiding Marion for the sake of the money, and suggests that if such is the case Marion is only *using* him. That remark strikes a particularly vulnerable spot in Norman's emotional makeup, as did Marion when she delicately suggested that he put his mother "away someplace." *Interrupting* the detective in a much more vigorous defense than he is accustomed to display, Norman insists he is not capable of being fooled, even by a woman. Arbogast's follow-up remark, "It's not a slur on your manhood," only aggravates the situation. The detective has stumbled upon a much deeper emotional sore spot than he anticipated. And it yields positive results for him. This time. But by exploiting Norman's vulnerability, Arbogast places himself in far greater danger than he realizes.

Norman recklessly undermines the lie he told earlier (that his mother was a virtual non-entity), which he told to conceal an even earlier falsehood (that there was no one else living in the house), which ironically turns out to be the truth. "She might have fooled me, but she didn't fool my mother," contradicts his assertion that he is incapable of being fooled. Norman's fragile male pride betrays him. The detective, convinced now that Mrs. Bates met with Marion, wants to question the old woman.

Norman can only back peddle so far without conceding final defeat. His resistance stiffens. He insists his mother is too sick to be questioned, and orders the detective to leave. Arbogast walks out of the camera frame as Norman watches him go. The play of light and shadow on Norman's face renders his gaze fierce, predatory. Certainly not nervous or vulnerable. Hitchcock holds on that image for a long time as we hear the detective's automobile engine start and see its headlights beam against the motel wall. Norman's black sweater appears especially stark against backlighting from the office window. One of the breast-shaped inkwells is clearly visible through the window's thin curtains. Norman swallows nervously, then smiles with overconfidence as the detective drives away. From insecurity to arrogance, meek passivity to aggression, Norman's mood swings are extreme and rapid.

Stopping at a roadside public telephone booth, perhaps near the diner a few miles outside Fairvale, Arbogast phones Sam's drugstore. Based on what he gleaned from his encounter with Norman, he now feels comfortable sharing information with Lila, to whom he offers several important conjectures: Marion stayed at the Bates Motel, in Cabin One, and spoke with the proprietor's sick old mother. And Sam did not know she was coming. He tells Lila he intends to return to the motel to interview Mrs. Bates, and be back at the hardware store within an hour.

The phone booth, albeit just a stage set, is dark, quiet and lonely. By not showing or even letting us hear Lila at the other end of the line, Hitchcock isolates Arbogast in that creepy setting, making him seem more vulnerable. Like our impression of Marion driving along a dark, deserted, rain-drenched country road before she spots the brightly lit Bates Motel sign.

A distant shot of Norman leaving the motel office provides an unusual juxtaposition of the motel and the house. Duality is emphasized by light emanating from both the office and from mother's upstairs room. But the house, with its own duality expressed in its half illuminated, half in shadow façade, visually dominates the lowly motel shrouded in the darkness of night. From the unusual camera angle, the house and the motel appear physically connected. And Herrmann's background music captures the lurking menace of that duality.

Norman, walking along the boardwalk as he continues to change linen, spots Arbogast's car approaching before we do, and slips out of sight between perpendicular rows of cabins. We don't realize until a later scene that there is a gap between those rows, leading to the back of the motel and up the hill to the Bates house. Where Norman will await the arrival of Arbogast. The detective's light-colored vehicle, eerily reminiscent of Marion's, enters the camera frame and stops in front of the motel. Arbogast heads for the office, his footfalls on the boardwalk and turning of the doorknob clearly audible, despite the quiet of the evening. Those sounds help accentuate our sense of his isolation and vulnerability.

Calling out to Norman but receiving no answer, Arbogast violates the privacy of Norman's parlor. Viewed in a reaction shot, his face largely in shadow, the detective's shining eyes bear a disturbing resemblance to those of Marion's killer when the shower curtain was yanked open. *Arbogast* is the intruder now, not to solve a murder and secure justice for Marion, but to spy on Norman for the purpose of catching up with a thief. The detective is startled to see Norman's collection of stuffed birds, including the Edgar Allan Poe talisman linked to another fictional character who exhibits an unhealthy obsession with a dead woman. The framed picture of angels positioned next to the stuffed raven is obscured by shadow. Only avian tokens of acute melancholy and predation (the owl) are visible this time.

Arbogast spots an opened safe on the floor. He searches inside and finds nothing incriminating, except the implication that something was recently removed from it. He snoops around the office a bit more before returning outside. Herrmann's music alerts us with its three-note madhouse motif as the detective climbs towards the house with the light on in mother's window.

Removing his hat in an empty, formal gesture of respect, Arbogast disrespectfully enters the Bates house without knocking or calling out for permission to do so. Just as Melanie Daniels will do at the Brenner home in *The Birds*. Except that the detective, with no legal warrant, enters the house in direct violation of Norman's earlier order to leave the Bates property. Window and door curtains visible behind the detective as he glances around the entryway recall the shower curtain through which Marion was attacked. Will the same maniac come crashing through the front door and attack Arbogast from behind?

The detective glances left down the corridor leading to the kitchen. Nothing. Just the meticulously maintained décor from a bygone era. He glances up the stairs. The door to Norman's bedroom lies straight ahead, down a short and obscure hallway. His mother's room is off screen to the left, but represented by a Victorian painting of a vibrant young woman dressed in white. An idyllic, misleading portrait of the woman Mrs. Bates might have been, many decades ago. To the right of the staircase, on the first floor, is another closed door. Next to it, on a pedestal, stands a black sculpture of Cupid shooting its love arrow. A more ominous *shadow* double of that sculpture appears on the door. The instinct to love perverted and turned violent?

A rear close-up of Arbogast's legs as he starts to climb the stairs encourages us to participate in his efforts to conceal his presence by making as little noise as possible. Likewise when he is shown in a backtracking shot from in front. But this visual empathy is disrupted by the next shot, a close-up of the door to Mrs. Bates' room. A door that opens slightly, quietly, emitting a sliver of light that illuminates the ornate, old-fashioned carpet on the floor. We return to the backtracking shot of Arbogast ascending the stairs, but this time with foreknowledge, which he lacks, of something very bad awaiting him at the top landing. The ornate wooden post at the bottom of the stairs looms behind the detective. So intimidating is the house to *us*, if not quite so much to Arbogast, we almost expect the post to attack him from behind.

An overhead shot from high above the second floor landing brings the two characters together for the first and last time. A gray-haired figure in a dress, and carrying a large knife, emerges from Mother's bedroom and closes quickly on the detective. Aside from the practical need not to give us too close a view of the attacker, this brutally objective shot counterpoints the highly intimate violence of the encounter and the passionate, screeching music that propels it into our brain and guts.

In close-up, from the assailant's point of view, we see a horrified Arbogast fall back, a bloody gash carved above and below one of his eyes. Reversing its previous movement, the subjective camera pursues him backwards (an awkward, uncomfortable movement) as he retreats back down the stairs, his feet audibly stumbling all the way.

The camera detaches itself again at the bottom of the staircase to show us the detective falling flat on his back, the bright whiteness of his shirt appearing extremely exposed and vulnerable against the backdrop of the ornate rug upon which he falls. Before he can defend himself, the dress-clad figure kneels at his side, raises the knife and plunges it into him, off screen. Through that flimsy white shirt and into his chest. Twice. A final scream of terror and pain is all we see or hear of Arbogast's final moments.

Visible behind the briefly upraised knife is another mirror, appropriately framed in elaborately carved wood. The mirror reflects two equally ornate glass lamps attached to the wall near the front door. Another duality, this time doubled. Both killer and victim, now below the camera frame, are frauds, in different ways. But at this lethal moment, Arbogast's fraud, like Marion's before him, seems so trivial compared to Norman's.

The mundane contents of the storeroom of a small town hardware store can look very dynamic in the right context, from the right angle, and in the right lighting. File cabinet, door frame, window, rake heads, window stickers, etc. Lila and Sam appear worlds apart as they silently await Arbogast's return. She sits in a chair at his desk, at foreground left, looking off to the left, her head resting on her hand as she silently worries about her missing sister. At background right, glancing in the opposite direction from Lila, Sam stands with his arms crossed while leaning against the office door. They share a concern about Marion, yet do not commiserate with each other. Together, yet alone.

"Sometimes Saturday night has a lonely sound. Ever notice that, Lila?" Sam comments, more on his own situation than on that of his missing girlfriend. Is he flirting with Marion's sister? Even if he's just trying to bridge the emotional gap between them, as Norman appeared to do more successfully with Marion in the parlor, Lila rudely ignores him. Shown now in a shot by herself, though interestingly accompanied by two of her own reflections (how many hidden sides does *she* have?), Lila turns towards Sam and expresses concern about Arbogast's tardiness. At the end of the same shot we hear Sam's reply, but we *see* him only from the chest down, checking his watch. Emotionally, the two characters are miles apart. Smiling, Sam urges patience. Is he *enjoying* his time alone with Lila, as a break from his customary Saturday night loneliness? If so, she does not reciprocate. Impatient, she wants to go to the Bates Motel and investigate matters for herself. By contrast, Sam's concern for his missing lover doesn't seem nearly as urgent.

Doubled, even trebled reflected images of Sam and Lila are evident in this scene, suggesting more happening than what is visible and audible on the surface. As characters, they are not explored to the depth that Marion and Norman are during *their* extended scene together. But they are not empty ciphers either. Lila approaches Sam and they are together again in the same shot. But not in outlook. Lila admits, "patience doesn't run in my family." Apparently not in Marion either. Could the undercurrent of hostility between Sam and Lila be a preview of the kind of relationship Sam and Marion might have had if they had married?

Sam argues against Lila's haste. She insists on it. Sam reaches for the phone, possibly to call the Bates Motel. Lila impulsively heads for the door. In the same shot Sam's larger figure supercedes hers as he angrily slams down the phone, grabs his jacket and heads out the office door, into the store proper. Lit only through windows from his back room office, the darkened store is now crowded with sinister silhouettes, including scythes and rakes and other domestic implements that suddenly appear dangerous. The mood between Sam and Lila has turned prickly too. In vividly lit profile, he orders her to stay behind while he goes to the motel. When she asks why she can't go with him, he fires back, "I don't know!" Then comes up with a lame rationale. It's clear he simply doesn't want her along. Possibly her impatience makes Sam feel guilty for not being equally so. Was his now pointless letter to Marion just a hollow concession to keep her in his life and alleviate his weekend blues, rather than a genuine profession of love? "Stay here!" Sam repeats emphatically as he walks out of the camera frame and out the door.

The last shot of the scene lingers and even closes in a little on Lila as she watches Sam depart. When he opens the door to do so, off screen, a cold breeze blows in, ruffling Lila's hair. She crosses her arms for warmth. The breeze is a passing remnant of the chilly relations between her and Sam. In a broader sense, it's a bracing token of the cold, lonely, indifferent and sometimes dangerous world outside. A row of pointy rakes, in silhouette, seems to menace Lila from behind too. Or are they tokens of *her* hostility towards Sam? With her eyes barely visible through the gloom of the store, she resembles an earlier portrait of Arbogast invading the privacy of Norman's parlor, and, in turn, our impression of Marion's killer from within Marion's shower stall.

The thin, rather fragile figure of Norman Bates stands looking into the swamp, where Arbogast's torn body has no doubt joined Marion's. Back at the motel office, Sam calls out for the detective. It's a desolate sound because no one answers. The front grill and headlights of Sam's truck are brightly lit in the gloom of night. They look like an angry, menacing face lurking behind an unsuspecting Sam, who faces the other direction. The effect is pure illusion, of course. But it contributes to the unsettling atmosphere of this scene, where the potentially hostile principals are kept far apart from one another.

Norman hears Sam's voice echoing from a distance. The camera, moving past a heavy black tree on the left, inches closer and closer to Norman's face as he turns to gaze directly into the lens, in the general direction of Sam's voice. The severe play of light and shadow renders Norman's facial expression brutally menacing, belying his fragile figure and taking over the ominous role visually played by the now absent tree off screen left. Without Norman speaking one word, we can read on his face the belligerence he feels towards yet another intruder into his pathologically private life. We sense how close Sam is to joining Arbogast and Marion in the black muck visible behind Norman. The dead branches of a stunted tree standing between Norman and the swamp speaks volumes for the sinister yet sad state of his life, as well as the fate of his victims.

At the hardware store in Fairvale, we see Lila from a great distance, seated alone and looking very fragile in Sam's office. Visible within the frame of the doorway, she and the small patch of light around her appear enveloped by the dark clutter of the sales floor from which the camera shoots. Compelled to practice the patience that is against her nature, sitting with hands folded on her lap and her head bowed, she is almost as forlorn a figure of entrapment as was Norman sitting alone at the kitchen table after failing to confront his mother about his feelings for Marion. Herrmann's music, carrying over from the brief motel scene, echoes the present passivity of both locations.

Hearing Sam's return, Lila rushes out of the office and directly towards the camera. Her face is completely in shadow, and for just a moment is reminiscent of the sinister image of Mrs. Bates after she pulled aside the curtain in Marion's shower. Our first image of Sam too, as he enters the store, is disturbing. Neither of these characters is violent by inclination. But Hitchcock's visual treatment of them suggests a *potential* for aggression, of one sort or another, that hovers around nearly every character in this movie.

Shown together in profile, Sam and Lila assess their meager information about Arbogast. And this time they agree. It isn't logical that Arbogast would phone Lila when he had few leads in the case, then just leave the area without a word if he got something more substantial from Norman's mother. Allies now, Sam and Lila depart for the home of the local deputy sheriff, Al Chambers. As she returns to the office to retrieve her coat, Lila briefly touches Sam with her hand. Not a sexual signal, it's more a token of growing trust between them.

Descending the staircase from his bedroom, securing his comfortable flannel robe around his waist, Al Chambers is clearly not pleased at the late night intrusion of Sam and Lila. Joining his wife and the visitors in the living room, he doesn't even speak until Sam is well into his explanation for the intrusion. The Chambers living room is very "normal," even quintessentially American for the period, with homey, sentimental pictures and sayings on the wall and bric-a-brac scattered about. It is an updated, less extreme, less sinister version of the Bate's home.

Alternating shots of Sam/Lila and Al Chambers include Mrs. Chambers in both. To some extent she is the mediary between the expostulating visitors and the silent, observant deputy sheriff. It is Mrs. Chambers who assumes the motel Arbogast referred to in his conversation with Lila is the Bates Motel, and that the woman Arbogast saw through a window in the house must mean Norman got married. The sheriff remains silent during this exchange, barely glancing at his wife as he lets Sam and Lila speak for themselves. The merest lowering of his eyebrows telegraphs his surprise at the notion of Norman taking a wife. When Sam corrects that impression by claiming the mystery woman to be Norman's sick old mother, Mrs. Chambers stares inquisitively at her husband, who again casts barely a glance in her direction. Theirs is an interesting marriage, judging from the brief glimpse of it we are afforded. Hitchcock seldom fills his movies with throwaway minor characters. Has Al Chambers grown accustomed to ignoring his wife's expressed thoughts? If so, what is *her* side of that equation?

Without questioning or correcting Sam's false assumption about Norman's mother, Al Chambers cuts directly to what is for him the heart of the matter — the reason for Marion's departure from Phoenix. A reason Sam and Lila have suspiciously avoided. In some respects, Chambers is as shrewd a judge of human character as was Arbogast. He gives nothing away yet, in terms of information, confirmation or contradiction, because he does not yet fully trust the story he's getting. Prompted by the skeptical sheriff, Lila reluctantly admits that Marion stole $40,000. But she has little patience for the sheriff's methodical, plodding approach to ferreting out the truth.

Just like Marion and Arbogast before him, Al Chambers has no clue how twisted and extreme the situation is surrounding the disappearances of Marion Crane and detective Arbogast. Rather smug in his conventional wisdom, and now shown separately from the other characters involved in this conversation, Chambers assumes two false premises: first, that Arbogast lied to Lila in order to keep her away from the Bates Motel while he pursued a hot lead about Marion and the stolen money; and second that, contrary to Sam's claim, Norman was not "out" when Sam stopped at the motel earlier. He just refused to come to the door to meet a stranger in the dead of night. Wrong on both counts.

Yielding to Lila's plea, the sheriff signals his wife to phone Norman for information. The four characters gathered in the living room are shown together in the same shot again as Al Chambers speaks with Norman over the phone. His pronunciation of "Ar-bo-gast" speaks volumes about his suspicious view of the detective/outsider. By contrast, he accepts without question Norman's explanation of the evening's events (Arbogast merely came and went, without returning) and repeats them matter-of-factly for Sam and Lila. And he possesses evidence to support his view. Norman's mother has been dead and buried for a decade. Mrs. Chambers adds, with hilarious attention to detail utterly irrelevant to the pressing case of two missing persons but very relevant to *her* priorities and values, that the burial dress she helped Norman pick out for his mother's funeral was periwinkle blue. She says this directly to Lila, who could not possibly care less about such trivia. A humorous example of what can divide people from each other.

The sheriff further explains the lurid facts, as he understands them, of the death of Mrs. Bates. The only murder-suicide in Fairvale history, it involved a married man with whom the widowed Mrs. Bates was involved. A slight pause before Chambers says the word "involved" discreetly conveys the sexual nature of that relationship. Mrs. Chambers compounds the effect by whispering, more enthusiastically, that Norman found the bodies of his mother and her lover together, "in *bed*." In their lighthearted, slightly ghoulish way, Al Chambers and his wife are minor league versions of the puritanical repression so viciously and dangerously evident in Mrs. Bates. Or at least in Norman's re-creation of her.

Sam, supporting Lila, with whom he is for the moment a full ally, insists he saw Mrs. Bates in the window while at the motel. Al Chambers then asks the logical question that is on *everybody's* mind, including the audience's, at this moment. If Sam and Arbogast really did catch a glimpse of Norman's mother, who is buried in her cemetery plot? The answer to that question is perhaps of most interest, emotionally, to Lila Crane. The scene ends with a big close-up of her.

The close-up of Lila dissolves into a close-up of the telephone in the office of the Bates Motel. Hitchcock's camera has transported us back to the place where we might get some answers to the mystery of Mrs. Bates. Following his conversation with Al Chambers, Norman sets the phone down. The return of Herrmann's music foreshadows the grimness of those answers. Still feeding his habitual sweet-tooth, Norman silently flicks off the light switch with his fist and exits the office. With an almost casual air of confidence he trots up the hill towards that monstrous Victorian edifice at the top, looming so stark and domineering against the night sky. Interestingly, we view both Norman, inside the office, and then the house from the same, intimidating low angle at the beginning of this scene.

With no trace of the hesitation he exhibited earlier, when trying to confront mother about his feelings for Marion, Norman climbs the stairs to the second floor of the house. There is a slightly feminine gait to his walk as we view him from behind. And the framed portrait of a woman at the top of the stairs, just outside mother's room, is prominently illuminated. In retrospect, we can see that Norman and the part of his personality that he has given over to the memory of his mother, are merging. As he ascends the stairs, Norman begins the process of *becoming* his mother.

Norman steps out of the camera frame and enters his mother's room, from which we hear the sound of their subsequent conversation. Another disagreement. Norman begins timidly, as expected. Mother disparages his timidity, mocking her "big, bold son" and his determination to take her, by force, out of the intense privacy of her room and hide her in the fruit cellar for a few days, until the threat of police detection has subsided. The sound of mother's voice is abrasive and aggressive, about as far removed from the conventional view of a mother's soothing, comforting voice as one can imagine.

With our ears riveted on the off screen argument between mother and son, Hitchcock's camera slowly climbs the stairs, angling towards the slightly open door of mother's room, tantalizing us with the promise of full entry and full disclosure. But the camera sails right past the door, rising to the ceiling and turning to look down on the landing from the same detached perch it occupied when Arbogast was murdered. Mrs. Bates continues to object strenuously as we watch, or *think* we watch, Norman carry the helpless invalid out of the room and down the stairs to the cellar. We cannot see her face. But the illusion of a living person, particularly enhanced by the sound of her voice, is strong. And Hitchcock exposes us to it only for a moment before fading to black and ending the scene.

Sunday morning. Services are just concluding at the Fairvale Church — a rather generic name that implies any or all religious faiths. The scene begins with a distant shot of the church as parishioners exit the building. A bell chimes. The church is visually bracketed and dominated by two objects much closer to the camera. A large tree on the left (Nature) and the front of Sam's pick-up on the right. The white grill on the front of Sam's black truck stands out boldly, even more so than it did earlier at the Bates Motel. And again it has the look of an angry mouth. Perhaps a metaphorical token of the lurking frustration and anger that haunt Sam's life but, unlike Norman, not his actions.

The camera cuts closer to the front of the church as Sam and Lila seek out Sheriff Chambers and his wife as they exit the building. They want to go with Chambers to the Bates Motel to find answers about the mysterious disappearances of Marion and Arbogast. But the Sheriff has already done so, before attending church. Mrs. Chambers, typically, is more concerned with the routine and, under the circumstances, more trivial aspects of life, inquiring if Sam and Lila have had breakfast yet. They ignore her.

Chambers, ever the man of law and order, ushers his little group away from the front steps of the church, so they don't interfere with emerging parishioners. Calm and self-assured, he insists he found nothing suspicious at the motel. And after searching the place he is convinced Norman lives there alone. Furthermore, he advises Sam and Lila to file a formal missing persons and theft report with the police. He has complete confidence in the official chain of law enforcement command. Yet *he* is part of that command, and *we* know that Norman successfully deceived him by hiding his mother in the cellar. The Sheriff's wife intercedes to suggest Sam and Lila file their report at the Chambers house, around dinner time, so it will be "nicer." She has no emotional comprehension of what her invited guests are going through. Mrs. Chambers is perhaps what the bank secretary Caroline will eventually become.

As they watch the Sheriff and his wife depart, Sam expresses self-doubt. "Maybe I am the seeing illusions type." Lila, not bothering to look at Sam, simply overrules him. "No. You're not," she replies firmly. By way of giving up on the search for Marion, Sam offers to drive Lila to her hotel. But Lila insists on seeing the Bates Motel in person. Sam half-heartedly concurs and they walk straight towards the backtracking camera as the scene ends. Lila Crane is clearly the dominating force in this relationship. We get the feeling that was also the case with Sam and his former wife. A relationship which ended in divorce and recrimination. If Lila and Marion are of like personality, would a marriage between Marion and Sam have similarly turned sour after a few years? Perhaps Sam has more in common with Norman than just physical appearance.

Throughout much of this scene, Lila and Sam are pictured between two

"Fairvale Church" signs, complete with white crosses, mounted on either side of the church entrance. The signs seem to visually confine the two characters. Yet Sam and Lila did not attend church. And now they, mostly Lila, refuse to be bound by Sheriff Chamber's faith in established legal procedure. If not for Lila's persistence and Sam's grudging willingness to follow her lead, would the disappearances of Marion and Arbogast ever be solved?

In Sam's truck on the road to the Bates Motel, pictured from the same flat, frontal angle as was Marion when she fled Phoenix and her crime, Sam and Lila discuss strategy. Sam asks the questions. Lila provides the answers. Grimly determined, she declares they will register as man and wife, be shown to their cabin, then "search every inch of the place, inside and out." Her loyalty to Marion is fierce and unqualified. Sam, by contrast, has neither her decisiveness nor her fervor. And this fact hints that his "love" for Marion is suspect. The only love that counts for much in *Psycho* is that of sister for sister and, on the perverse side of that coin, of a son for his mother.

Sam and Lila arrive at the Bates Motel to the revival of Herrmann's passively ominous background music. The Bates house, perched on a hillside, metaphorically advertises its extreme duality with one wall reflecting bright sunshine and another shrouded in shadow. The house visually dominates the low-roofed motel and the arriving pick-up.

Norman peeks out at the unwelcome visitors from between the curtains of his mother's second story bedroom. Predictably, it is the keenly observant Lila who spots him, and informs the typically clueless Sam. Norman saunters down from the house to greet them. Wearing a bright white shirt and light-colored trousers, with his hands tucked in his pockets, he appears non-threatening. But his *attitude* is less shy, cooler and less open than when he greeted Marion Crane on that rainy night so long ago. "Well? I suppose you want a room," he inquires in a casual manner that smacks more of indifference than courtesy. Sam complains about the prospect of an approaching storm (but there isn't a cloud in the sky!) as a lame excuse for wanting a cabin so early in the day. Norman half-smirks to himself and replies with a flippant "Okay" before trotting past his guests and heading for the office. No polite escort or "Go ahead in, please" this time, as there was with Marion.

Inside the office, Hitchcock's camera angle provides us with a double image (one a reflection in the mirror at the end of the service counter) of Sam and Lila rather than Norman. *They* project a false impression this time, as Marion and Arbogast did before them. Norman gives them Cabin #10, located far from the office. He desires no intimacy with them. But Sam insists on registering and getting a receipt first, for his non-existent boss. A camera shot from behind Lila shows her head directly below the key to Cabin #1, Marion's cabin, hanging from a hook on the wall behind the counter. As Sam and Norman go through the pretence of registration, Lila's eyes dart here and there, keenly exploring Norman and his surroundings. Including the back parlor. But she is careful to offer a pleasant smile when Norman looks directly at her.

"I'll get your bags," Norman says in a perfunctory manner. Just doing his job. Until Sam's quick reply, "Haven't any," abruptly changes the tenor of this scene. Big close-ups of the characters echo the intensification of their relations. Norman's hesitation and surprise are quickly followed by a tight shot of Sam looking somewhat guilty, or rather *pretending* to be trying *not* to look guilty. Norman then fakes *not* being suspicious, and offers to show his guests their room.

Like Arbogast before him, Sam tells just enough of the truth, or in this case fake truth, to make Norman uncomfortable, and perhaps careless. He remarks how uncommon it is for a motel desk clerk not to demand payment in advance for a room rented by a man and a woman without luggage. Of course, the sometimes indecisive and dispassionate Sam is in his element here. How often did he register at the Phoenix hotel so he and Marion could enjoy an afternoon rendezvous?

Caught in a careless mistake and not wanting to appear naïve or unusual, Norman demands ten dollars prepayment for the cabin, then flashes Sam a big smile intended to convey his understanding of the situation (Sam and Lila engaged in an illicit affair) but instead unwittingly betrays his momentary lapse of confidence. Sam's return glance, as he hands Norman the money, expresses more hostility and suspicion than it does empathy between two men of the world. Norman starts to move out from behind the desk to show his guests to their cabin. Sam interrupts him to request a receipt. Struggling to maintain self-control and a façade of nonchalance, Norman obliges.

A facial resemblance between Anthony Perkins and John Gavin is most noticeable in this scene, and in particular during the exchange of close-ups in the office. If Norman Bates is *Psycho*'s most prominent concealed monster, Sam exhibits a hint of the same potential. Previously not very engaged in, and at times annoyed by, Lila's determined hunt for her sister, Sam *becomes* engaged in this scene. There is a predatory quality about him as he methodically peels away Norman's façade of confidence, normality and innocence. He is significantly taller than Norman, and his dark suit contrasts with Norman's white shirt, in the same way Arbogast's dark suit counterpointed Sam's white shirt when they first met at Sam's hardware store. In spite of our conscience and the memory of Marion Crane, we feel empathy for Norman's increasingly threatened situation.

Lila, also in close-up, and unusually passive during the tense face-off between Sam and Norman, takes the cabin key from Norman, announces "I'll go on ahead," and quickly leaves the office. Norman watches her go with a suspicious, predatory look in his eyes. the equal of Sam's gaze at Norman a few moments earlier. It is remarkable how this little fragment of a scene, with no physical or verbal violence to speak of, illustrates so subtly the darker shades of human nature. Sam Loomis, so wishy-washy in the previous scene, suddenly displays a capacity for deception and aggression matching the metaphorical anger of the grill on his truck and the frustrated anger he expressed about his dead father and ex-wife in *Psycho*'s first scene. Bullying Norman is *his* route to power.

Alone outside the office for a moment before Sam and Norman join her, Lila tries the door to Cabin #1 and discovers it's unlocked. Closing it quickly, she "casually" heads for Cabin #10. From the office doorway, Norman glances suspiciously after her, but is blocked by the larger, black-attired, somewhat intimidating figure of Sam, who informs Norman that he and his "wife" don't need any further assistance. "Don't bother yourself, we'll find it" falsely implies that Sam and Lila are doing Norman a favor. He need not *bother* himself to help them. But we see Norman's worried expression, then observe from his point of view as the suspicious guests make their way to the distant Cabin #10, at the far end of the motel. Far from his observation. Perhaps he *should* have given them Cabin #1, spied on them through the peephole in the back parlor, and thereby discovered the details of their plot against him.

Inside Cabin #10, Sam sits on the bed with his back to Lila as she urges the case for investigating Cabin #1, "no matter how much it hurts." Surprisingly, he agrees. But he continues to face away from Lila as she builds a rational argument for their invasion, An argument based on simple, conventional, desperate financial need. A logical reason for Norman to have disposed of Marion in order to steal her stolen $40,000. Sam finally turns to face Lila, but only to *challenge* her. He doesn't argue against the motive she attributes to Norman, a motive that turns out to be completely false, but rather against their ability to *prove* it. Ever since *Psycho*'s first scene, in a Phoenix hotel room, Sam has been a defeatist at heart, convinced he can do nothing to improve his or anyone else's situation. Even the letter of reconciliation he was writing to Marion when Lila interrupted him at the hardware store offered his lover the prospect of as much shared misery as happiness.

Lila is no defeatist. Despite her misunderstanding of Norman's real reason for killing Marion, her dedication to finding proof against him overwhelms Sam's passive pessimism. She moves closer to Sam to plead her case further, explaining that Arbogast's mysterious disappearance strongly suggests the detective discovered something about Marion and was somehow stopped from returning to Fairvale to share that information. A lingering tight shot of Sam's face captures the new fire of determination Lila has stoked within him. We can see it especially in his eyes. And the facial resemblance between Sam and Norman is now disturbingly pronounced. No, Sam is not on the verge of becoming a homicidal maniac. But when he gets off the bed he moves and speaks with new passion. He tells Lila if they are spotted by Norman while heading for Cabin #1, "we're just taking the air." As we saw briefly in the motel office moments earlier, Sam is once again taking an *active* role in the investigation, not just reluctantly following Lila's lead.

The camera observes Sam and Lila from approximately what *was* Norman's last known vantage point as they stroll along the boardwalk from Cabin #10 to Cabin #1. Herrmann's passively sinister music reminds us of the lurking though unseen homicidal menace at the Bates Motel, but also the threat Sam and Lila pose to *Norman's* security. Sam checks the office to make sure Norman is absent before he and Lila enter Cabin #1 and begin to search it. Their search is ironically reminiscent of Marion's search for a hiding place for the stolen money. They, albeit in the fraudulent guise of a married couple, or an unmarried couple *pretending* to be married, seek to uncover evidence of a crime. Marion sought to conceal one.

Lila is the first to enter the bathroom, to which Norman previously closed the door, as if to block out the memory of what happened there. Sam follows her. They now perform as a team. Not a romantic couple, as in Hitchcock's *North by Northwest*, *The Thirty-Nine Steps* or *The Lady Vanishes*, but as an investigative team. A worthy substitute for the missing detective Arbogast and the incurious Sheriff Chambers. Hitchcock's overhead camera makes of them almost a single unit as they simultaneously discover separate clues about what happened to Marion. Sam notices the unusual absence of a shower curtain while Lila retrieves a scrap of paper from the toilet. A scrap on which is written the amount 40,000. Of course, by having Sam visually overlap Lila for a moment, Hitchcock was also able to conceal Lila physically reaching into the toilet bowl to fish out the evidence — something to which the overly sensitive movie censors of the day might have objected.

Whether because Lila is still the dominant member of their team, or the evidence she discovers is more compelling than Sam's, the two of them ignore the missing shower curtain and focus on the scrap of paper. Carefully preserving that scrap in his wallet, Sam prudently dampens Lila's enthusiasm for what it might prove. As he points out, Norman never disputed the fact that Marion stayed at the motel. Though, unbeknownst to these two characters, he did initially try to conceal it from Arbogast. The number written on the scrap of paper is circumstantially suspicious, but it doesn't prove Norman stole the money.

Never discouraged or diverted, Lila quickly concludes that Norman's mother must have revealed something to Arbogast. Something Lila is determined to learn. Sam cautions her. "I don't like you going into that house alone" makes him sound a bit like a concerned lover. "I can handle a sick old woman," Lila fires back. But their conversation has now moved outside the bathroom. And Lila's over-confidence is visually counter pointed by pictures of birds on the wall behind her. Reminders of the potential for extreme violence that lurks somewhere, in someone, on the Bates property.

Sam prudently offers to divert Norman's attention while Lila searches the Bates house. Equally prudent is his advice that she head straight back to Fairvale, without informing him, if she learns something. Lila keeps Sam motivated. Sam brings caution to their team effort. Out of what began as mutual hostility and suspicion emerges something positive and effective, though by no means romantic.

They exit Cabin #1, Sam heading for the office to engage Norman in diversionary conversation while Lila heads back towards Cabin #10. But Sam, and we, are startled to discover Norman standing just inside the office doorway as Sam passes by. "Looking for me?" Norman asks in a confident, suspicious manner. A stuffed bird is visible above and behind his head. It could be another token of menace, except that it looks more like a game bird than a bird of prey. And Norman *is* the victim here, in a sense. Sam deceives him with a lie about his wife needing sleep, then physically blocks the doorway when it appears Norman wants to exit. He suggests a conversation inside, to which Norman agrees. Then Sam surreptitiously signals Lila to proceed with their plan as he follows Norman into the office.

Herrmann's music resumes in a more tense vein now as Lila slips behind the motel and heads for the intimidating house on the hill. The back of the motel, which we have never before seen, is a dump site for discarded objects. Visually evocative remnants of the Bates family past. Empty packing crates, never used by Norman to pack up and leave this desolate place. An old box spring from a bed. Which bed, and used by whom? Mrs. Bates and her lover? An abandoned mop, though not the one Norman used to clean up the bloody mess following Marion's murder. *That* mop is buried even deeper, in the trunk of the car at the bottom of the swamp, even *further* out back of the motel.

Most striking of all the garbage is an ancient, rusting, dilapidated automobile, half concealed in shadow and half mercilessly exposed to the glare of the midday sun. Its prominent headlights and grill vaguely resemble a face, like the front of Sam's truck in two earlier scenes, or the automobiles that seemed to follow Marion's as she guiltily fled Phoenix. There is something unsettling about it. From a dramatic standpoint, the old wreck is a tangible relic of a distant family past that weighs so heavily on Norman's life in the present. Dead, yes. Inert, definitely, But not gone, and certainly not forgotten. Like old memories that lurk in the backwaters of Norman's sad and lonely life, exerting a corrosive influence on everything he sees, hears, feels and does. It is Norman's nightmarish version of Charles Foster Kane's sled, Rosebud, in *Citizen Kane*. Not a (false) reminder of better times long past, but a ghostly echo of past events too horrible for Norman to fully confront in the present. And the dead "eyes" of that ancient ghost seem to pitilessly observe an unsuspecting Lila from behind as she advances up the hill towards the house. The house where past and present overlap and intermingle in an even more disturbing, dangerous manner.

Hitchcock employs his practically patented mix of subjective forward tracking and partly subjective (movement matching the character's even as the camera observes her) backtracking shots as Lila climbs the hill towards the Bates house. From this frontal angle the house still looks sinister, but also more noticeably rundown than in previous scenes, when we viewed it from more oblique angles. The exterior is unpainted and badly weathered, exposed to the elements. What passes for a front lawn is overgrown, uncared for, with unpruned trees. The silhouette of an ancient birdbath stands far to the right. But there are no birds in sight. And we *hear* no signs of life either. In retrospect the birdbath, like Norman's collection of stuffed birds, seems to foreshadow Hitchcock's next movie, *The Birds*. But in *Psycho* the birdbath is a dead, unused structure. It's as though the Bates house and grounds have sucked out of the very atmosphere the life, joy and animation a sunny day might otherwise bring.

Lila approaches the house rapidly and fearlessly, at first. The backtracking camera cuts closer and closer to her face, and her extraordinary eyes, which beautifully tell the story of her intense, probing curiosity. A curiosity reflecting her devotion to her missing sister, but also quite threatening from the perspective of the reclusive, secretive Norman Bates and his mother, for whom the retreating camera is virtually a stand-in. For a moment Lila's determined approach to the Bates house seems to menace *us*. But as she nears the house, Lila's expression shifts from curiosity and determination to wariness. Her pace slows, then stops as she confronts the building's inhospitable façade, with its antiquated, ornate front steps, porch and door. Herrmann's music accompanies Lila all the way up the hill, one set of notes ascending with her, but another set, played simultaneously, *descending* as she nears this joyless heart of darkness. Lila's modern hairstyle and clothing (circa 1960) contrast vividly with the old fashioned house and its unkempt yard. She seems surrounded by an alien, hostile environment.

Her determination revived, Lila quietly enters the Bates house, into which she has *not* been invited. Domestic invasions, of various types and for various reasons, are a recurring theme in this and the other two movies discussed in this book. In *The Birds* Melanie Daniels surreptitiously invades the Brenner house. And is eventually attacked in that very house by invading birds. In *Halloween* the audience invades the privacy of the Myers home in the first scene, in subjective company with a character who has every right to be there but whose actions violate the even more private space of his sister's bedroom.

In dead silence Lila glances around the entryway, then prudently closes the front door behind her, leaving the camera and us outside as we nervously watch her (we're now emotionally *with* Lila rather than threatened by her), through veiled curtains, advance deeper into the house. The house where Mrs. Bates, presumably concealed there earlier by her son, awaits.

Inside the motel office, Sam engages Norman in conversation. The desk separates them. Sam sits in near the duplicitous mirror, playing his phony role as married traveling salesman and trying to draw out Norman on the topic of loneliness. But Norman begins their conversation saying very little, revealing even less, and looking very relaxed, with his hands concealed in his pocket and one foot propped up as he leans against the parlor doorframe. "Drive me crazy" Sam postulates about the emotional effects of isolation such as Norman has experienced. "I think that would be a rather extreme reaction. Don't you?" Norman casually replies. He can deal with this type of intrusion from the outside world. But Sam keeps needling him to elicit a confession.

On the second floor landing of the Bates house, Lila approaches the door to Mother's room. The same door from which Arbogast's killer emerged with a knife not long ago. The camera initially observes Lila from the bottom of the stairwell. She appears as a small, vulnerable figure of modernity surrounded by old world décor: heavy wooden railings, ornate worn-out wallpaper, and a thickly framed portrait of a woman in frilly Victorian dress. The black shape of the Cupid statuette, in extreme foreground on the first floor, seems to point its sharp arrow menacingly at the intruder. True enough, the *real* danger to Lila in this scene comes from Norman's pathologically repressed and perverted romantic impulses.

Lila knocks lightly on the door to Mrs. Bates' bedroom and calls out her name. The camera cuts from an extreme long shot to a big, nearly subjective close-up of the back of Lila's head as she opens the door and enters. Herrmann's music resumes on a note of hushed, pulsing anticipation. Something dark and sharp appears over Lila's head. But it's only the wing of a stuffed bird mounted on the far wall.

We observe Lila glancing around the room before we share her view of it. And it is a breathtaking sight. An enormous, ornate bed frame. Victorian style clutter everywhere, yet immaculately tidy. Seemingly a lived-in room, but unoccupied at the moment. Our minds immediately place Mrs. Bates downstairs, in the cellar, towards which we saw Norman carrying her a few scenes ago.

Lila seems curious and amazed at the room's appearance, especially after the seeing the house's unkempt façade and yard outside. A sink with a cake of soap and a half-filled glass of water confirms recent occupation. Among other furnishings are an elegant, half-nude statuette of a woman, classical lyre at her feet, seemingly poised to take flight. But the same object casts its shadow double on the wall behind it. Advancing further into the room, Lila takes note of the richly carved fireplace, recently used if the wood in it is any indication. Lila opens the door to an armoire containing old-fashioned women's dresses, again testifying to a living occupant. Then her eyes are attracted to a mirrored dressing table crowded with personal grooming items. At the center of those items lies a statuette of elegantly posed, ruffle-sleeved, folded female hands resting serenely on a pillow. Curiosity draws her and us (we share in Lila's illicit entry and investigation) towards the unusual object. The camera zooms in to a close up of the hands, which because they are so convincingly rendered make a somewhat disturbing impression. They appear *severed* from their owner's body. In addition to being another example of Victorian style, the hands may be Hitchcock's grim reference to the historical inspiration for Norman Bates. The Wisconsin serial killer Ed Gein, who butchered some of his victims.

Glancing into the mirror atop the dressing table, Lila is frightened by its reflection of yet another reflection, of her own back, from a free-standing dressing mirror located behind her. All we have to fear is ... ourselves? Recovering quickly from this illusion of danger, Lila's interest turns elsewhere, off-screen, then abruptly changes direction again, to something different. By keeping his camera on Lila, Hitchcock keeps us as attuned to the character's somewhat impulsive behavior (like her sister's) as he does to the objects of her curiosity. The latest object to capture her attention is the mattress on the bed, which is badly indented in the shape of a reclining human body. Lila starts to examine the indentation, but is distracted yet again by something else off-screen before drawing any conclusion about the disfigured mattress.

Back at the office Sam and his mirrored reflection face off in profile against Norman, on the other side of the desk. Sam, standing now and appearing both taller and physically stronger than Norman, moves in for the kill, half-accusing Norman of being willing to do anything to escape his failing business and lonely life. Norman's calm and self-confidence have eroded. He carelessly refers to "this place" as "my only world," insisting aggressively that he led a very happy childhood in the care of his mother. His defense is unraveling, as it did under Arbogast's slyly ruthless inquiry.

In the house, Lila finds her way to Norman's bedroom. Herrmann's music, pausing during our brief cutaway to Sam and Norman, resumes on the same note of suspenseful anticipation as Lila enters the cramped confines of Norman's inner sanctum. He hasn't even appropriated the master bedroom for himself during the years since his mother's death. His memories of her are stronger than his regard for his own life in the present.

The room is divided against itself, containing tokens of both childhood and adulthood. Among the former are toys and a variety of stuffed animals, including a rabbit sitting on Norman's cramped, unkempt bed. Only a cot, really. So different from the grandiose bed in his mother's room. The rabbit wears a perpetual frown, betraying the sadness that plagues Norman's life but that he tries very hard to conceal. Herrmann's background music for Lila's surreptitious tour of Mrs. Bates' and Norman's private sanctuaries evokes melancholy as well as suspense. There is an acute sense of tragic waste in what Lila and we discover. Almost forgotten, for a moment, are the tragic losses of two lives who had to pay for that waste.

Elsewhere in the room Lila finds objects more associated with the adult Norman's interests. A record player and its LP recording of Beethoven's 3rd Symphony, the "Eroica." Or Heroic. Does Norman fancy himself a "hero" sometimes, in his daydreams? An atmosphere of acute failure permeates this little room. Images of old-fashioned sailing vessels speak of a desire for escape and adventure that obviously eluded Norman in real life. Lila finds a book with no printing on the spine. She opens it. Unlike the record player, Hitchcock doesn't show us what is inside the book. Only Lila's reaction to it. A diary? Unlikely, since Norman is not inclined to explore his own demons, except briefly with Marion. Perhaps a diary "with nothing there, for an empty life" (Durgnat, p. 205). Some critics have suggested the book is pornographic. But we cannot tell from Lila's brief reaction to it.

Back in the motel office, our profile in confrontation grows more intense. The index finger of Norman's left hand taps nervously on the counter and his jaw muscles clench as he tries to evade Sam's now open accusation that he did something criminal in order to liberate himself and his mother from their dying motel. Norman tells Sam to leave, then more aggressively orders him to "Shut up!" Not a typical outburst for the reserved motel keeper, and something we've only heard him say once before, allegedly to his mother, when she railed against him and Marion Crane.

At the mention of Marion's 40,000 dollars, about which Norman knows nothing, Norman retreats for safety into his parlor. Sam pursues him there, relentlessly pressuring him to confess. In a shot of both characters in the same camera frame, with Norman facing away from his tormentor, their faces are rendered equally menacing by shadow. Hitchcock encourages us to feel Norman's fear of Sam as well as the danger posed by Norman himself. Sam threatens to get the truth about the missing money from Norman's mother. Norman panics, making *him* more dangerous. Imagining the worst, he demands to know the whereabouts of Sam's companion. Glancing out the parlor window at the house above, Norman suddenly understands the purpose of Sam engaging him in conversation. It's a diversionary tactic. Simultaneously, Sam looks off-screen in the opposite direction, hoping that Lila has obtained some information and departed in his truck.

Inside the house, Lila returns downstairs after snooping in the bedrooms of mother and son. At that same moment, Sam and Norman struggle in the parlor. Norman picks up a decorative jar from an ornate table and bashes the bigger man over the head with it. Sam collapses, unconscious. Background music returns, no longer passive and contemplative, but now an active participant in violent action. Norman rushes out of the office. Lila sees him, from the entryway, approaching the house. She hides on the stairs leading down to the cellar, directly under the main stairwell. Another double image. Norman enters through the front door, glances briefly down the hallway in Lila's direction, his head tilting like a bird's listening for its prey, then races upstairs. Lila is about to ascend the cellar stairs and wisely flee the house when her own curiosity, the cat killer, draws her back down, deeper into the Bates darkness.

Through windows in the cellar door, Lila can see a clutter of stuff on the other side. The possibility of more clues to Marion's disappearance? Like her sister, Lila is impulsively impatient and recklessly brave. She opens the door quietly and enters the cellar, where we, though not she, expect to encounter Mrs. Bates. Passing through a dimly lit room full of junk, she enters yet another, buried even deeper inside the Bates house. A room in which Norman's deepest secret resides. Though better lit than its predecessor, this one is lower, and if possible more dank and creepier. In the way of many unfinished cellars. Illumination comes from a single light bulb fixture hanging from the ceiling. Norman has thoughtfully left a light on for his mother, who sits in a chair in a corner of the room, with her back to the entrance and to us.

Mrs. Bates wears a shawl over her shoulders, evoking age and fragility. But we saw her move quickly and violently when motivated to do so. Her potential threat to Lila permeates the atmosphere of this cramped room, and fuels the background music. Mrs. Bates' gray hair is done up in a bun, old-fashioned and prim. In contrast to Lila's, but reminiscent of Carlotta's and Madeline's in *Vertigo*, another complex story about the past weighing heavily on the present. And foreshadowing Lydia's in *The Birds*, another character haunted by past tragedy and corrosively affecting the life of her son in the present.

Believing Mrs. Bates to be alive and in possession of information about Marion, Lila calls out her name and touches her on the shoulder. Audiences watching *Psycho* for the first time, and knowing nothing of its secrets, might expect a reaction of lethal proportions. In a vivid close-up of the back of her head, the old woman turns to her right. But it is a purely physical reaction, albeit exaggerated for dramatic purposes, to the slight pressure from Lila's fingers. Mrs. Bates turns to face her intruder, jerking to a stop that mocks the animation of a true living being. Her face is nothing more than desiccated, wrinkled flesh stretched tightly over a skull. Grotesquely large white teeth protrude from a lipless mouth, forming the hideous approximation of a smile.

Lila screams at this shockingly unexpected apparition. A full-throated, prolonged scream of terror. Her right arm reflexively recoils up and back, striking the light fixture and setting it in motion. Another shock follows closely on the heels of the first. Approaching footsteps draw Lila's attention to the doorway. Norman rushes in, wearing a gray wig and one of his mother's old dresses, and brandishing a large kitchen knife. He wears a maniacal grin on his face, as cheerless as the one on his mother's. Herrmann's music too goes insane, repeating the shower cue as Norman attacks Lila. This is, in dramatic terms, a tricky moment. A man wearing a woman's dress and wig is not a conventional figure of menace. An audience not caught up in the story, not inclined to think about the depth and nature of the monster's pathology, could easily laugh at Norman's bizarre impersonation, But in more than one respect *Psycho* thwarts expectations and ignores convention.

Sam arrives in the nick of time to grab Norman from behind, restraining him. Norman twists and turns to escape his grasp and fulfill his obsessive, contradictory need to both protect his mother and vent his sexual fury. In his writhing, he knocks the wig off his own head. Hitchcock's camera closes in on the struggle, then backs away to give us a more comprehensive view of Norman's horrifying facial and bodily contortions as he is forcibly separated from his disguise and deprived of his goal. It is a spectacle both frightening and tragic. How far this young man has descended from the figure of intelligence, compassion and shy flirtation we first encountered with Marion.

For Lila, the spectacle of Norman's psychotic tantrum, almost childish in its extremity, is merely terrifying, not compelling. The scene ends with a huge close-up of Mrs. Bates' mask-like face, the wavering light from off-screen lending her eyeless sockets and lipless grin a false, ghoulish semblance of movement and life. As her psychotic son tried to do using his inadequate taxidermy skills and by conceding to his memory of her much of his own life.

The county courthouse. A crowd of curious onlookers and a television crew are gathered outside. The private lives of Norman Bates and Marion Crane have suddenly become public fodder. Inside the Office of the Chief of Police, Sheriff Chambers speaks with Sam and Lila as they all await the arrival of a psychiatrist who is interviewing Norman. And once again the Sheriff's investigative skills prove inadequate. He admits his failure to get any information out of Norman, despite their long acquaintance. Long perhaps. But intimate, no. Marion probably learned more about Norman during their brief conversation in the parlor behind the motel office than Chambers did in years of "knowing" Norman. Does he really know *anybody*, even his own wife, intimately? Still, his intentions are good. Seeing Lila pull her coat around her shoulders, he inquires if she is warm enough. Such trivial matters are of little concern to her at the moment. She sits up with eager anticipation as the psychiatrist enters.

The psychiatrist and his explanation of Norman's psychosis have frequently been criticized as one of *Psycho*'s few failures. I disagree. As he settles into his story, derived from an interview with Norman, he is shown in a frontal medium shot backed by various objects in the Chief's office. A black filing cabinet, perhaps filled with official forms and case records. A map of the area, hanging on the wall. An electric fan, with its potentially dangerous blades encased in the usual safety cage — a neat little metaphor of human nature, as depicted throughout this film. Photographs of men on motorcycles. Is the Chief of Police a closet rebel? Outlaw? A Marlon Brando wannabe from *The Wild One*? But the motorcycle riders in the photographs are all policemen. Now there's a chilling thought. Massed policemen with the mentality of thugs but the authority of the law to back them up. Gestapo? Not in this movie, fortunately. That's a *different* sort of nightmare.

Actor Simon Oakland was a curious choice to play the psychiatrist. Typically cast as a tough guy, even a villain, he brings an intensity to his performance that gives the character a strong personality. A far cry from the bearded, grandfatherly, German-accented psychiatrist more typical of Hollywood movies at the time. Oakland's black hair and intense eyes recollect both Sam's and Norman's. With confidence, authority, a theatrical flair and even a trace of smugness, the psychiatrist provides his fascinated audience with a clinical and believable explanation of Norman's bizarre relationship with Mrs. Bates. It's the tale of a boy thoroughly dominated by his tyrannical, demanding mother. A young man consumed by jealousy when his mother takes up with a strange man. Norman kills them both, then out of unbearable guilt gives over a sizable portion of his own personality in an effort to sustain the illusion that his mother still lives.

Everybody has his or her own agenda. The psychiatrist seems fascinated with Norman Bates, the case study. Less so with the moral and emotional consequences of Norman's crimes. The psychiatrist's narrative is interrupted by Lila, who briefly re-focuses his, and our, concern on what is for *her*, and presumably for Sam, the most important question. Did Norman kill Marion? Yes. Then the District Attorney interrupts, thinking ahead to a possible trial. He challenges what he assumes is the psychiatrist's attempt to justify an insanity plea by Norman. But the doctor deftly sidesteps that challenge. "A psychiatrist doesn't lay the groundwork. He merely tries to explain it." "Merely" is an interesting choice of words, perhaps unwittingly downplaying the many potential ramifications, including legal, of his professional explanation.

In addition to filling in gaps with new information, the psychiatrist's narrative seems to fit the facts of Norman's life, as we know them, even if his re-creation cannot match the emotional depth or understanding that Hitchcock's camera and soundtrack gave us. Concluding his presentation, the psychiatrist lights up a cigarette. A sly little joke by Hitchcock? Lighting up a cigarette is, or was, a movie cliché signaling post-coital satisfaction, especially back in the days when movie censorship prevented anything close to on-screen intercourse. Being the center of attention, solving a mystery and having his expertise accepted almost without question is an emotionally satisfying experience, even for a man trained to dispassionately study the human mind. When a policeman enters the office to ask if he can give Norman a blanket to ward off a chill, the psychiatrist replies offhandedly, "Sure." Neither Norman's comfort, Lila and Sams' grief nor the District Attorney's trial tactics are of immediate concern to him. And it probably adds to his self-esteem that the Chief of Police waits for *his* okay before giving the policeman permission to take the blanket to Norman. This short scene not only helps clarify Norman's story, it is also a dramatic little addendum to the much larger and more detailed story of self-esteem, frustration and power played out earlier among the film's major characters.

Leaving behind the self-satisfied psychiatrist, the placated Chief of Police, the grieving Lila Crane and the who-knows-what Sam Loomis, we follow the blanket down a corridor, stopping just outside the door to Norman's holding room. From outside that doorway, we *hear* the voice of Norman's mother, or rather Norman's re-creation of it, politely thank the policeman for the blanket. The policeman returns to the corridor. The door is locked. Norman is alone again. Or maybe not. At any rate, there is a police ban on access to him. The cop carrying the blanket to Norman shooed away two people standing in the corridor before he entered Norman's room.

Cutting to a long shot of Norman seated inside the holding room, the camera allows us to defy the police ban, bypass the locked door and invade Norman's privacy. Wrapped in a blanket, his small figure stands out starkly against the white, almost featureless institutional wall behind him. A closed, locked, barred window is visible at the far right of the camera frame. But even that token of entrapment disappears as the camera, and we, slowly close in on Norman, who at the beginning of this shot isn't even pictured at center screen. He's off to the left. Beside the point. A pathetic, vulnerable, lonely figure seated on a chair, huddled beneath a blanket. Herrmann's music returns after being absent throughout the psychiatrist's tale. It restores emotional life to what was, for the doctor, just an interesting clinical case, and perhaps an opportunity to flex his own power in the world.

Slowly, inexorably, Hitchcock's camera advances on Norman, its pitiless gaze examining him at closer and closer range ("The cruel eyes studying you," Norman once described it) as we listen to Norman's re-creation of his dead mother's voice condemn him for crimes he committed in her name. In the history of film has there been a more dramatic portrait of a personality divided against itself? Norman shakes his head and pouts slightly as his dominant mother persona verbally rejects him. The worst kind of rejection. "They'll put him away now, as I should have, years ago. He was always *bad*." And she does so in order to protect *herself* from police scrutiny and guilt over the murders of Marion, Arbogast and others.

Of course, Norman *is* the murderer. And his first victim was his *mother*. But he condemns himself now, in her voice and in her name, in order to protect his hopelessly fantasized, idyllic memory of *her*. A memory that does not square with the psychiatrist's probably accurate description of a "clinging, demanding" woman who warped Norman's childhood beyond recovery. It is painful to watch Norman, in striking full-frontal close-up, sacrifice himself on behalf of his not-so-sainted mother. Especially after we saw and heard glimpses of the sensitive, intelligent and kind young man he seemed capable of being with Marion Crane, who was nothing like Mrs. Bates.

Norman's eyes dart around suspiciously as mother's voice speaks of the outside world (which includes everyone, now that he/she has terminated all intimate contact with other people) spying on him with evil intent. "Let them see what kind of a person I am," she declares defiantly. She deliberately, deceptively shows her best face to the world. Another mask. Then she glances down at a fly crawling across Norman's hand. A fly like the two she violently exterminated back at the Bate's Motel and house. But not this time. Norman's mother persona, manufactured out of desperate need and desperate guilt, must be preserved in his mind as innocent of all crimes attributed to *him*. Of course everyone else knows the story, or enough of it, to identify the guilty parties. This pose of innocence, this final triumph of mother's memory over son, occurs solely inside the mind of Norman Bates.

"Why, she wouldn't even harm a fly," crows Mrs. Bates in her most soothing old lady voice as Norman slowly raises his head and looks straight into the camera, his previously shy smile now transformed into an aggressively malevolent grin. We are face-to-face with madness. The reassembled horror of a shattered mind that once seemed worthy of better things. The psychiatrist's clinical, dispassionate explanation of madness is now displaced by our chillingly intimate proximity to a living example of it. The human potential for self-deception and violence stares directly at us. Norman Bates is now a mirror image of the very worst in ourselves. And it is not a comforting moment.

All of *Psycho*'s reflected images coalesce into this single face-to-face encounter. And I cannot think of a more terrifying image in the history of film. It offers two shocks in one: a chillingly intimate, mirror-image-he-could-be-us encounter with "the irretrievable annihilation of a human being" (Wood, p. 149), and Hitchcock's "Gotcha!" moment (Thomson, p. 90), when the director wrings one last fright, albeit from a position of passivity, from a monster who is now exposed, captured and subdued. Norman looks *through* the camera and directly at *us*. Seeming to breech the invisible cinematic barrier that shielded us not only from the kind of violence he inflicted on Marion and Arbogast, and tried to inflict on Lila, but from the recognition of Norman's all-too human origins. If Alfred Hitchcock suffered from his own demons, including worries about his appearance and weight, maybe he relished rubbing our collective noses in the possibility of malevolence and madness merged with youthful good looks and boyish charm. Sometimes the boogeyman is conveniently hideous. Sometimes not.

Everything about the next-to-last shot in *Psycho* is beautifully executed. The dark shadow surrounding Norman's piercing stare. The black, slightly tousled, boyish hair. The same open collar that helped make Norman appear so friendly and welcoming when Marion arrived at the motel. The sheltering blanket around his unevenly sloped shoulders, suggesting a fragility sharply contradicted by his malevolent, insanely *in*vulnerable stare. The blank wall behind him, giving us nothing else to which we might more comfortably divert our attention. The madness motif that creeps back into Bernard Herrmann's extraordinary music, laying out Norman's twisted psychological guts for us one more time.

As if Norman's horrific grin and predatory stare were not enough, Hitchcock briefly overlaps it with the toothy death mask of Mrs. Bates. Revealing the mask behind the mask, so to speak. It's Mrs. Hyde lurking behind Mr. Hyde, Dr. Jekyll having fled the scene entirely. The shock of seeing, for the first time in the same shot, Norman's youthful charm blended with and thoroughly corrupted by the homicidal hostility of his re-creation of Mrs. Bates.

The camera dissolves to another gruesome disinterment of the violent past. From a position overhead, we watch a clanking, heavy metal chain pull Marion's white car out of the black muck of the swamp in which Norman buried it. Repressed memories resurfacing. Concealed crimes regurgitated and exposed to a world that likes to think better of itself. Herrmann's musical score growls out the madness motif once more, this time at full volume. Another slap in the face of human complacency. But in resurrecting Marion's muddied/bloodied automobile, Hitchcock also reminds us of Marion Crane, whose life and untimely death still matter. And the loving devotion of a sister whose determination, persistence, deception (of Norman) and illegal entry (of the Bates house) led to the mystery of Marion's disappearance being solved and to the recovery of her body from the foul muck in which it was cruelly buried.

"The End" title appears in white letters, matching Marion's car (which, when she traded in her darker car for it, was itself an attempt to avoid the *appearance* of guilt), but is a moment later eradicated by invading black lines that slash across the screen and soon blot out everything. Herrmann's music concludes with a double, stabbing downbeat. *Psycho* ends, in visual terms, by savagely re-burying the evidence of guilt it dug up. Few films pursue the emotional vulnerability and fallibility of human beings as relentlessly as does this one. There is not a single character in it that provides the audience with a simple, easy way out of that final, mirror image confrontation with Norman

Bates. Sam, Caroline and her husband and mother, Cassidy, Lowery, the car salesman, Sheriff Chambers and his wife, the psychiatrist. Even Lila. None of them are as self-deluded or violent as Norman. But none of them are without some degree of flaw either, and with at least the potential for worse. Even Marion Crane, the film's most likable character, experiences a moment where she *relishes* the vengeful impact of her crime on its principal victim (Cassidy), who is hardly innocent himself. And at that moment Hitchcock gives us a portrait of Marion that foreshadows the final portrait of Norman, his madness now fully, unreservedly expressed by his face.

But *Psycho* is not merely a relentless expose of human delusion, selfishness and cruelty. That depressing portrait is balanced by moments of understanding and compassion that transform violence and cruelty into tragic loss rather than a mere parade of horrors. Most notably the parlor scene between Marion and Norman. Lila's tireless efforts to find Marion. And her exploration of the profoundly melancholy world of Norman's and his mother's bedrooms in the Bates house, with their terrible evocations of loneliness and waste. The highway patrolman's routine concern for Marion's safety, before he begins to suspect her of some misdeed. Even the infamous shower scene and its prolonged aftermath contribute to the film in this regard. The violence done to Marion. The desperate hopelessness of her final moments, dying alone in a strange motel bathroom. The indifference with which her body is subsequently disposed. All of these things emphasize the fact that her life *mattered*. And that it is shocking to see her treated so callously. Even Norman's desperate attempts to protect his mother, or at least his fantasy of her, by so painstakingly concealing her crime, is an example, deeply ironic to be sure, of the human potential to care passionately for others. And like *Psycho*, Hitchcock's other horror film, *The Birds*, offers the audience some glimpses of human warmth and compassion that make deliberate cruelty, unreasoning fear and unlucky accident a shocking waste of what should make life worth living.

# 2

# Hitchcock's *The Birds*
## *Hidden Talons*

Clouds of black smoke billow across a movie screen, enveloping a pattern of straight, vertical lines formed by the metal wall of a munitions plant. Chaos displacing order in 1942's *Saboteur*. Black smoke belches from an approaching train, hovering ominously over the vulnerable figure of a small boy standing on a railway platform in *Shadow of a Doubt* (1943). The train brings the boy's uncle, a serial killer, from urban to small town America. Massed, rigid formations of soldiers, tanks and missile launchers parade through Moscow streets to the grimly enthusiastic strains of a military march in *Topaz*, a Cold War thriller from 1969.

Apocalyptic impressions lurk within many of the films of Alfred Hitchcock, but seldom dominate on the surface. The shocking shower scene in *Psycho* (1960) is apocalyptic in its intensity, but only on a deeply personal level, for victim Marion Crane. Unless one views the scene in broader terms, as a game changer in the history of how violence is portrayed in the movies.

*Personal*. That's the key. After the munitions factory conflagration, *Saboteur* settles down to its hero's desperate efforts to clear his name of sabotage charges, stop Nazi sympathizers from wreaking further havoc on America's military defenses, and romance a reluctant heroine who doesn't quite believe in his innocence. *Shadow of a Doubt* focuses on a single family's, and more especially one teenage girl's, reactions to the presence of evil in their midst. And following a very public display of Soviet saber-rattling in *Topaz*, Hitchcock switches gears to explore the fortunes of a much smaller cast of characters enmeshed in Cold War intrigue.

*The Birds* (1963) is Hitchcock's most overtly apocalyptic movie, containing many memorable images and sounds conveying the potential for doom on a large scale. Yet at the same time it is one of his most intensely intimate stories, involving us in the developing relations among a handful of lead characters who, conversely, behave less violently or criminally than many of their counterparts in other Hitchcock films. Not a spy, thief or killer among them.

The film's blending of extremes, of relatively normal people working out their anxieties in the midst of a growing external threat of mass destruction, renders *The Birds* unique in Hitchcock's output. That and the almost seamless way in which the director and his writer, Evan Hunter, interweave these seemingly disparate stories into a dramatically potent whole.

Despite their relative normalcy, each of the four major characters in *The Birds* is caught in a private trap, to continue a theme broached in *Psycho* by Norman Bates during an intimate supper conversation with Marion Crane. None of these traps are as extreme in terms of legality or lethality as those of Norman and Marion. They are, instead, closer to what most of us might experience, and for that reason of equal dramatic importance when juxtaposed and interwoven with larger threats. For upon the resolution of those traps depend the characters' happiness. The bird attacks in Hitchcock's follow-up to *Psycho* are, among other things, amplified metaphorical echoes of the private traps of the film's human characters. As Norman's is of Marion's. As those of Fran and Adamson, a pair of homicidal kidnappers, are of bungling con artists Blanche Tyler and George Lumley in *Family Plot* (1976). In the absence of human perpetrated physical violence in *The Birds*, the bird attacks fulfill Norman's *second* observation about the human condition: "We all go a little mad sometimes."

But the bird attacks are not exclusively reflections of dark human anxieties and urges. They are also the mysterious phenomena of an unpredictable natural world, completely independent of human emotions. In other words, avian violence in *The Birds* both reflects and radically alters the lives of the film's major characters. And on an even broader level of interpretation, they echo Cold War tensions and communal reactions to those tensions, like the massive military parade in *Topaz*. Beginning modestly, then building to a terrifying crescendo, the bird attacks threaten to overwhelm all human endeavors, if not human life itself, in the same way Norman Bates snuffed out the intriguing, private story-in-progress of Marion Crane. It is as though the stuffed raven whose beak pointed at Marion's throat in Norman's parlor while she spoke of escaping the trap she laid for herself suddenly came alive and flew into Hitchcock's next movie, carrying out a literal attack it merely foreshadowed in *Psycho*.

The Daphne du Maurier short story from which Hitchcock's *The Birds* was adapted is an apocalyptic tale with roots in the science fiction of H. G. Wells' *The War of the Worlds* and the very real London blitz of World War Two. Though intimating a large scale catastrophe engulfing London, Europe and possibly the world, du Maurier focuses her reader's attention on two farm families living near the coast of England. One of them takes the threat of bird attacks seriously, and may or may not survive their ordeal. The other does not, and pays dearly for it.

None of du Maurier's characters reappear by name in Hitchcock's film. Nor do they bear much resemblance to their movie counterparts. Perhaps the short story's lead character, a disabled war veteran named Nat Hocken, shares a solitary defensiveness with the movie's lead character, the emotionally abandoned and wounded Melanie Daniels. But du Maurier does not probe much into pre-existing tensions within the Hocken family.

What short story and movie do have in common are the bird attacks themselves: their unexplained cause, their progression from singular to massed, their locations, their linkage to Cold War fears, and the aesthetic means employed to convey the horror they inflict. Nat Hocken notes the *silence* of birds circling overhead prior to an attack. Hitchcock repeats and expands on that silence, at the school playground and inside the Brenner house. Du Maurier includes hawks, falcons and buzzards among the attacking birds, mixing major predators with what are generally viewed as lesser threats, such as seagulls, crows, wrens and sparrows. Hitchcock limits his avian cast to gulls, crows and sparrows, either to emphasize the shock of less obviously predatory species turning on humans or because of practical safety concerns.

Where movie and short story greatly diverge is in their conclusions. Du Maurier ends her tale in the midst of a relentless series of bird attacks on the crumbling defenses of the Hocken farm house. All radio and physical contact with the outside world has ceased. The fate of the entire world seems, by extension, hopeless. How Hitchcock retains that apocalyptic mood without yielding to it entirely is dealt with at the end of the following journey into darkness.

The opening credits of *The Birds* set a style and tone for the rest of the movie. Birds in black silhouette flutter rapidly across a blank white screen. Overlapping them are sky blue credits printed in tidy letters. Visual representations of Nature and human mix. But the credits do not displace each other in standard fashion. Instead of dissolving into or cutting directly to the their successors, each credit breaks up in ragged fragments, imitating the frenzied flapping of bird wings visible behind it. Human names and job titles disintegrate piece by piece. Robin Wood describes the birds in Hitchcock's movie as "a concrete embodiment of the arbitrary and unpredictable, of whatever makes human life and human relationships precarious" (Wood, p. 154). The curiously mechanical feel of the break-up of names and job titles approximates, though is not identical too, *Psycho's* fragmenting and splitting opening credits. Both films deal with emotional turmoil and the breakdown of human order. But *Psycho* does so in starkly private terms. *The Birds* deals with individuals and groups who adhere more closely to social norms, then integrates their stories with a tale of Nature gone mad in a way that both echoes and exacerbates the precariousness of human relations. Andrew Sarris contends, "Hitchcock requires a situation of normalcy, however dull it may seem on the surface, to emphasize the evil abnormality that lurks beneath the surface" (Sarris, p. 87) Before returning to that placid and dangerously complacent surface, the opening credits of *The Birds* foreshadow emotional and moral disintegration to come.

On the soundtrack during the credits we hear various bird calls mixed with the sound of beating wings. Close your eyes for a moment and listen. The beating wings sound like distant gunfire. An eerie token of human warfare in an era of Cold War tension, and an aural blending of bird and human behavior that reinforces the visual mix. That *The Birds* contains no background music is an indication of the importance Hitchcock attached to sound effects as a medium for telling his story. Bird cries resembling human screams and flapping wings that mimic small arms fire could not have done their job with opening title theme music. Not even music as memorable as Bernard Herrmann's for *Psycho*, though Herrmann did have a hand in the sound effects for *The Birds*.

Bird calls carry over into the first scene, set in downtown San Francisco. A distant billboard advertising British Airlines continues the opening credits' analogy between avian and human activities. Other than general urban background noises, the first authentic human sound we hear in the movie is an anonymous whistle directed by a street worker at the film's attractive protagonist, Melanie Daniels, as she walks along a sidewalk. She turns and smiles, flattered by the male attention. The whistle resembles a bird call, and is, after all, something of a human mating call. Albeit a safe, restrained expression of sexual attraction, far removed from Norman's surreptitious spying on and rape-like murder of Marion in *Psycho*. Immediately after acknowledging the whistle, Marion spots a large flock of seagulls circling overhead. Nothing menacing, but unusual enough to strike her as odd. A hint of more disturbing things to come, and an unsettling echo of the bird metaphor in Hitchcock's previous movie.

As Melanie enters Davidson's Pet Shop, Hitchcock himself, making his customary cameo appearance, exits while holding two dogs on leashes. Animal nature restrained by man. Inside the shop all the animals for sale are caged. And in terms of physical appearance, Melanie Daniels conforms to civilized fashions of the day. Her blond hair, make-up, dress, shoes and purse are in perfect order. So much so that she is a striking portrait of elegance. In *Rear Window* (1954) a caged bird in one of the apartments surrounding the central courtyard serves as a metaphor for the various residents, including protagonist L. B. Jeffries. The railings on the apartment balconies add to that impression of confinement.

If the animals in the pet shop are physically restrained, their voices are not. Quite the opposite, their various vocalizations (mating calls? protests? cries of alarm?) are loud and raucous at times. Heading for the bird department on the second level, Melanie questions a sales clerk named Roberta about the peculiarly large flock of seagulls gathered in the sky over San Francisco. Roberta speculates that a storm at sea drove them inland, offering a rational and safe explanation for their atypical behavior. Barring any evidence to the contrary, who would suspect otherwise?

Melanie has ordered a mynah bird, and is disappointed to hear it hasn't arrived. Her reaction to this minor delay informs us that she is accustomed to getting what she wants, when she wants it. Though her impatience is not expressed in an inordinately uncivil manner. She reluctantly agrees to wait while the clerk makes a telephone call to check on the cause of the delay. During their brief conversation, Roberta is pictured against an orderly backdrop of file cabinets, boxes of bird seed and a framed portrait of a bird — the accoutrements of running a pet shop. Melanie, by contrast, is shown against a backdrop of colorful, living, caged birds. And she subsequently proves to be a vibrant, willful personality, trapped less by social convention than by emotional cages in her own mind. Cages which impel her to defy social convention to some degree. The mynah bird she seeks to purchase is, we discover later in the story, one instrument of that defiance.

Mitch Brenner, dressed in a conventional suit and tie befitting his profession as a lawyer, enters the shop and climbs the stairs to the bird sales floor. Hitchcock's camera angles, framing and movements in this scene are as controlled and smooth as is the outward appearance of his characters. Mitch glances at a black bird in a cage, then at Melanie Daniels, dressed in a black dress and black shoes, standing at the sales counter, writing her delivery address on Roberta's notepad. Melanie and the caged bird appear side by side in the same shot.

Understandably, or so it seems at first, Mitch mistakes Melanie for a sales clerk and asks her for help finding a pair of lovebirds. Reacting to his request, Melanie rises into a medium close-up, her movement into the camera frame and the subtle expression of mischief on her face conveying her immediate interest in the handsome stranger. Like the first meeting of Bruno and Guy in *Strangers on a Train* (1951), this chance encounter has far-reaching consequences for the characters involved and several of their acquaintances.

Playing a practical joke on Mitch, she pretends to be the sales clerk he thinks, or seems to think, she is. Their subsequent conversation about birds is a flirtatious game of cat and mouse. But who plays which part? Initially Melanie appears to be the cat, toying with Mitch for her own amusement. Their banter is the stuff of screwball comedy. A lighthearted battle between the sexes. But *The Birds* is not a screwball comedy. And the consequences of the characters' actions are not always amusing.

Mitch seeks a pair of lovebirds as a birthday gift for his eleven year old sister. "Not too demonstrative" yet "not too aloof" either, he specifies, in view of his sister's tender age. Again there is tension between emotional control and emotional fulfillment, or civilized restraint and self-indulgence. Mitch wants a pair of PG-rated lovebirds. Love stripped of the passions of sex. As events in the film develop, the caged lovebirds are about the only characters that fit that safe description.

The camera lingers inquisitively on Melanie as she leads Mitch around the sales floor, looking quite smug while making up lies about what she knows almost nothing. Dialog turns verbal sparring match, with Mitch asking leading questions intended to expose Melanie's ignorance and Melanie supplying what she hopes are plausible answers. It is a subtle, civilized power struggle. When Melanie misidentifies a pair of yellow canaries (whose color, not by coincidence, complements Melanie's golden hair) as lovebirds, Mitch challenges her, then adds, "Doesn't this make you feel awful?" Is the jig up? By now he obviously knows she is a fraud. But no, when she asks him to clarify his question he prolongs their duel, rather than claim victory, by changing the meaning of his question. Instead of asking Melanie if she is ashamed of deceiving him about her identity, he asks her if it doesn't make her feel bad to keep "these poor little innocent creatures caged up like this." Which is a bit hypocritical, considering how much he enjoys putting Melanie in a tight spot and watching her squirm. Melanie answers, "We can't just let them fly around the shop." Oddly enough, free-spirited Melanie plays the disciplinarian while law and order man Mitch defends the free-spirited individual. Neither character appears conscious of the film's thematic contest between restraint and indulgence, yet their amusing banter touches on it. There is no philosophical integrity to their remarks. Both characters assume moral poses only as a means of manipulating each other.

Diverting Mitch's attention from her ignorance about lovebirds, Melanie tries to interest him in the canaries. He asks to see one. She tries to remove one from its cage, but loses her grip on it. The bird flies frantically around the shop. Amused by the chaos he caused, Mitch calmly observes Melanie and Roberta vainly attempt to recapture the creature. He succeeds where they fail, trapping it under his hat when it lands, and returning it to its cage. "Back in your gilded cage, Melanie Daniels," he says as he does so, revealing his knowledge of Melanie's true identity and the fact that he has been playing his own prank on her from the moment they met. He rather arrogantly assumes the role of society's law enforcer, punishing Melanie for her own failed prank. The "gilded" remark suggests that he regards her as a spoiled rich girl who lacks self-discipline.

The bird Mitch traps under his hat, though not the one he returns to the cage, is clearly fake. Perhaps this was a technical necessity for Hitchcock, but it nevertheless suits the character of Mitch, who is a bit too smug about his ability to control things — especially free-spirited creatures so unlike himself. His understanding of Melanie is shallow at best. And his knowledge of his own shortcomings is equally lacking.

Mitch brings to the surface, in a superficially lighthearted manner, the bird/human analogy implied by Hitchcock since the film's opening credits. And he wields it against Melanie, who is angered to have her prank exposed and upstaged and her character insulted. The prevailing veneer of civility wears thin as Melanie challenges Mitch's claim to have encountered her earlier, in court. In a precise, arrogant, lawyerly manner, Mitch "re-phrases" his statement, claiming now he merely *saw* her in court when she was charged with breaking a plate glass window. "Judge should have put you behind bars," he adds, passing judgment on her while we see her pictured next to a birdcage similar to the jail cell to which Mitch would like to see her confined.

Melanie's defense quickly turns to aggressive offense. She accuses Mitch of lying about wanting to buy the lovebirds. He insists otherwise. She points out that since he knew all along who she was, he deliberately deceived her, making him guilty of the same crime of which he accused her. He counters by claiming moral justification for his prank. He only wanted to teach her a lesson by giving her a taste of her own medicine. Yet he so obviously enjoyed manipulating Melanie, perhaps as compensation for the manipulation he has endured, we learn later, at the hands of his mother, that it undercuts his claim. Descending the staircase to leave the store, Mitch too appears briefly aligned with a bird cage. He too is emotionally trapped, without being aware of it.

Melanie angrily refers to Mitch as a "louse," another animal/human analogy, just as he compared her to an unruly bird that should be caged. A louse feeds off the blood of other animals. Mitch has just emotionally fed off Melanie's well-publicized legal troubles, and leaves the pet shop feeling very superior about it. Determined to regain the upper hand, as she prefers to possess in all her relationships, Melanie asks Roberta for the name of her departed foe. The sales clerk doesn't know. The camera closes in on Melanie's face as she ponders her options. She has the look of a predator, though within the relatively genteel limits Hitchcock has established thus far in the movie. Quickly formulating a plan of action, she runs down the stairs in pursuit of her prey. Her elegant, rather tight dress and high heeled shoes seem confining, unsuited to her haste. She attracts the attention of other shop patrons who are mildly disturbed by her behavior.

Reaching the pet shop exit just in time to spot Mitch's car pull away from the curb outside, Melanie takes note of his license plate and phones an employee at her father's newspaper to request the name and address of its owner. Invading Mitch's privacy is not exactly an ethical use of her father's journalistic power. Melanie's fingernails, polished red, are suggestive of the talons on a bird of prey. But they are also decorative, like a bird's plumage. And colorful plumage is usually a device for attracting a mate. Melanie's interest in Mitch, and his in her, involves more than mere domination through pranks and the teaching of moral lessons. Their budding relationship already involves a complex, contradictory mix of mutual attraction, mutual hostility and compulsive, emotionally driven behavior.

Melanie summons the sales clerk and orders a pair of lovebirds. As with the mynah bird, she wants them "immediately," but has to wait for their delivery. Patience is not one of her virtues. Persistence is. Delivery of the lovebirds by the following morning is soon enough. Relaxed now, she contentedly anticipates the execution of her scheme. The gift of lovebirds is both a prankster victory over and a romantic overture to Mitch. Though Melanie may not yet be fully aware of, or willing to admit to herself, the latter.

Attired in a green dress partly concealed by a blond fur coat, and carrying a pair of green lovebirds in a cage (is the color analogy between lovebirds and herself Melanie's conscious choice, intended to plant a romantic seed in Mitch's mind, or only Hitchcock's?), Melanie sets out the next morning to conquer her conqueror. The camera focuses initially on her legs and the caged birds, capturing the confidence of her brisk stride, perhaps resulting from the tactical advantage she now believes she holds over Mitch. But when she enters an elevator in Mitch's apartment building, we see a pair of men's legs next to hers. The camera tilts up to reveal a balding, portly man who casts curious and mildly disapproving side-glances at her. Possibly, like Mitch, he is both attracted to Melanie and also familiar with tabloid accounts of her outrageous behavior. Or maybe he just disapproves of her lively demeanor. In any case, Melanie is oblivious to or maybe even, judging by the expression on her face when the camera rises to that level, willfully defiant of his disapproval. The stranger, played by actor Richard Deacon, is an Alfred Hitchcock look-alike, and may be the director's wry comment on his own conflicted personality: fastidiously conventional and even snooty on the surface, but rife with contradictory impulses beneath that façade. Not the least of which, apparently, was a growing romantic obsession with actress Tippi Hedren.

The camera tracks with Melanie and the man as they walk down a hallway, revealing their sly glances as she searches for Mitch's apartment in order to complete her prank and the stranger pursues both his interest in and mild suspicion of this attractive young woman. Melanie sets the bird cage down outside the door to Mitch's apartment and attaches an envelope with his name on it. To the stranger, who knows nothing of the pet shop duel, it might appear simply that Melanie is leaving a gift for Mitch. But if we can believe later evidence supplied by Melanie herself, the envelope contains a note insulting Mitch. She is leaving him a typically mixed message.

All politeness on the surface, the stranger, who resides nearby, courteously informs Melanie that Mitch has left for the weekend. He also tells her where Mitch has gone. He even says he would take care of the birds himself if he too were not leaving. He apologizes to Melanie and enters his apartment, but then casts one final glance of mild contempt in her direction. Hitchcock makes so much out of these brief, seemingly innocuous encounters between major and minor characters. There are few wasted scenes in his movies. The stranger's mild display of disapproval in this scene prefigures a more intense, collective moment of suspicion later directed at Melanie by a group of people in Bodega Bay.

That Melanie is willing to pursue her practical joke/flirtation all the way to Bodega Bay, a small town up the coast from San Francisco, is one measure of her emotional need to beat him in a test of wills. So too is the reckless speed with which she drives her sporty, convertible car along the winding coast road. Like Alicia Huberman in *Notorious* (1946), but not drunk and not so dangerously. Or Frances Stevens in *To Catch a Thief* (1955), but not merely as a way of showing off to the man in whom she is interested. Melanie's haste is at odds with the immaculate, well-ordered elegance of her appearance, including dress gloves and a scarf to preserve the careful arrangement of her hair. Yet she seems more than capable of controlling the vehicle at such a speed around sharp curves. And that control complements rather than contrasts Melanie's physical appearance.

A close-up of the lovebirds leaning left and right in their cage as Melanie's car careens along the road reinforces the movie's link between human feelings (in this case the driver's compulsion to go fast and to outsmart Mitch Brenner) and birds, who are also forces of nature sometimes acting without conscious direction. On a more literal level, this one shot strikes a false note, since birds pushed this way and that by centrifugal forces would instinctively flap their wings to maintain balance. The two obviously fake birds Hitchcock uses do not. An insignificant quibble. The point is, the green lovebirds react involuntarily to Melanie's reckless driving. And in the same shot we see Melanie's green high heeled shoe alternately pressing down and easing up on the accelerator as she navigates the winding road to Bodega Bay. It's what she must do to serve an emotional need that drives *her*.

Viewed from a great distance, Melanie's sleek sports car races towards the tranquil seaside village of Bodega Bay. A noisy intrusion on a sleepy paradise? That initial impression, not surprisingly, proves deceptive. Bodega Bay's peaceful façade conceals a fair amount of emotional turmoil, as did that of another small town, Santa Rosa, in Hitchcock's *Shadow of a Doubt*. In *The Birds*, Santa Rosa is mentioned several times as a neighbor of Bodega Bay, and a secondary target of attacking birds. Like Uncle Charlie, the killer who seeks sanctuary in *Shadow's* Santa Rosa, Melanie Daniels is a stranger who stirs up the deceptively calm waters of Bodega Bay society. Though without the threat of physical violence brought by Uncle Charlie. That ingredient is supplied by the marauding birds, who act as both agents of violent human passions and as a destructive force indifferent to and independent from human affairs.

## 2. Hitchcock's *The Birds*

Small communities and rural settings are for Hitchcock a playground of disturbing contrasts. A little boy plays with his toy gun in a bucolic New England landscape at the beginning of *The Trouble with Harry* (1956). Then from off screen comes a shot from a real gun. The surface contrast between Melanie's sleek sophistication and Bodega Bay's lack thereof is particularly striking when she parks in front of the town's very plain general store, Brinkmeyer's. Watched by curious, puzzled passersby, all of whom are dressed plainly, Melanie enters the store. In long shot she appears surrounded by a clutter of canned goods, pots and pans, hardware and a wide variety of other merchandise. But certainly nothing like the fur coat she wears. In appearance, Brinkmeyer's General Store is reminiscent of Sam Loomis's small town hardware store in *Psycho*, though not rendered menacing by black and white photography, stark shadows and, in one shot, a chilling breeze.

Fred Brinkmeyer, the store's owner, sits inside a kind of metal cage, from where he also serves the community as postmaster. The cage, perhaps supplied by the federal government, is less a restraint on Brinkmeyer than on his patrons, limiting their access to mail before he officially sorts and distributes it. A sign advertising "Dog Licenses Issued Here" speaks of another type of social regulation. But the cage is no barrier to friendly communication between Brinkmeyer and Melanie. As a relatively exotic looking stranger ("bird?") in town, Melanie has the potential to either puzzle, intrigue or arouse suspicion among the local residents. Fred Brinkmeyer exhibits the first two reactions when Melanie asks him where Mitch Brenner resides. In this he is an older, harmless variation on Norman Bates reacting to the arrival of attractive stranger Marion Crane in his drab little world in *Psycho*.

Brinkmeyer seems boyishly smitten as he interacts with Melanie. But their slight miscommunication as they converse about Mitch is symptomatic, if only in a mild and subtle way, of the barriers to understanding between strangers. As a long time resident of Bodega Bay, Brinkmeyer erroneously presumes Melanie shares his knowledge of the town's layout. Twice she has to repeat her question, "Where?," before he walks her outside and points to a large white house visible between two large trees across the bay. And when he says the "Brenners" occupy that house, Melanie incorrectly assumes, to her obvious distress (betraying her romantic interest), the shop owner refers to Mitch and a wife. Brinkmeyer corrects that false impression, referring to "Lydia and the two kids," meaning Mitch and his younger sister. Melanie is relieved and amused. She does not think of Mitch as a "kid," returning home to mother on weekends. At this point in the movie she understands no more of Mitch's domestic situation than he does of hers. And that mutual ignorance will lead to more trouble than the trivial misunderstanding between Melanie and Brinkmeyer.

Three times Melanie has to explain to Brinkmeyer that she wants to approach the Brenner house indirectly in order to surprise the family. Each time he waits for further details of her intention. Inquiring minds want to know. But Melanie is defensive by inclination, and politely declines to elaborate. Brinkmeyer, in turn, politely suggests she rent a boat and approach the Brenner farm from the bay. By his tone of voice and the way he looks her up and down, he obviously doubts the ability of so elegant a woman to handle a boat. Like most of us, he makes assumptions based on superficial evidence.

While Brinkmeyer telephones a local boat rental business from within his postmaster cage, Melanie, impatient as usual, interrupts him to ask for the name of Mitch's sister. It's a mildly inconsiderate action, since Brinkmeyer has to put on hold the person he is speaking with over the phone in order to do yet another favor for Melanie. He thinks the name of Mitch's sister is Alice. Melanie politely but rather demandingly wants a more definitive answer. So Brinkmeyer asks a store employee named Harry, all but hidden among the rows of merchandise. We never even knew he was there. Harry's disembodied voice fires back, "Lois." Ignoring the opinion he solicited, Brinkmeyer now *insists* the girl's name is Alice. Having his opinion challenged, worse yet by his own employee, impels him to claim more certainty than he originally asserted. Even local residents can disagree over what might be considered common local knowledge. As it turns out, both men are wrong, however confident they pretend to be. Mitch's sister is named Cathy. But at least Brinkmeyer is considerate enough to direct Melanie to Cathy's school teacher, Annie Hayworth, for confirmation, though he also suggests she save herself the trouble and take his word for it that Alice is correct.

The camera lingers on Brinkmeyer as Melanie, thanking him for his help, leaves the store. His brief encounter with the beautiful, exotic and somewhat mysterious stranger is probably the highlight of his day. But that will not be the reaction Melanie gets from every Bodega Bay resident she meets.

Following directions supplied by the postmaster, Melanie drives past the two story Bodega Bay School, pausing for a moment to confirm its identity, then spins her wheels on the gravel road and speeds towards her destination up the hill. The school is a substantial, slightly sinister looking building reminiscent of the Bates house in *Psycho*. But it harbors no lurking psychopaths. Just a few children playing audibly in the school playground. But the school *does* embody Bodega Bay's emotional hold on Annie Hayworth, and is therefore a kind of haunted structure visually dominating the surrounding landscape, including Annie's house just up the street. In the same way the Bates house, haunted by memories of Mrs. Bates, dominates the nearby motel where Norman struggles in vain to lead some semblance of an independent life.

Annie's house is a modest, plain structure, especially when juxtaposed with Melanie's car from the same flat camera angle Hitchcock used to compare the car with Brinkmeyer's storefront. But the house's façade doesn't do justice to its complex, sophisticated owner. A white picket fence in front of the house constitutes another metaphorical cage. Annie Hayworth, like her surprise visitor, is something of a prisoner to her emotions. A red mailbox, like Melanie's extravagant car, speaks to the passionate nature of its owner.

Standing on the porch, Melanie rings the doorbell. Annie's off screen voice answers from the nearby garden. "Who is it?" "Me," replies Melanie, as irrationally as Brinkmeyer describing to Melanie the location of Mitch Brenner's house with a vague, "Here in Bodega Bay." "Who's *me*?" Annie inquires, understandably still in the dark about her visitor's identity. Another of the film's many examples of every individual's rather myopic perspective of the world. A quick, face-to-face introduction and this particular, minor confusion is cleared up.

Greeting Melanie on the porch, Annie is a study in visual contrast with the elegant stranger from San Francisco. Dressed in casual work clothes, her cheek smudged with dirt, her raven hair disheveled, she looks pure Bodega Bay. But she doesn't talk like it. Her red sweater, like her red mailbox, counterpoints her placid looking house, hinting at the passionate underpinnings of her life. Something she has in common with Melanie are her red fingernails; along with youth, beauty, sophistication, a fair amount of bluntness and a taste for cigarettes, which she cordially shares with the stranger.

The interaction between Melanie and Annie in this and subsequent scenes is one of the underappreciated highlights of this complex and often subtle film. Hitchcock himself, in pre-production conversation with Tippi Hedren, said of this first encounter: "So it's a nice scene ... I'll photograph it to get the benefit of these looks, but we should observe every nuance ... because every look and every pause ... you can see in every beat and give us a meaning, you see. And I'm sure when you get together with Miss Pleshette, you'll be able to work out the timing which is so important" (Auiler, p. 399).

Annie resolves any debate about the name of Mitch's sister. It's Cathy. Brinkmeyer's confusion, she remarks with a slight smirk, explains why mail never gets delivered to the right people in Bodega Bay. From that comment we surmise Annie's dissatisfaction with life in this small town. The reason she resides here is hinted at when the focus of her conversation with Melanie turns to Mitch. Clearly they share a romantic interest in him. And from that point of mutual discovery, their conversation becomes a contest, with Annie probing for information about Melanie's intentions and Melanie defensively withholding it. The tone of their interaction changes, without becoming blatantly hostile. Annie tends to turn her back on the stranger when asking about anything related to Mitch, as though she were ashamed of snooping or perhaps afraid of what she might learn. Her interest in Melanie's relationship with the Brenners is much stronger than was Fred Brinkmeyer's passing curiosity.

Responding to an inquiry about whether she and Mitch are friends, Melanie replies, "No, not really," which for the moment reassures Annie, who turns back to face her guest and chats pleasantly about a seemingly neutral topic: her competing compulsions for gardening and cigarettes. She confesses that gardening helps her fill her spare time. In *Psycho*, Norman remarked to *his* guest that a hobby (his is taxidermy) should help *pass* the time, not fill it. Both he and Annie are unhappy characters who yearn for what they cannot have. But unlike Norman, Annie deals with her loneliness and frustration in a relatively positive way.

Turning away again from Melanie, Annie compulsively returns, if indirectly, to the topic that interests her most. Mitch. She asks if Melanie intends to stay long in Bodega Bay. "Just a few hours" sounds hopeful to Annie, bringing them face to face again. "Then you're leaving right after you see Cathy?" she inquires, rather intrusively seeking clarification. Melanie understands the nature of Annie's interest in her plans, and declines to clarify them further. The façade of politeness between the two women is never overtly breeched. Melanie apologizes for being so "mysterious." Annie reciprocates by admitting that Melanie's plans are none of her business anyway, shrugging her shoulders as though it doesn't matter much to her, but then flashing Melanie a straight look proving it does. Mutual courtesy masks a brewing rivalry.

The scene is beautifully performed by both actors. Intelligence and candor are delicately balanced by unspoken suspicion and resentment. When Melanie compliments Annie's garden, she doesn't sound phony. Nor does Annie's "Thank you" in response. The hint of a potential friendship between these two bright and passionate women, despite their interest in the same man, shows through despite their verbal sparring.

Annie walks Melanie to her car and assumes a deliberately casual pose by leaning against her red mail box, which by its bold color contradicts her pose. Then she *not* so casually asks if Melanie met Mitch in San Francisco. No longer apologetic or mysteriously evasive, Melanie stops, looks straight at Annie, and replies with a firm, defiant "Yes." We see them in separate camera shots now, emphasizing the emotional divide between them. Until Annie backs away from their confrontation a bit, remarking rather sadly, "I guess that's where everyone meets Mitch." Melanie challenges her to be more forthright, "Now *you* sound a bit mysterious, Miss Hayworth." Leaning nonchalantly on the passenger door of Melanie's car, Annie reveals in thinly veiled terms that she had and lost a romantic relationship with Mitch. Her tone of voice sounds resigned rather than challenging. Noticing the caged birds in Melanie's car, she innocently inquires what kind they are, as yet ignorant of their connection to Mitch. "Lovebirds," Melanie reveals. No longer casual, returning the direct look Melanie gave her a few moments earlier, Annie replies with a touch of cold sarcasm, "I see. Good luck, Miss Daniels." Her tone of voice undermines the literal content of her good wishes and the deceptive indifference of her posture.

The scene concludes with Melanie asking for directions on the easiest way to get back to town and Annie providing them. But Annie's voice is cool now. And in the final shot we observe her unsmiling face, black hair fluttering in the breeze like the wings of a bird, as she watches Melanie drive away. Annie's red mail box, red sweater and red lipstick all reinforce our impression of her lurking fear and resentment of Melanie. By contrast, visible in the background are the white school house and a white church: both institutions ostensibly designed to curb, or cage, the more reckless of human passions. But later in the movie, that same school house will be the scene of a tremendous outbreak of violence. And in Hitchcock's universe, no institution is immune from appropriation by all manner of human passion.

Armed with the correct name of Mitch's sister, Melanie makes a brief return to Brinkmeyer's store to pick up a birthday card for Cathy. Improvising within her overall scheme, she addresses a new note to Cathy. Driving a short distance down to the docks, she parks her compact, silver speedster between two larger, inelegant and more utilitarian local vehicles. The visual contrast is striking, as it is again between Melanie and two local fisherman who stare at her curiously as she steps onto the dock with her birdcage in hand. And yet again between Melanie and the boat rental proprietor in his work clothes. She ignores his quizzical looks as he prepares a small boat for her and helps her into it. Like Fred Brinkmeyer, he seems to doubt Melanie's ability to handle the vessel, though he is unfailingly courteous to her. To his surprise, she proves more than competent as she starts out across the bay on her private mission.

One thing Melanie, the proprietor and most characters in the movie have in common is the propensity to confine both animals and the animal within themselves. As she walks along the dock, Melanie's caged lovebirds are matched by rows of lobster cages. We've already seen the many caged animals back at the pet shop in San Francisco, as well as two dogs held on leashes by Hitchcock himself. And the sign referring to dog licenses for sale at the general store. So far the movie has shown us nothing of the danger of such caged forces unleashed, or confined so tightly that they become pent-up and explosive.

In two extreme long shots, Melanie in her small boat appears tiny and vulnerable as it motors across the vast bay. Nature as a potentially overwhelming and hazardous environment. The Bodega Bay School is visible in the distance behind her, reminding us of Annie Hayworth's unscripted (from Melanie's point of view) role in Melanie's private mission. And if Melanie willfully disregards Annie's feelings, she as yet knows nothing of the emotional forces at work inside the Brenner family whose home she is about to invade.

Back at Brinkmeyer's store, she laughed in surprise and relief when informed that the Mrs. Brenner with whom Mitch resides is his mother, not his wife. But she has no understanding of the complicated relationship between Mitch and his mother, or the challenge that relationship will pose to her own troubled pursuit of him. Just as Mitch knows nothing of Melanie's family background, having based his assumptions about her character on newspaper accounts of her ungoverned public behavior. Melanie and Mitch are virtual strangers to one another: mutually attracted yet hostile to and mutually ignorant of each other. There's a lot of emotional baggage residing in that little boat crossing the wide bay in that much bigger ocean. And even more in the house towards which that little boat sails.

Melanie approaches the Brenner farm by sea instead of by road because she wants to surprise Mitch, whether to enhance the flirtation between them or to regain a tactical advantage in their contest of pranks after her defeat at the pet shop. She cuts the boat motor while the vessel is still a ways from the Brenner's private dock, and silently spies on the family as Lydia and Cathy head for town in a pick-up truck while Mitch, rather enthusiastically (is it good to be liberated from mother, if only for a short time?), heads for the barn. Melanie is L. B. Jeffries spying on his neighbors in *Rear Window*, except that she intends to intrude in their lives. Seen from Melanie's point of view, the Brenners appear as small and vulnerable as Melanie did moments earlier when viewed from a distance. But appearances are often deceptive in a Hitchcock movie.

With the Brenners either gone or out of sight, Melanie rows to their dock and secures her boat. Alternating tracking and traveling shots depict her surreptitious approach to the house and her watchful eye on the barn. It's a classic Hitchcock device to create suspense. No, the fate of the country or the world is not at stake here, as it is in similar shot selections in *Notorious* and *North by Northwest* (1959). Nor is her life at risk as was Lila's when she surreptitiously approached the Bates house in *Psycho*. But on her own level, Melanie is just as naïve about the Brenners, and especially Mrs. Brenner, as Lila is about Mrs. Bates. And Hitchcock achieves remarkable dramatic potency in depicting Melanie's reluctant and difficult journey towards love.

With neither a knock nor an invitation, Melanie enters the Brenner house through an unlocked front door. It's a mildly shocking moment, and one measure of her brazen character. Melanie invades the private residence of a person (and a *lawyer* to boot) she has only met once, under less than friendly circumstances. Strictly speaking, she is committing a crime. She didn't even know Mitch's name until she employed questionable methods to find it out. *The Birds* is not a story of theft, deliberate deception or murder in the manner of *Vertigo* (1958) and *Psycho*. But Melanie's reckless, selfish actions betray longstanding emotional problems no less than Marion stealing $40,000 or Scottie obsessively re-creating Judy Barton in the image of his deceased lover.

Inside the house, Melanie deposits her lovebirds in the living room and leaves the note for Cathy. Then she tears up the note she wrote earlier for Mitch. Circumstances have changed, perhaps as a result of her encounter with Annie Hayworth. Melanie now knows she has competition for Mitch. And as we discover later, her note to Mitch was hostile and petty, expressing the revenge aspect of her lovebirds mission. By tearing up that note, Melanie chooses to emphasize the flirtatious and maybe even apologetic aspects of her mission. But circumstances and emotions change quickly in a Hitchcock movie. Melanie will soon find reason to reveal the mean-spirited content of that shredded note to the man from whom she now conceals it.

Returning to the boat, Melanie rows away from the dock and stops at a discrete distance to crouch down and observe Mitch's reaction to her little stunt. We observe that reaction, at first, from her distant vantage point. And it is as enthusiastic as she hoped it would be. After discovering the lovebirds inside the house, Mitch runs outside and searches for Melanie. He spots her boat offshore, at which point she tries to start its motor and depart. Her slight difficulty in doing so gives Mitch time to retrieve a pair of binoculars from the house, return outside and get a closer view of the woman who just invaded the sanctity of his home. The grin on his face conveys his pleasure at Melanie's unexpected intrusion. Romantic attraction triumphs over any potential outrage he might have legitimately felt over her illegitimate invasion.

The boat motor finally catches and Melanie heads back out into the bay. Mitch jumps in his car and follows her back to Bodega Bay by way of the coast road. The chase is on. Melanie is pleased, judging by the warm smile on her face. It appears that both participants in an originally hostile encounter are now intrigued with each other. The fast pace of Mitch's pursuit is visible proof of his strong desire to become better acquainted with Melanie. And the elaborate steps she took to deliver the lovebirds testify to her interest. But there are many emotions at play in this second encounter between these two characters, who as yet know very little about each other. And some of those emotions run counter to their flirtation.

Mitch, predictably, arrives in Bodega Bay first. Melanie had no intention of eluding him. He runs to the end of the dock to greet her, but then *casually* leans against a post there as if to mask his passion, in the same manner Annie leaned casually against her mailbox while verbally sparring with Melanie. Mitch's posture is at odds with the reckless speed at which he navigated the coast road. And Melanie matches him in this little game of deception, her warm smile of greeting changing to a mask of cool indifference as she nears the dock. Suddenly she doesn't want Mitch to know how interested in him she is. Both characters endanger their budding romance by playing power games, being dishonest with themselves and each other. And at that precise moment of defensive, somewhat self-destructive behavior, Melanie is struck on the head by a swooping seagull.

On one level, Melanie is a victim of her own extreme need to control situations and manipulate other people. In short, to maintain power and security she lacked as a child, which we discover later. The gull attacks her when she puts up a false front in order to manipulate Mitch Brenner and shield her own fragile emotions, rather than openly acknowledge her attraction to him.

On another level, the bird attack is a shocking surprise. Not unlike Norman's murder of Marion Crane, though less extreme, which violently tore us out of her private drama and plunged us into his. Hitchcock himself said of this first bird assault: "You see, this gull should strike when her mood is cozying itself up for another meeting with him. That's all she's thinking of ... then boom, this thing arrives" (Auiler, p. 401). Andrew Sarris notes (Sarris, p. 84) that all of the major characters in *The Birds* are initially complacent, self-absorbed in their private concerns and narrow perspectives. The gull attack on Melanie is a blow to that complacency, an objective intrusion on a largely subjective scene in which we, the audience, were caught up in Melanie's little flirtation/competition with Mitch.

These two somewhat different interpretations of this first and all subsequent bird attacks are not necessarily contradictory. As Robin Wood remarks, not all moments of self-destructive behavior by human characters in *The Birds* are accompanied by a bird attack. Therefore the attacks are "not a straightforward *punishment* for complacency" (Wood, p. 158). In dramatic terms, the bird attacks are both shocking reminders that our precious private lives are not lived in a void, and sly stand-ins for the potential violence of human passions even in those of us who are not inclined to rob, stalk, kidnap, harass, torture or murder our fellow humans.

The seagull's attack rips off the masks Melanie and Mitch donned moments earlier. Her expression of indifference is replaced by one of surprise and pain. Mitch drops his casual pose and races to her aid. She is unsteady on her feet as he helps her out of the boat. Her previously immaculate hair is now a bit less so. And a single trickle of bright red blood running from her blond scalp down her pale face mars an otherwise carefully cultivated appearance. A jarring contrast between surface elegance and underlying passion, between civilized veneer and brutal undercurrent.

Mitch explains to a passing local fisherman what happened to Melanie. The surprise and disbelief in the fisherman's voice as he reacts to the news is a measure of how rare and unexpected such an attack is. Even when bird attacks grow more frequent, massive and violent, the people of Bodega Bay will feel the need to come up with a conventional explanation. *Any* explanation that will help them cope with the consequences.

Mitch gallantly escorts Melanie to the Tides Restaurant, prudently reminding her she might need a tetanus shot as a precaution against infection. She replies that she had a booster just last year. Everything appears to be under control again. Institutional safeguards are in place to minimize potential medical complications of such an attack. But as Melanie and Mitch approach the restaurant, they pass by a public telephone booth that will soon play a role in the destruction of that impression of security, especially as it relates to Melanie herself, who is to some extent the film's Everywoman. Us.

Inside the Tides, Melanie draws stares from curious patrons and employees. As both a stranger in town and an injured person, she becomes an object of special interest to local residents. But they stare mostly out of concern, not suspicion, for the time being. Deke Carter, the café owner, and a waitress named Helen are very attentive, fetching peroxide and cotton to treat Melanie's wound. But altruism is never completely divorced from survival instincts. Deke, concerned about a potential lawsuit because he was previously sued by an injured patron (his selfish worry is not entirely paranoid), delicately inquires if Melanie sustained her injury on the restaurant premises. Mitch, slightly annoyed by Deke's misplaced concern, assures him Melanie will not sue. But Mitch, as we learn later, is a lawyer who has defended some pretty shady clients. If this incident did not involve an old friend (Deke) and a new romantic interest (Melanie), would he hesitate to pursue a lawsuit on behalf of the injured party? Little hypocrisies, real and potential, lurk in the background of this movie.

Melanie uses a cloth to dab the trickle of blood from her forehead, gracefully eliminating all visible evidence of the bird attack. Meanwhile, Mitch cleans out the cut concealed beneath her hair. Immaculate again, she puts on another mask of emotional invulnerability. The two begin to spar, resuming their verbal duel from the pet shop scene. Deke provides Melanie with ammunition by revealing that Mitch is a lawyer. She utters the word as though it denoted a dishonorable profession — a point of agreement between she and Deke. Her previous experiences with attorneys have not been pleasant. Mitch emphasizes that he is a *criminal* lawyer, aggravating the situation further. Melanie accuses him of wanting to put *everyone* behind bars. He insists otherwise. "Only violaters and practical jokers?" she asks. "That's right," he affirms, implying, at least within the context of their playful duel, that Melanie is a likely candidate for incarceration.

Cleaning out Melanie's wound with peroxide is a prudent precaution against infection. But it also causes her a moment of pain. Mitch quickly apologizes, twice, and backs off. Verbal sparring aside, his concern for her is genuine. But this otherwise trivial incident is a subtle reflection of Mitch's impulse to judge and reform the rebellious Melanie Daniels. An impulse based largely on lurid and dubious newspaper accounts of her bad behavior, and perhaps indirectly on his own self-sacrifice on behalf of his emotionally dependent mother, and the resentment he may feel against another woman who seems to indulge her selfish desires so freely, with no regard for anyone else.

Both characters are attracted to each other, but neither is willing to admit it first. Pictured now in separate shots emphasizing their enmity, Mitch interrogates Melanie about why she brought the lovebirds all the way to Bodega Bay. Evading the truth, which would make her emotionally vulnerable, she claims to have done so only for Cathy's sake. Then she compounds that fib with another, contending she came to Bodega Bay primarily to see Annie Hayworth, whom she insists is an old friend from college. The camera pulls back to show both characters as Mitch sits down opposite Melanie, crosses his arms, and challenges her directly to admit the truth. "I think you came up here to see me." Of course it's only *her* truth he wants to expose, not *his* own. He speculates, logically, that she must have gone to a good deal of trouble to get his name and address. She retorts, accurately, that by exploiting the resources of her father's newspaper it cost her very little effort, implying that Mitch is not worth much effort.

"You really like me, huh?" Mitch teases, cutting right to the heart of the matter. Melanie vehemently denies it. "I *loathe* you. You have no manners, you're arrogant and conceited." In her eagerness not to admit her romantic interest in Mitch, she reveals the existence of her insulting letter to him. The same letter she tore up and returned to her purse while delivering the lovebirds to the Brenner house. The spirit of conciliation and flirtation (spurred on by her discovery of romantic competition from Annie Hayworth) in which she destroyed the note has, for the moment, been displaced by a renewed spirit of conflict. And yet, paradoxically, she refuses to disclose the contents of the note when Mitch asks her to do so. She doesn't want him to feel *too* offended.

In her growing irritation with Mitch, Melanie heaps on him some of the blame for her recent injury by referring to *"your* seagulls." This is nonsense, at least on a literal level. Mitch came to her aid after the bird attack. Melanie's inclination to blame Mitch, and later the entire community of Bodega Bay, for her troubles is typical of human perception under stress. Mitch does the same to Melanie by judging her harshly and by occasionally baiting her. Later in the film, when the bird attacks grow more massive and violent, Melanie will become a similar victim of *communal* distress and misplaced aggression. So even though Mitch and the residents of Bodega Bay are not literally responsible for the bird attacks on Melanie, figuratively speaking those attacks are a metaphorical reflection of human fear, suspicion and hatred.

"I came all the way up here to [bring you the lovebirds]..." Melanie starts to tell Mitch, recklessly building on her impulsive attempt to make him feel guilty about the bird attack. Mitch, ever the lawyer, catches her in another lie. "But you were coming up anyway," allegedly to see Annie. Melanie cannot think of a quick reply. Advantage to Mitch, whom we see, from her subjective vantage point, seated across the table, grinning triumphantly at her/us. For all the tactical maneuvering and bickering in this encounter, there is still a strong element of flirtation between them. That element is abruptly dispelled when Lydia Brenner, in the background, enters the restaurant and approaches the table. In a shot of all three characters, Lydia positions herself between her son and Melanie. Ignoring the stranger, she turns immediately to Mitch, who politely brings Melanie back into the equation by introducing the women to each other. Isolated close-ups of all three characters subsequently emphasize that this scene is now a *three*-way contest. Separate shots of Lila, Sam and Arbogast bickering about Marion at Sam's hardware store in *Psycho* convey the same mutual hostility.

Mitch informs his mother that Melanie brought a gift of lovebirds for Cathy. "Oh, I see," Lydia responds, in the same words and tone of voice as did Annie when she learned of Melanie's gift. Both Lydia and Annie stand to lose in the transaction. Mitch invites Melanie to dinner at the Brenner home, ostensibly to meet Cathy, for whom Melanie ostensibly brought the birds. So many polite yet false facades. When Mitch inquires what time dinner will be served, Lydia replies, "Seven, the same as usual," implying that Melanie's attendance will not make it a special occasion and will not be allowed to disrupt family routine. Family routine on which Lydia is more emotionally dependent than we or Melanie yet realize.

Emotionally this is a complicated scene. The contest of wills between Mitch and Melanie is interrupted and modified by Lydia's arrival. Mitch uses his mother's presence to pressure Melanie into accepting a dinner invitation. How can she refuse, without appearing rude to a woman she's just met and has no reason to insult?. Yet it is obvious Lydia opposes the idea, though she cannot say so without appearing rude herself. Lingering close-ups of Lydia convey the hostility she politely refuses to verbalize. Mitch comes off as a master manipulator in this scene. But in time he will prove much less in control of Melanie, of Lydia and even of himself.

Mitch cleverly exploits one of Melanie's own fibs, about spending the weekend with Annie, to trap her into having dinner with him. Melanie protests that Annie may have made other plans for the two of them. But it's a weak ploy. The best she can do is reassert a measure of independence by insisting on driving herself to the Brenner farm, instead of letting Mitch pick her up at Annie's, which he offers to do. "I can find my own way" is both an attempt to keep Mitch away from Annie, so they don't compare notes and expose Melanie's lie, and a more general declaration of self-reliance by a person who dislikes depending on others.

Mitch delivers a final, sarcastic jab, advising Melanie not to come by boat. Nevertheless the unresolved duel between them ends on an outwardly polite note, with him asking about her injury and she insisting it feels much better. Melanie explains about the gull attack to Lydia, whose lack of sympathetic reaction hints that she secretly wishes the attack had been more successful. In retrospect, Lydia too now participates figuratively in the movie's first bird attack. The scene's final shot lingers on Lydia's unhappy gaze. She's not quite Mrs. Sebastian, despising and eventually conspiring to murder Alicia Huberman for stealing her son's heart and devotion in *Notorious*. Lydia's jealousy, as we shall see, is rooted in her own emotional fragility. As for Melanie, she is made of sterner stuff than Annie Hayworth, and will not back down after one or even several cool encounters with Lydia. In the words of Hitchcock himself, "I don't think Melanie would give a damn" (Auiler, p. 404).

Brazenly, perhaps thoughtlessly, because she knows about Annie's feelings for Mitch, Melanie returns to Annie's house and asks if she can rent for a single night a room Annie intended to rent for a longer period of time. (Does Annie need the money or the *company*?) She not only used Annie as a phony excuse for her trip to Bodega Bay, and for avoiding commitment to Mitch's dinner invitation, she now, in effect, asks for Annie's help to achieve her confused romantic goals. It is an amazingly selfish act by Melanie, and an equally amazing act of generosity by Annie to let her get by with it.

As usual, Melanie appears stylish and sophisticated in her elegant attire, though the brown paper bag containing overnight provisions makes an odd visual juxtaposition with her fur coat. Slumming in Bodega Bay. Annie is dressed more casually and comfortably, though no longer appears unkempt by comparison, as she did in their earlier encounter. In her own way, she is now every bit a visual match for Melanie. She leans comfortably against the front door frame as she and Melanie converse. Though reluctant to rent her room for only one night, she quickly relents. Both women seem friendly as they joke about Melanie's "utilitarian" luggage. The underlying tension between them returns briefly when their conversation touches on the reason for Melanie's overnight stay. But only briefly. Like a squall, it soon passes.

As they enter the house, both women turn back and look up to see a large flock of birds flying by overhead. "Don't they ever stop migrating?" Annie asks rhetorically. The same question could be applied to Melanie, whose search for happiness has led her from San Francisco to Rome, back to San Francisco, and now to Bodega Bay. Perhaps there is a wistful trace of envy in Annie's comment, since she has stopped migrating and planted herself in Bodega Bay in the vain hope of renewing her broken romance with Mitch, or perhaps just surviving emotionally on the crumbs of their friendship. In any case, a frontal medium shot of Melanie and Annie watching the birds fly by is the first of a series of striking double portraits of the two characters emphasizing both their differences and similarities. Blond versus brunette.

Blonde fur coat versus dark gray blouse and pants. Yet both women are intelligent, beautiful and share a dissatisfaction with their lives.

Melanie arrives at the Brenner farm. Wanting to make a good impression, whether she admits it or not, she checks her make-up before ringing the front door bell. No more illegal entries for her. Mitch, Lydia and Cathy approach the porch from the direction of the barn. As a family, they have lives and routines separate from Melanie's. But their manners of greeting her are diverse. Cathy, after confirming that their guest did indeed bring her the lovebirds, breaks away from the family group, runs to Melanie and gives her a big hug. A typical, unfiltered, impulsive reaction from a child. Very different from the evasive, often contradictory relations among adults. Cathy knows nothing of Melanie's ulterior motive for bringing her the lovebirds. But if Cathy is only a subsidiary recipient of that gift, Melanie seems genuinely pleased by her warm reception, returning Cathy's hug with enthusiasm.

A tracking shot of Lydia, approaching the porch much more slowly than did Cathy, captures her singular, more reserved reaction to Melanie's arrival. Though not overtly rude, she is obviously suspicious of the stranger. A smiling and clearly pleased Mitch then enters the same shot, visually and verbally counterpointing his mother as he cheerfully greets Melanie. As all four characters enter the house, Lydia complains that her chickens won't eat and blames Fred Brinkmeyer for selling her bad feed. Her displeasure with Melanie, which for the sake of propriety and her son's feelings she cannot express directly, is channeled into displeasure with the proprietor of the general store. And she will not be put off by her lawyer son's defense of Brinkmeyer: "Caveat emptor," meaning "Let the buyer beware." "Never mind the law," Lydia retorts. When it is convenient for her to do so, she will whistle a different tune.

On the surface Lydia is all politeness to Melanie, assuring her, "This won't take long, Miss Daniels" while venting her annoyance on Fred Brinkmeyer over the telephone. Pictured in the foreground while Mitch, Cathy and Melanie appear relaxed with each other in the background, Lydia's black mood once removed is visually complemented by the black shade of a nearby table lamp. She scolds Brinkmeyer for selling her bad chicken feed. Their conversation reveals that another local farmer has had the same problem with his chickens, but used a different brand of feed. This odd phenomenon recalls the unusual presence of so many seagulls over San Francisco, noted by Melanie at the start of the film. That mystery was quickly, if dubiously, explained away by the pet store saleswoman. The present scene ends with mystery lingering in the air. After Lydia hangs up the phone, Cathy parrots what *had* been her mother's claim, blaming Fred Brinkmeyer's defective feed for the problem. The first of several instances in the story where Cathy parrots her sometimes very judgmental mother. But Lydia, based on evidence provided by Brinkmeyer over the phone, has changed her mind. And for the moment, she is no longer concerned about venting her displeasure with Melanie onto someone else.

While Lydia is preoccupied on the phone, Mitch and Melanie engage in pleasant small talk in the background. One important fact revealed by their conversation is that a painted portrait of Mitch's late father, Frank, hangs over the piano. Their casual comments about that portrait convey nothing of the emotionally charged role the dead man played and still plays in the relationship between Mitch and Lydia, and in Annie's troubled connection to the Brenner family. Mitch, Lydia, Cathy and Annie are linked together in a somewhat stable though dysfunctional set of relationships. Perhaps "longstanding" is a better description than "stable." Melanie arrives as an agent of radical change in their stagnant lives.

After dinner, the atmosphere in the Brenner living room appears more relaxed and congenial. Melanie seems comfortably integrated into the family's evening routine, playing a tranquil Debussy piece on the piano and chatting with Cathy while Mitch and Lydia remove dishes from the dining room table. But tension is never far from the surface in this film. Lydia casually probes for information about how Melanie became acquainted with her son. Melanie characteristically reveals very little as she smokes a cigarette — always a stress reliever. Then Cathy changes the topic of conversation by describing Mitch's San Francisco law clients as "hoods." Is she echoing disapproval once expressed by her mother? If so, Lydia is embarrassed by the bluntness of Cathy's remark, cautioning her daughter, "In a democracy, Cathy, everyone is entitled to a fair trial." Funny, she wasn't so scrupulous about the presumption of innocence when it came to Fred Brinkmeyer's suspect chicken feed. But in that instance she had an ulterior motive for browbeating the defendant, who was an unwitting substitute for Melanie.

Cathy, undeterred, refuses to buy into her mother's "democracy jazz" argument. Lydia gives up the battle, but Cathy presses on, embellishing her own argument by citing the case of one of Mitch's clients who shot his wife six times in the head. Amused, Melanie asks Mitch why. Equally amused, Mitch explains that the man was watching a ball game on television and his wife changed the channel. As though that were an adequate explanation of why a man would commit such an atrocity. Typical of Hitchcock, this little discussion is a deceptively lighthearted treatment of a very dark subject. As after-dinner conversation, the human capacity for rage and violence can be funny and entertaining. But that veneer of lightheartedness barely masks the potential heart of darkness lurking beneath it. Consider the little deceptions Miss Gravely and Captain Wiles practice on each other during their otherwise pleasant luncheon in *The Trouble with Harry*. Or the seemingly blunt, revealing supper conversation between Norman Bates and Marion Crane in *Psycho*. It may be therapeutic for Marion, but Norman leaves much more unsaid about his private life than he reveals. As the shower scene bears out. In *Dial M for Murder* (1953), Tony Wendice and Mark Halliday carry on an amusing, hypothetical conversation about the perfect murder, while Wendice secretly plots one (against his wife) and Halliday would like to (against Tony).

None of the characters in *The Birds* are even close to being closet killers. But they are certainly capable of other, subtler forms of aggression and destruction often veiled by their superficial good manners. The man who shot his wife six times in the head for what seems to the rest of us a shockingly trivial reason is an example of man's usually hidden potential for violence, and the misunderstanding (of each other and of one's self) and miscommunication that can trigger it. Of course on a much bigger scale that occasionally dwarfs the private affairs of individuals, the husband who suddenly and inexplicably explodes into murderous rage foreshadows an eruption of violence in the animal kingdom that will soon engulf all of the characters who in this scene sit and contemplate so comfortably, from so physically and emotionally remote a perch, the darker side of human nature. There is no Uncle Charlie (*Shadow of a Doubt*) in their midst, harboring a criminal secret that could shatter their family. *Their* Uncle Charlie is gathering on telephone lines outside the Brenner home.

Cathy begs Melanie to return the next day for her birthday party. Surprisingly, in spite of the mostly warm welcome she has received thus far from the Brenners, Melanie declines. Habitual defensiveness creeps back into her behavior, endangering the progress she made with Cathy and Mitch, if not yet with Lydia. Melanie claims she must get back to San Francisco. After describing in advance the "surprise" party she isn't supposed to know about, but with no clue about the surprise bird attack that will abruptly end that party, Cathy pleads once more, openly and unashamedly, for Melanie to attend. Glancing discretely in the direction of the kitchen, where Mitch and Lydia have gone, Melanie sadly declines, again. Perhaps anticipating rejection by a second mother figure, before we even learn about the first. Cathy, in her direct, childlike way, tries to make sense of her new friend's rejection. "Don't you like Bodega Bay?" she asks. Typically, Melanie avoids giving a direct answer, claiming she doesn't know yet.

Though her directness is refreshing compared to the evasiveness of many adults, Cathy is inclined to take what those adults say at face value. And in a Hitchcock movie, that is often a mistake. Mitch, she claims, prefers Bodega Bay to San Francisco and therefore returns home from the "anthill," as Mitch describes the big city, every weekend. Only with hindsight, after we learn more about Mitch's reason for returning to Bodega Bay so often, can we speculate that he describes San Francisco in such unflattering terms in order to make his obligatory returns to Bodega Bay seem more tolerable. Cathy understands nothing of this.

Melanie's tranquil piano music continues from the living room as we move to the kitchen, where Lydia and Mitch wash dishes while discussing their guest. The contrast between cooperative domestic routine and a thinly veiled contest of wills between mother and son is amusing. Lydia probes for more information about how Mitch met Melanie. Information she could not get from Melanie herself. Mitch stops her short, exposing her suspicious interrogation for what it is by asking her where she went to law school. Lydia apologizes, then goes right on talking about Melanie in unflattering terms. Deriving her evidence from gossip columns (from, as it turns out, a newspaper that is a rival to the one owned by Melanie's father), she comments on Melanie jumping naked into a public fountain in Rome. Mitch does not refute her claim, and is clearly uncomfortable discussing an incident which violates the rather strict sense of propriety he apparently inherited from his mother.

Lydia presses her tactical advantage, even as she veils her attack in terms of denial. "Of course, it's none of my business, but when you bring a girl like that..." Mitch interrupts her, claiming rather smugly that he can handle Melanie Daniels. Can he? Lydia backs off, for the moment, claiming respect for Mitch's wishes in the matter.

In the wake of defending Melanie, sort of, against Lydia's prosecutorial efforts in the kitchen, Mitch surprisingly reverses roles while escorting his guest to her car in the peaceful twilight, after what seemed to be a reasonably successful first date. No sooner do he and Melanie make plans to see each other again in San Francisco then Mitch turns prosecutor himself and adopts the same argument Lydia used to question Melanie's moral character. Think of Devlin in *Notorious*, slowly warming to Alicia, even defending her honor to his skeptical bosses, then with no justification other than petty jealousy turning on her when he learns that Sebastian, the target of their mutual espionage efforts, was once in love with her. Mitch perhaps unwittingly resents the spoiled rich girl he sees in Melanie because he has had to sacrifice so much of himself in order to care for his needy mother. Hitchcock seems to confirms this: "His [Mitch's] anger, therefore, with his mother is taken out on Melanie as she leaves" (Auiler, p. 405).

Mitch casually and thoughtlessly questions Melanie about the alleged Roman fountain affair. Melanie defends herself by claiming she was pushed rather than jumped into that fountain, was fully clothed when it happened, and that the story was falsified by a rival of her father's newspaper.

Backed by the as yet unobtrusive croaking of birds, who echo his deceptively playful aggression, Mitch intensifies his attack, treating Melanie like a hostile witness in court, interrupting and mocking her explanation. "You're just a poor, innocent victim of circumstances." She effectively rebuts, "I'm neither poor nor innocent. But the truth of that particular incident..." Again Mitch interrupts to twist her reasonable explanation into a further condemnation, accusing her of running around with a wild crowd. Compounding that maneuver, he gets her to confess to lying about knowing Annie Hayworth prior to her arrival in Bodega Bay. She even confesses tearing up her insulting note to Mitch "because it seemed stupid and foolish." But in his rush to undercut her credibility, Mitch punishes Melanie for being honest, vulnerable and even apologetic about the note. "Stupid and foolish," her description of and reason for destroying the note, is redeployed by Mitch to describe her allegedly scandalous behavior in Rome. Not only does he refuse to acknowledge that she was pushed into that fountain, he doesn't stop his assault on her character for one moment to acknowledge that by tearing up her insulting note to him Melanie did something responsible and nice. Mitch's surprisingly vicious attack on Melanie, despite its phony lightheartedness, seems driven by some mysterious compulsion. Does he lash out at Lydia by using her tactics on Melanie?

Much of the contest of wills between Mitch and Melanie occurs while she is seated in her car and he leans against the car door, looming above her like a prosecuting attorney cross-examining a defendant sitting in the witness box in court. A visual reflection of his attempt to dominate her. Angry and defensive again after Mitch's surprising rudeness, Melanie shuts him out emotionally. "I don't give a damn what you believe!" Mitch makes matters worse by flippantly suggesting they see each other again because it "might be fun." He treats her almost like a prostitute for hire, the titillation factor of her supposedly bad behavior being her primary allure for him. But Melanie wants none of that, insisting that while such a relationship might have been good enough in Rome, it isn't now. "It is for me," grins Mitch, adding insult to insult. "Not for me!" Melanie fires back, then speeds away angrily in her car. The car whose sleekness and power has been an emotional escape for Melanie for quite some time.

Still smiling and clueless about how badly he hurt Melanie, Mitch watches her depart. But before returning to the house, he glances up and sees nearby telephone wires covered with birds. Fluttering and squawking, the mere gathering of so many birds in one place feels vaguely ominous. Mitch is puzzled by their presence. He is equally, not coincidentally, clueless about why he treated Melanie Daniels so badly at the end of their first date. Clearly he is attracted to her. Yet he also judges her harshly, as his mother did in the kitchen, and punishes her for it. There is just a touch of Norman Bates in him. Just as Marion Crane's phony name and hometown both aroused and angered Norman, Melanie's bad girl reputation arouses and angers Mitch. As we soon discover, Mitch himself has never, if for honorable reasons, been able to assert the kind of independence that Melanie sometimes asserts too recklessly. The birds gathered overhead at the end of this tense scene are, of course, an unrelated force of Nature about to overwhelm and trivialize the petty bickering between Mitch and Melanie. But those same birds are also a reflection of the blind compulsions that sometimes compel two human characters to act destructively against each other and even against themselves.

Melanie returns to Annie's home for the evening. Annie's living room contains numerous fine art reproductions, books and classical music record albums. Her tastes are sophisticated, like Melanie's. Hitchcock himself notes that Annie's house, like Annie, combines elements of San Francisco and Bodega Bay (Truffaut, p. 254). One record album prominently displayed is a recording of Richard Wagner's *Tristan und Isolde*. Its tale of love and death intertwined is a theme explored by Hitchcock most thoroughly in *Vertigo*. In *The Birds*, Annie plays a role roughly equivalent to Midge from the earlier movie. Midge is in love with longtime friend Scottie Ferguson, who in turn becomes romantically obsessed with a new woman in his life, Madeline Elster. By the end of *Vertigo*, Midge is no longer a part of Scottie's life. Annie's role in Mitch Brenner's life experiences an even more radical change. But in the present scene, Annie's home has the look of a private sanctuary in what has become a very lonely existence for her as she waits in vain for some hopeful change in her life.

Midge and Madeline/Judy never meet face-to-face in *Vertigo*, though Midge sees her once, with Scottie, from a distance. By contrast, Annie and Melanie do meet, and for sufficient time to get to know one another a little. Annie not only graciously allows her romantic rival to spend the night in her home, she greets Melanie warmly upon the latter's return from dinner with Mitch. Noticing that something is troubling her guest, Annie inquires if the cut caused by the bird attack is the reason. It is not. She offers Melanie a brandy, a sweater and a quilt to ward off the coastal chill of Bodega Bay. And her show of compassion seems genuine. Melanie accepts the brandy, then reciprocates that kindness by asking Annie to call her Melanie rather than Miss Daniels.

This is one of the most memorable, intimate and underrated scenes in any Hitchcock movie, performed with great emotional subtlety by Tippi Hedren and Suzanne Pleshette. Their interaction balances precariously between empathy and hostility, developing friendship and lingering competition. The two characters have much in common, including intelligence, perceptiveness and sophistication. If not for their conflict over Mitch, they could be what Melanie falsely claimed they were when trying to deceive Mitch about her reason for coming to Bodega Bay. Old college buddies. Pleshette invests Annie with a casual, easy, slightly melancholy demeanor spiked with an occasional, sardonic glance or smirk betraying darker passions.

Just as she was about Melanie's relationship with Mitch during their previous encounter, Annie is understandably curious about Melanie's evening with the Brenners. "Did you meet Lydia?" she inquires, touching on the bitter experience that both links and divides them. Both women have felt the sting of Lydia's rejection. But at the same time, Lydia's hostility towards Melanie presumably keeps Melanie from getting closer to Mitch, which is something at least a part of Annie also wants to prevent. Noticing an expression of anger come over her guest's face, Annie backs off and graciously offers to change the subject. She then inquires how Melanie likes "our little hamlet." If Shakespeare's *Hamlet* is a template for dramatic presentations of complicated love/hate relationships, Annie's characterization of Bodega Bay is appropriate on two levels. "I despise it!" replies Melanie sharply. Obviously the topic of conversation has *not* changed, in spite of Annie's offer to do so. Melanie's resentment of Lydia's veiled hostility and Mitch's not-so-veiled cruelty is channeled into her negative opinion of Bodega Bay, about which, in the previous scene, she told Cathy she had not yet made up her mind. That was before Mitch taunted her about her Roman scandal and her lies to him. Melanie's opinion of Bodega Bay hinges on her relations with the Brenners. Just as, it will turn out, Bodega Bay's communal opinion of Melanie, a stranger, will hinge on larger events that just happen to occur while she visits their town.

Annie laughs off Melanie's expression of loathing for Bodega Bay, while at the same time curiously echoing it by describing the town as a "collection of shacks on a hillside." And we've already heard Annie's negative opinion of the local postal service. She and Melanie are big city girls at heart. Pictured in separate camera shots, across the room from one another, Annie and Melanie segue quite comfortably into a conversation about how Annie moved from San Francisco to Bodega Bay several years earlier to be near Mitch. The romantic conflict between the two young women seems to melt away as they discuss with remarkable frankness their current and past relationships with the Brenners. Melanie, seeking Annie's friendship, insists there is nothing romantic between herself and Mitch. And after her unpleasant exchange with him outside the Brenner house, she may believe that to be true. But it will take only a single phone call to repair the damage between them and transform into a lie her reassurance to Annie.

Annie responds to Melanie's claim by expanding the scope of their conversation. "Maybe there's never been anything between Mitch and any girl." Melanie is curious, and wants more information. Something she seldom supplies when other people are curious about *her*. Before spilling her emotional guts to her new confidante, Annie joins her in a brandy, bracing herself for the painful revelations to come. She also moves closer to Melanie as she divulges her history with Mitch and Lydia. A history that parallels but does not exactly duplicates Melanie's.

Through Annie, we and Melanie learn of Lydia's excessive dependence on Mitch after her husband's death. When Mitch brought Annie with him from San Francisco to Bodega Bay for a weekend, Lydia did not welcome her with open arms. And Mitch was too worried about his mother's delicate mental health to risk endangering it for love. So his romance with Annie died a slow death in San Francisco. But Annie, unable to let go, moved to Bodega Bay and became a schoolteacher in order to remain close to Mitch. What a sad, pathetic, prolonged situation for so bright and capable a person as Annie Hayworth. With great insight, she clarifies Lydia's jealous attachment to Mitch as being rooted in fear of abandonment rather than on some bizarre Oedipal fixation between mother and son. By strange coincidence, as we discover in the next scene, Lydia's traumatic experience of abandonment by her husband (death of a loved one can *seem* like abandonment to the person left behind), parallels Melanie's experience with her mother. But that similarity drives Lydia and Melanie apart rather than brings them together. Melanie tries to put a hopeful spin on Lydia's neediness, suggesting she would gain a daughter rather than lose a son if Mitch were allowed to have a romantic relationship. Annie laughs with bitter, though understated, humor at such naive optimism. "No, she already has a daughter," refers to Cathy, whom Lydia had at a rather advanced age. But Cathy *seems* more like Mitch's daughter and Lydia's granddaughter. Emotionally too, familial roles overlap in a confusing and sometimes dysfunctional manner.

Annie notes that since she is no longer perceived as a threat by Lydia, the two have become good friends. In fact, however, Annie's repressed love for Mitch has not diminished, as she makes clear to her new rival when she declares, looking straight at Melanie, "You see, I still like him a helluva lot. And I don't want to lose that friendship. Ever." Melanie gets the message. Struck by the force of Annie's words, if not by their literal meaning (Friendship? Who is Annie trying to fool, Melanie or herself?), Melanie pauses for a moment while lighting a cigarette. The intimacy that had been building between she and Annie throughout this scene suddenly encounters a roadblock.

The telephone rings. It's Mitch. The warmth in Annie's voice as she speaks with him cools a trace when he asks to talk with Melanie. As the two women pass on the way to and from the phone, they pause and lock eyes. Shown in profile, they become another in a striking series of double portraits of these two characters. We sense their mutual, wordless understanding of each other and of their changing relationships with Mitch. There is a hint of a smirk on Annie's face after Melanie breaks eye contact and walks on by. She knows Melanie's assurance that nothing romantic exists between herself and Mitch is an empty claim. In *Marnie* (1964) the title character and her mother just sit and look at each other, like two worn out boxers, after an exhausting and painful trip down memory lane. Though Melanie and Annie have known each other for a much shorter period of time, they understand each other very well.

Annie, with a pacifying cigarette in her hand, reclines in a chair while Melanie, seated at Annie's desk, talks with Mitch over Annie's telephone. We listen to some of the ensuing conversation from a camera position near Annie, whose emotional future hangs in the balance. Though we never hear Mitch's side of the conversation, Melanie's responses make it evident that he was concerned about her getting back to Annie's house safely, that he is sorry for his rudeness to her, and that he wants her to come to Cathy's birthday party. Though, as always, reluctant to commit herself, Melanie eventually agrees to attend. But this minor triumph over her often self-destructive defensiveness is a *major* blow to Annie, who in a terrific profile shot turns her head away from Melanie, Mitch and the camera lens immediately after the unintended blow is delivered. Her deceptively relaxed posture and the casual way in which she holds her cigarette beautifully mask and thereby dramatically emphasize the passion of this moment for her. Melanie's acceptance of the party invitation marks the probable death of Annie's vain hope of renewing her romance with Mitch, possibly by outlasting Lydia.

When Melanie hangs up the phone, Annie turns back to face her. Smiling, she puts a good face on her heartbreak. With phony nonchalance she remarks that she'll be at the party too, to help out. "It should be fun," she lies. The appearance of casual intimacy between the two women is restored when Melanie, announcing her departure for bed, shows Annie her nightgown, a rather plain flannel thing she purchased at Brinkmeyers, and probably very different from her customary attire. "My luggage," she jokes about the single item she retrieves from a plain paper shopping bag. Annie remarks, "That's pretty." Maybe she's a bit more acclimated to Bodega Bay standards than she admits. At any rate, this brief conversation about an emotionally neutral topic is comfortable and friendly, with no trace of sarcasm from either woman.

In the spirit of restored friendship, Melanie asks a direct question about a sensitive topic that does divide them. "Do you think I should go?" refers to Mitch's invitation. Melanie is obliquely asking for Annie's permission to attend the party, exhibiting a degree of respect for Annie's lingering feelings for Mitch. Annie's response is evasive, "That's up to you." Melanie, matching Annie's avoidance of direct confrontation, re-phrases Annie's reply. "No, it's really up to Lydia, isn't it" makes an absent third party the primary obstacle between Melanie and Mitch. Annie fires back, in a firm voice, "Never mind Lydia. Do you *want* to go?" Melanie admits she does. "Then *go*," Annie adds, in what appears to be a sincere expression of support and approval, which Melanie gratefully acknowledges with a heartfelt "Thank you."

Annie's motives for granting Melanie permission to attend Cathy's party are complex. Compassion for her new friend and confidante? A secret desire to avenge herself, through Melanie, on Lydia Brenner, who has thwarted her passion for Mitch for the past three years? Or maybe she does it for Mitch, whom she realizes is now more interested in Melanie than in herself. If so, Annie sacrifices her own happiness for his. The point is that *many* emotions and motives are at play in this scene.

A moment after Annie encourages Melanie to attend the party, something strikes the outside of her front door. Annie goes to the door and opens it. The two women find a dead seagull lying on the doorstep. Annie speculates the bird got lost in the darkness. But Melanie points out the brightness of the full moon. In yet another double portrait of the two characters, Melanie and Annie stare at each other in puzzlement. The same puzzled expression Mitch wore at the end of the previous scene, as he stared at bird-covered telephone lines near his home. They cannot think of a good reason why a seagull struck Annie's well-lit front door so violently that it killed itself.

On a literal level, this bird attack is a natural abberation, like the one preceding and those following it. No wonder the humans are confused. But on a different level of interpretation, the attack occurs on the heels of Annie giving Melanie permission to attend the party, and is perhaps Annie's attack on herself (her own home). The act of self- sacrifice that may bring happiness to Melanie and Mitch condemns Annie to loneliness and sadness. On the other hand, Melanie is closer to the door when the attack occurs. Perhaps the gull's aggression is a product of the lurking hostility Annie still bears for Melanie, despite consciously giving her permission to pursue Mitch. More than likely the bird attack encompasses all of these interpretations. It certainly concludes the scene on an ominous note, contradicting the newfound spirit of friendship that had been developing between Melanie and Annie.

Annie Hayworth's reference to Bodega Bay as "our little hamlet" is unwittingly descriptive of herself. Because Annie *is* Bodega Bay's Hamlet, unable to tear herself away from Mitch, yet unfulfilled by her mere friendship with him. "To leave or not to leave. That is the question." The answer will be imposed on Annie, violently, by outside forces wholly ignorant of her dilemma.

The following day, at the Brenner farm, Cathy and the other children play games in the yard while Mitch and Melanie, drinks in hand, climb a nearby hill overlooking the bay to converse privately. Annie, Lydia and several other adults supervise the children. We hear Annie's voice off screen as Mitch and Melanie seek out a private retreat. Atop the hill, he points out the beauties of the bay, now half empty at low tide and looking tame. The sky appears likewise. The overall mood is relaxed and non-threatening. But some things carry over from previous scenes. For one thing, Melanie's insistence that she must return to San Francisco.

Mitch is surprised to hear that Melanie has a job with Travelers' Aid at the airport. Did he assume she, as a wealthy heiress, led a life of complete indolence? "Helping travelers?" Mitch inquires, with a trace of doubt if not outright sarcasm in his voice. "No, *misdirecting* them. I thought you could read my character," Melanie responds, but with a smile. Both characters are now capable of joking about matters that might have divided them the previous evening. Melanie, in an unusually expansive, non-defensive mood, reveals that she is taking a course in General Semantics at Berkeley. "Finding new four-letter words," she adds with a grin, anticipating Mitch's critique of her reason for taking the class and beating him to the punch. A whiff of their previous antagonism lingers in the air, despite the congeniality of their chat. But they are making progress overcoming the causes of that antagonism by learning more about each other.

Melanie also reveals that she belongs to an organization that raises money to help put a Korean boy through school. Such altruism, she explains, turning away from Mitch and the camera (us) because she is broaching a painful subject (the way Annie, in their first encounter, turned away from *her* when inquiring about Melanie's interest in the Brenner family), is partly the consequence of her lost, directionless summer of rebellion in Rome. Turning back to Mitch, Melanie re-lives a bit of that Roman defiance as she describes her scheme to give her very "prim" and "straitlaced" Aunt Tessa a mynah bird she has taught to say a few naughty words. Her casual manner of describing the prank suggests her lighthearted attitude towards it now. Reciprocating that light touch, but also revealing a bit of his still lurking Puritanism, Mitch mockingly offers a stern admonition. "You need a mother's care, my child." But because he is still ignorant of Melanie's family history, Mitch treads on thin ice here.

Melanie's smile disappears, her voice turns cold and she abruptly turns away again from Mitch and the camera. "Not *my* mother's," she insists. Mitch, trying to back away from his unwitting offense, apologizes. "What have you got to be sorry about?" Melanie challenges him, forgetting for a moment, in her own pain, what Annie told her about Mitch's struggles with Lydia. Anger tends to promote insensitivity. Revealing that her mother deserted the family, for a tycoon out east, when Melanie was only eleven, she again hurls an angry challenge at Mitch. "Do you know what a mother's love is?" Hesitating for a moment, Mitch replies that he does. Melanie interprets that hesitation as an unexpected moral conclusion. "You mean it's better to be ditched?," she asks incredulously. Mitch pauses again, as though still uncertain of his answer, before responding, "No, I think it's better to be loved." In those two brief pauses lie the burden of Mitch's complicated relationship with Lydia, whose extreme dependence on him since Frank's death has kept him from attaining the independence that was thrust on Melanie at much too early an age. The same age, perhaps not coincidentally, that Cathy has become on this very day. The gap between Melanie's and Mitch's very different experiences of family life is as wide as the bay they currently overlook.

Melanie turns away again, nearly in tears, as she admits not knowing where her mother currently resides. Fighting off those tears, she walks away from Mitch, in effect breaking off their painful conversation, while remarking, "Maybe I ought to join the other children." In such a remark she anticipates what she assumes will be Mitch's harsh judgment of her weakness. But this time Mitch exhibits none of the condemnation or cruelty he did the night before.

Returning to the party below, Melanie and Mitch are observed keenly though separately by Annie and Lydia, who both stand to lose from their growing romantic attachment. But Annie, who reacts with a resigned smirk, also glances back at Lydia, as Lydia peers apprehensively at the approaching couple. Annie, far more than Lydia, is capable of seeing and acting beyond her own immediate emotional needs. She is saddened by the relationship between Mitch and Melanie, but also, maybe, concerned about Lydia's potential interference with it. And this visual impression of the similarity and contrast between Annie's and Lydia's points of view is supplemented by Annie's simultaneous assistance to Cathy. In a sense, Annie plays mother to Cathy while Mitch plays father to both Cathy and Lydia. An odd and unsatisfying familial relationship which has gone on for at least three years.

Cathy and her friends play a game of Blind Man's Buff. As a child, Cathy is largely ignorant of the hidden emotional dynamics of the adults who supervise and protect her: Mitch, Lydia, Annie and soon Melanie. And at that precise moment of wordless group tension, a flock of seagulls attacks the children, who often suffer when adults are emotionally torn. Fittingly, Cathy is the first to be attacked. Blindfolded, she has no idea, at first, by whom or what. In the chaos that follows, party balloons are burst and a birthday cake is overturned. Little tokens of normality destroyed in seconds by an unexpected intrusion of violence.

The bird attack in this scene is more persistent and on a larger scale than the two preceding it. Swooping seagulls chase after scattering children. Adults, led by Annie's rallying cry, snap into action to rescue and protect Cathy and her friends. They are all good people with noble impulses to do the right thing, in spite of the compulsions that sometimes rule their actions. Melanie fits right in with this impression of adults acting responsibly as she removes her green dress jacket and uses it to shoo away a bird attacking a fallen child. One layer of her private defensive shield discarded in order to defend someone else.

After the children are gathered inside the house, Mitch and Melanie stand alone in the open doorway, watching the gulls depart as mysteriously as they arrived. Annie, briefly visible in the background still comforting children, disappears from view. Lydia too is nowhere in sight. Mitch learns from Melanie about the second bird attack, at Annie's house the previous evening. Puzzled and concerned, he asks Melanie to stay for supper. Or is he using the bird attack as an excuse to extend their time together? She agrees, with none of her usual hedging this time. A crisis of Nature originating from outside themselves brings them closer together. As the scene ends, two small children huddle together between Mitch and Melanie and gaze up fearfully at the departing menace. The camera closes in on the children's faces, reducing Mitch and Melanie to larger, anonymous figures of adult authority. In the visual absence of Annie and Lydia, Melanie and Mitch form a kind of parental couple.

A light supper is served at the Brenners' home later that night. Lydia, Mitch and Cathy function as a team again, while Melanie sits on the couch, being served like a guest. Cathy's caged lovebirds are chirping. Lydia, no fan of that sound, covers their cage with a sheet, just as she will try to stifle the romance between her son and Melanie. Cathy asks why Annie didn't stay for supper — the implication being that she has on many previous occasions. Mitch explains that Annie returned home to take a phone call from her sister out east. A convenient and possibly phony excuse for Annie to avoid the pain of watching Mitch and Melanie grow closer.

Lydia encourages Mitch to hurry with the serving of supper, assuming, or more likely hoping, that Melanie is eager to be on her way back to San Francisco. Cathy, unaware of her mother's real motive for such an assumption, encourages Melanie to spend the night in the spare bedroom upstairs. The four characters sit around a central coffee table: Melanie and Lydia on the couch, Cathy and Mitch in chairs facing them. Curiously, their seating arrangement matches the superficial alignment of their arguments for and against Melanie's quick departure. Melanie and Lydia argue for it, though for very different reasons. Cathy and Mitch argue against it, again for different though not unrelated reasons. The caged lovebirds continue to be heard as well. Alerting us to another, impending attack? Or speaking (chirping) for the veiled human passions *really* at work in this debate.

Of the four human characters in this scene, Melanie spots the danger first. Noticing a single sparrow on the fireplace hearth, she quietly calls out to Mitch in a tone of mild inquiry. Before anyone else can act, all hell breaks loose. Hoards of sparrows pour down through the chimney and into the living room, silencing all debate about Melanie's departure and disrupting all semblance of family routine. Curiously, it is Melanie who shields Cathy from the bird attack, while Lydia fends for herself, and Mitch, warning the others to cover their faces and eyes, acts aggressively to stem the attack. Accustomed to playing family guardian ever since the death of his father, he makes a vigorous effort to block the birds' point of entry and chase out the invaders who have already gotten inside. Without much success. Hitchcock's 1963 special effects do quite a successful job of creating the illusion that the Brenners' living room contains more flapping, screeching sparrows than it really does.

Melanie, acting as protective mother alongside Mitch's protective father, sees Lydia in distress and pulls both the older woman and child out of the house, to safety. Mitch finally bails out too, temporarily abandoning the house to chaos.

In the aftermath of the fourth bird attack, the Brenners' living room is a mess. The local sheriff has been summoned to inspect the damage. But because he has neither witnessed nor been a victim of the bird attacks, he downplays and seeks a conventional explanation for them, blaming the children for provoking the latest one. Because *we* have witnessed several, the sheriff's dismissive attitude strikes us as willfully ignorant and therefore annoying. Mitch challenges the sheriff's complacency. Lydia, predictably, supports her son's assertion. But they are not allies in everything.

During conversation with the sheriff, Lydia walks around the room tidying up, trying to restore a semblance of order to her home. She picks up pieces of broken china, which in this and subsequent scenes becomes a virtual symbol of her fragile sense of order, control and well-being. She straightens the portrait of her sainted husband hanging on the wall over the piano. While doing so she dislodges a dead sparrow, which falls to the floor and frightens her. Melanie, still comforting Cathy on the other side of the room, observes Lydia's actions with an expression of sympathy. She compassionately takes charge of putting Cathy to bed and offers to stay the night. Another signal of her increasing ability to commit to Mitch and Cathy. Mitch gratefully accepts her offer. But it is, like the broken china and the falling bird, another blow to Lydia's delicate world order. She watches Melanie leave the room, arm around Cathy's shoulder, to fetch some things from Melanie's car. It cannot be easy for Lydia to watch a virtual stranger and rival play mother to Cathy. The scene's final image is of Lydia's unhappy facial expression silently protesting her loss of status within her own family.

The following morning begins with a feeling of normalcy restored to the Brenner residence. Dressed in her rustic Brinkmeyer nightgown while getting ready for the day in her room, Melanie seems more acclimated to life on the farm. Outside, having begun their morning earlier than the city dweller (Melanie is not yet *fully* integrated into Brenner family routine), Mitch burns a pile of dead birds down by the shoreline, getting rid of the remnants of disorder, while Lydia announces she is taking Cathy to school and then driving to Dan Fawcett's farm, presumably to inquire about his problem with chickens that won't eat. Melanie seems comfortable, even happy, as she watches and listens to the Brenners outside.

Lydia enters the Fawcett farmyard in a pick-up truck as bulky, utilitarian and inelegant as the one Melanie parked beside at the Bodega Bay docks in an earlier scene. Informed by George, a hired hand, that Dan Fawcett is presumably still in the house, Lydia knocks at the front door but gets no answer.

She walks inside, calling out Dan's name. Superficially, her action is analogous to Melanie surreptitiously entering the Brenner house to deliver the lovebirds. But Lydia is a neighbor and friend of Dan's. And she has just been informed that Dan is inside. So Lydia's entry is neither improper nor illegal, and perhaps intended as a point of contrast to Melanie's unannounced, uninvited entry into a private home she knew was unoccupied.

The lack of background music accentuates an oppressive silence inside the house. In Dan's kitchen Lydia finds the remnants of broken china cups hanging from the bottom of a cupboard. The first tangible indication of disorder, especially in the wake of Lydia's experience the previous day. She proceeds cautiously down a hallway towards Dan's bedroom. And the way Hitchcock shoots that brief trek renders the hallway ominous and Lydia vulnerable. Inside the bedroom, Lydia and we are exposed to a series of escalating shocks. A framed picture hanging askew on the wall. A dead seagull stuck in a shattered window. A dead crow in the disheveled bed. Then Dan Fawcett himself, lying dead in a corner of the room. First his bloody, naked feet, sticking out of pajama legs, looking pathetically vulnerable. He was attacked in his own bed, equivalent to Marion Crane being murdered in a shower. Then his face, eyes gouged out, sockets now just empty black holes. He scarcely looks human. Quick camera cuts force us closer and closer to that gruesome image of violent death.

Terror amidst dead silence. Terror *producing* silence. Horrified, Lydia flees the room, dropping her purse in the hallway, then lurches and stumbles out of the house. Stopping briefly when she reaches George, she cannot describe what she saw inside. She cannot utter a single word. If miscommunication and misperception are at the root of much that is evil in *The Birds*, fear and panic only make them worse. Lydia's inability to explain her panic to the hired hand is shown in a low angle shot that also includes an antenna on the roof of the house. An ironic juxtaposition of her inability to communicate and an instrument of communication. Jack Sullivan writes, "Hitchcock viewed music in extremely broad terms," and that his definition of it "included silence, the sudden, awesome absence of music, capable of delivering the most profound musical frisson of all" (Sullivan, p. xv). The music of silence speaks eloquently for Lydia's paralyzing terror in this scene, as does her dropped, discarded purse.

Rendered mute by what she saw, Lydia flees to the safety of her truck and then flees the farm, at top speed. Viewed in the same extreme long shot that began the scene, the truck kicks up a cloud of dust in its wake that speaks volumes for Lydia's panic. Rash reactions are not typical of her. She tends to repress her feelings, expressing them indirectly. But not now. Her terror and shock sustains the truck's reckless speed all the way home.

As she enters her own farmyard, we and the subjective camera look out through the truck's windshield. From Lydia's point of view we see Melanie and Mitch leaning on a fence in the yard, huddled together and looking quite cozy. For a fleeting moment it seems as if Lydia's truck might slam into them. A homicidal expression, unleashed in a moment of reckless panic, of Lydia's lurking resentment of being abandoned by Mitch and replaced by Melanie. Think of Richard Blaney in *Frenzy* (1972), sneaking into the apartment of the man whose murderous crimes he has been falsely accused of committing, "killing" him by repeated blows with a tire iron, then discovering his victim to be the already dead victim of the man he wanted to kill. So in the end, Blaney did *not* commit murder. But clearly *tried* to.

Lydia is neither Richard Blaney nor Norman Bates. Her truck veers away from its potential targets and screams to a halt. She exits the vehicle and slumps weakly in distress. Mitch and Melanie rush to her aid. Mitch asks his mother what's wrong. Still unable or unwilling to speak, Lydia rudely shoves aside both her unfaithful son and her rival for his attention, then flees to the sanctuary of her house. Terror may not have reduced Lydia to a killer, but it elicits from her an uncharacteristically rude and direct expression of anger. And the residents of Bodega Bay will soon follow her example.

Later. Mitch and Melanie are in the kitchen. Melanie prepares tea for Lydia, who is recovering in her bedroom. Mitch announces his departure for the Fawcett farm, to which he has been summoned by the sheriff. Grateful for her attention to his mother, he kisses Melanie on the neck. She embraces him in return, urging him to be careful. For the first time in the film, they behave openly like a romantic couple. The emotional defensiveness and verbal sparring between them is over. In the words of Robin Wood, "the moment conveys perfectly the beginning of sincerity in the characters, their acceptance of the human need for a relationship grounded in mutual respect and tenderness. It reveals the essentially positive bent of an undermining and ruthless film" (Wood, p. 165). True. But this honest display of affection occurs in the absence of two other characters who have a contrary stake in the relationship: Lydia and Annie.

After Mitch's departure, Melanie brings a tray of Lydia's precious china into Lydia's room, playing the gracious host Lydia would normally play in the Brenner home. Another displacement, however well-intentioned, of Lydia's role in the family. Lydia lies in bed, recuperating from her shocking experience. Hearing a knock at the door, she mistakenly assumes it's Mitch, coming to check on her. She *wants* it to be Mitch. Seeing that it is Melanie, she asks for her son. Informed that Mitch has gone to the Fawcett farm, Lydia assumes everyone doubts her story about Dan's death. Feeling vulnerable for a host of reasons, including her husband's death several years earlier, the two bird attacks on her own home, the discovery of Dan Fawcett's mutilated body and the recent intrusion of Melanie into her jealously guarded family life, Lydia is understandably a bit paranoid. Soothing away some of that paranoia, Melanie assures Lydia the deputy sheriff phoned Mitch from the Fawcett farm and therefore knows the grim truth of her story. Not quite. In a later scene we learn that the stubbornly skeptical sheriff attributes a different cause to Dan's death than does Lydia.

Lydia's bedroom is *not* the oppressive Victorian nightmare of Mrs. Bate's bedroom in *Psycho*, haunted by horrible deeds and memories dating back to Norman's childhood. In the absence of Mitch and Cathy, Melanie and Lydia have a chance to get better acquainted. The prevailing mood between them is friendly, and communication relatively open. When Lydia expresses concern for Cathy at the school, where large windows render the children vulnerable to bird attack, she half apologizes for sounding "foolish." Melanie, having grown up *without* a mother's care, assures her she is not, in a voice full of conviction. She and Lydia have a potential affinity that Mitch and Lydia lack, because he has experienced too *much* "foolish" maternal attention.

Just as Melanie, in the growing atmosphere of trust between them, revealed more of her private pain to Mitch during the birthday party scene, Lydia now admits some of her own emotional weaknesses to a sympathetic Melanie, after having had time to recover from the shock she suffered at the Fawcett farm. She admits to not being strong since the death of her husband. And that Frank understood their children much better than she did, possessing the knack of entering into their private worlds. "I miss him," she confesses wearily, explaining how difficult it has been adjusting to his absence. How many mornings she woke up motivated to make breakfast for him and anticipating their conversations together, then sadly remembering he was gone. Frank's death left Lydia feeling alone, useless and without purpose, lacking an intimate companion with whom she could discuss such matters as she now discusses with Melanie. Listening to Lydia's tale of sadness, Melanie is sincerely moved. She glances at an old family photo, on the mantle, of Mitch as a boy with his parents, apparently enjoying the kind of childhood she lacked. But she sees and assesses that childhood through the eyes of her own experience, not Mitch's. For him it was, perhaps, not so ideal.

Lydia's loneliness cannot be fully ameliorated by her children. Cathy is too young to offer the kind of conversational intimacy Frank did, and Mitch "has his own life." Not exactly, as Lydia unwittingly acknowledges with her next line, "I'm glad he stayed here today. I feel safer with him here." Lydia's extreme dependence on Mitch prevents him from leading that independent life she claims he does. Her feelings will always be contradictory on that point. But in a new spirit of generosity she at least *tries* to respect Mitch's unspoken desire for independence. Lydia says she wants to understand Melanie better. And in an extraordinary, uncharacteristic display of candor, Lydia admits she doesn't even know if she *likes* Melanie. Something she would never have said to Melanie earlier in their brief acquaintance, when Lydia clearly *disliked* Melanie.

Melanie turns away from Lydia, and the camera, in the face of such emotional pressure. "Is that so important? Your liking me?" she replies in a shaky voice, having already endured rejection at the deepest emotional level by her own mother. Lydia's reply sounds reasonable. "Mitch is important to me. I want to like whatever girl he chooses." Yet that was clearly not the case three years earlier with Annie Hayworth, when the pain of Frank's death was still too fresh to overcome. Melanie turns back to face Lydia and asks tentatively, as though afraid of the answer, "And perhaps if you don't?" Lydia's subsequent claim, made in a voice full of resignation, that her opinion of Melanie won't matter much to anyone but herself and that Mitch has "always done exactly what he wanted to" is pure self-delusion. She has no clue how much Mitch has tailored his life to suit her needs, or that she indirectly destroyed his romance with Mitch and Annie.

Despite her talk of conciliation with Melanie and consideration for Mitch, Lydia relapses into weakness and dependence at the end of the scene. Sobbing, she admits she could not bear to be alone. Her apology for that weakness, "Forgive me," is followed immediately by a demonstration of it: "I don't know what I'd do if Mitch weren't here!" No wonder Mitch feels trapped. But Mitch is not presently at his mother's side. Melanie is. And it is Melanie who supplies comfort and reassurance, encouraging Lydia to lie down and sleep, and offering to fetch Cathy from the school when Lydia, for the third time, worries aloud about her daughter's welfare. Worry that Lydia is unable to act on herself. As Melanie leaves the room, taking with her the tray of fragile china, Lydia thanks her for the tea in an almost childlike voice. Melanie assumed the role of protective mother to Cathy during and after the recent bird attack. Now she begins to share in Mitch's role as *Lydia's* protector. But adjustments to new and healthier relationships are seldom seamless in a Hitchcock movie. There are setbacks, complications and regressions. Norman Bates seemed to be a better person after his supper chat with Marion Crane. But that proved a dangerous illusion.

Melanie arrives at the Bodega Bay School while the students inside are singing a strange nursery rhyme about a new bride who combs her hair only once a year and appears to be something of a social pariah. There is a slightly creepy feel to the chant-like performance, especially in the disembodied voices of children. Heard from outside the schoolhouse, from Melanie's perspective, it sounds like a ritualistic purging masking itself as a lesson being taught to students. A school is, after all, an institution of social conditioning as well as, hopefully, a place for children to learn critical thinking. But if the nursery rhyme is all about a strange woman who becomes a social pariah, it eerily foreshadows the role Melanie will be forced to play a couple scenes later, in the minds of Bodega Bay residents. And has already played within the Brenner family.

Melanie enters the schoolhouse. Annie's classroom is a testament to American tradition and normalcy, complete with an American flag and a portrait of George Washington on the wall. Both of which render the nursery rhyme a slightly disturbing juxtaposition. Melanie pokes her head inside the classroom. Cathy turns in her desk and smiles at her. But Annie, not about to interrupt her classroom routine for an intruder (she has already yielded the Brenner home to Melanie), signals Melanie to wait outside for a few minutes. Melanie respectfully complies.

Melanie finds a seat on a bench near the playground. The day is beautiful and peaceful. Melanie seems relaxed. But she lights up a cigarette, perhaps slightly impatient with the delay in fulfilling her promise to Lydia, whom she wants to please in her struggle for acceptance. Then, on the playground equipment visible behind Melanie, crows begin to gather. Slowly. Inexorably. Silently. Melanie is unaware of the growing danger. But curiously, as the bird menace grows, the children's song drones on and on, straining Melanie's patience. Add that frustration to Melanie's intrusion on yet another of Annie's territorial claims (first Mitch, then Annie's home, now Cathy), and you have a human subtext for the impending bird attack. Perched on playground equipment, where the school children would *like* to be right now, the crows are also a reflection of pre-adolescent students who are, in a sense, caged within a fortress of civilization, subject to the adult discipline of their teacher. The avian violence about to be unleashed is both destructive and self-destructive, like a child's tantrum, resulting in harm to the teacher and to the children themselves. And if the children resent adult restraint, and their teacher resents Melanie's intrusion on her authority, Melanie herself has reasons to resent Annie, both for thwarting her "rescue" of Cathy on behalf of Lydia and for remaining a lurking rival to her growing romance with Mitch. None of these characters are likely to act on their resentments with violence. They are not Bruno Anthony in *Strangers on a Train*. But resentment can manifest itself in tricky, subtly destructive ways. The gathering crows echo that potential threat, as well as constitute an independent, inexplicable threat of their own. An extraordinary threat arising from the appearance of the ordinary. After all, birds perching on playground equipment in a schoolyard is in itself a common and hardly alarming sight. Birds *massing* on playground equipment in the wake of previous attacks on humans *is* alarming.

Melanie catches sight of a single crow flying overhead. Following its flight path, her gaze settles on playground equipment now covered with birds. Hitchcock treats us to a close-up of Melanie's stunned expression as she rises up off the bench and into the camera frame. However annoyed she may have become with the song Annie insisted the children finish before being dismissed for recess, Melanie now acts to protect those children. She quickly returns to the classroom, where Annie is enforcing discipline on children eager to go outside and play. This mild imposition of authority coincidentally saves them from a greater disaster than what soon occurs. Melanie too protects the children by telling Annie to close the door, which Annie earlier opened, that leads out to the playground. In a small way, Melanie's *defiance* of Annie's authority contributes to the children's welfare too.

Annie seems momentarily irritated at Melanie's interference. But at Melanie's urging, she looks out one of the large classroom windows that justifiably worried Lydia, recognizes the danger to the children, and quickly forms an alliance with Melanie. As Melanie gives voice to their joint mission, Hitchcock gives us another memorable double profile shot of the two women as they gaze out the window in alarm and before they turn back to the children. This shot emphasizes their unanimity of purpose and resolve rather than their superficial differences. Performing in concert, they herd the children out of school and down towards the town. Annie exercises considerable authority over her students by falsely characterizing their evacuation as a fire drill — something for which they have already been prepared. Annie takes the lead while Melanie guards the rear as the students make their way out of the classroom.

A silent shot of hundreds of crows perched on the Jungle Jim in the playground is counterpointed by the off screen *sound* of many pounding feet striking the ground. The birds take flight. Then follows an extreme long shot of the school, taken from down the street towards the town. A herd of schoolchildren, guarded by Annie and Melanie, runs towards the foreground as a hoard of screeching crows rise up over the now fragile-looking school and swoop down on their victims. Through the illusion of perspective, the birds seem to emerge *from* the school itself, like some ghastly specter of collective madness. It is an awesome display of menace, and one of Hitchcock's most apocalyptic images. In aesthetic and thematic terms, the film now enters territory as much public as personal, informed by such then current events as the Cold War and the prospect of nuclear obliteration.

Each bird attack is more violent than the last. The crows draw blood from cuts they inflict on the children. One very effective shot shows a girl turning to look back at the camera, subjectively aligned with the attacking birds, and screaming in terror. Yes, some of the images involve actors running on a treadmill combined with back screen projections of their pursuers. But the overall impression of panic and violence is dramatically convincing. One of the smaller children trips and falls to the pavement, breaking her eyeglasses. She calls out to Cathy for help. And Cathy responds, playing the same protective role for the younger child that Melanie, Mitch and Annie play for her. Perhaps she had to learn an early lesson in independence because of a weak mother, just as Melanie learned the same lesson because of an absent one.

Melanie steps in to hustle both Cathy and the injured child, who now lag dangerously exposed behind the rest of the group, into a nearby parked car. She rolls up the windows to keep the birds out. But there is no key in the ignition. They are trapped. Attacking crows surround them. The fallen girl's face is badly bloodied. Melanie honks the car horn several times to scare off the birds. Gradually the attack subsides and the crows depart. But it is more of a natural winding down, like the subsiding of an earthquake or a storm, than a consequence of anything Melanie does. As the attack ends, Melanie rests her head on the car's steering wheel, exhausted and feeling much less confident than when she was behind the wheel of her own car as she approached Bodega Bay two days earlier. Still, she successfully rescued two children from probable death, and fulfilled her promise to Lydia. Mission accomplished, for the moment.

A scene in the Tides Restaurant, like the bird attack on the school, fleshes out the larger, communal dimension of the story. Relations among Melanie, the Brenners and Annie temporarily take a back seat to a more populous group of café employees and customers, many of them strangers to one another, who offer a wide range of explanations for the bird attacks. Explanations that reveal as much or more about the people who offer them as about the attacks. The Tides, in this scene, is a microcosm of diverse human perspectives and personalities. Interaction among the characters sways back and forth between serious and comic, agreeable and disagreeable, cooperative and uncooperative, rational and hysterical. In his fascinating book *The Moment of Psycho*, David Thomson describes the first forty minutes of Hitchcock's *Psycho* as the portrait of a modern America that is grasping and devious, permeated by a "nastiness [that] can be felt like sandpaper" (Thomson, p. 22). There is at least a bit of that potential for communal nastiness on display in the Tides Restaurant. Especially towards the end of this scene.

Melanie, observed with interest by café owner Deke Carter and some of his patrons, speaks to her father in San Francisco by telephone and describes the crow attack on the school. As part owner of a newspaper, he can help spread the word to the wider world outside Bodega Bay. But apparently he, like Bodega Bay's sheriff in an earlier scene, is skeptical of bird attack reports, and consequently slow to appreciate danger from so unexpected a source.

Deke is inclined to believe Melanie's story, and is frightened by it. At the other end of the spectrum, an elderly woman named Mrs. Bundy, who by chance stops in to buy a pack of cigarettes and overhears Melanie's phone conversation, does not. An ornithologist possessing considerable scientific knowledge, she is very sure of herself on the topic of birds. To the point of arrogance. Inserting herself, without invitation, into the phone conversation, she answers a question Melanie directs to her father. Yes, there is a difference between crows and blackbirds. And she supplies more information than

Melanie requested, giving the scientific, Latin names of both species. She also disputes Melanie's claim that the crows "attacked" the schoolchildren, insisting that birds possess insufficient intelligence to mount such a coordinated action. Mrs. Bundy's expertise and self-assurance resembles that of the psychiatrist who explains Norman's violent behavior to a police station full of interested spectators at the end of *Psycho*. Both characters are supremely confident in their dispassionate, scientific knowledge. Emotionally secure in their lofty, professional perches. The psychiatrist is not made to pay for his arrogance and complacency, though we the audience soon confront the terrifying emotional reality behind his clinical explanation of Norman's madness. Mrs. Bundy will not be so fortunate.

But for now Mrs. Bundy defends birds in general against Melanie's accusation, insisting they are inoffensive creatures who bring beauty into the world. And that it is instead mankind who makes life on earth difficult. By coincidence, her point is interrupted, to her annoyance, yet given humorous credence by a waitress calling out an order for fried chicken. If man is only rarely on the menu of birds, birds are frequently on the menu of man. None of the characters acknowledges the waitress's unintended contribution to the debate, which continues. In Hitchcock's *Rope* (1948), the murderer Philip is revealed to have once strangled chickens. An early indication of his cruel disposition? In *Foreign Correspondent* (1940), the brutally tortured old scientist Van Meer comments to the film's hero that people feeding birds is a good sign for peace. And in *Halloween* the monster kills two dogs.

Mrs. Bundy's lecture and Melanie's attempt to phone Mitch at the Fawcett farm are interrupted by a new contributor to the debate. A change in camera angle introduces us to a drunkard seated at the end of the bar, declaring "It's the end of the world!" while pointing to the heavens. Simultaneously, the waitress calls out an order for Bloody Mary's. Religion rears its apocalyptic head as the drunk quotes Biblical passages about God's vengeance on the world. Undercutting his argument is a large "Lager" sign behind him. The waitress challenges him more directly, quoting Bible versus warning against the consumption of liquor. A bit hypocritical considering the shelves of liquor bottles for sale in her place of employment. No one takes the drunk seriously. Yet *he* takes perverse delight in the prospect of divine punishment unleashed on all mankind. What is *his* grudge against the world? Hitchcock told Francois Truffaut he based his doom-spouting drunkard on playright Sean O'Casey (Truffaut, p. 69). But the character doesn't require an outside, historical source to be an interesting example of an emotionally skewed perspective.

Mrs. Bundy scoffs at the idea of Armageddon, doubting whether "a few birds" could bring about doomsday. Melanie counters that the attack consisted of more than a few birds. But her argument is cut short by the man who previously defended her. Deke Carter sidetracks the debate by questioning whether or not crows even reside in Bodega Bay at this time of year. Mrs. Bundy compensates for his ignorance by informing him that crows are permanent residents throughout their range. The sheer variety of opinion, knowledge and motive, plus the constant shifting of specific topic, on display in this scene is remarkable. Democracy in action, though not always shown to best advantage. Interplay among characters in the restaurant is reminiscent of an early scene in *The Lady Vanishes* (1938), where a diverse group of travelers stranded at a central European inn converse and bicker, displaying much bigotry and national snobbery, while only a short distance away a street singer is murdered. No one appreciates the larger danger looming over them all.

Mrs. Bundy's response to Deke's inquiry, which interrupted Melanie's point, is in turn interrupted by a local fisherman named Sebastian Scholes, seated in a far corner of the restaurant. Each participant added to the discussion comes as a surprise to us and to the previous participants, as though we hadn't even noticed their presence in the café before they speak. Sebastian questions the ornithologist about seagulls that recently plagued his fishing boats. Before Mrs. Bundy can reply, Deke intrudes a comment about the first seagull attack on Melanie. The waitress then interrupts *that* interruption to complain that she is still waiting for an order of Bloody Mary's. Then a woman seated at a table complains to the waitress that all this talk about bird attacks is frightening her two children. The waitress relays the mother's complaint to Sebastian, who ignores it as he joins the other debaters and describes in detail how gulls attacked members of his crew. Deke echoes the mother's complaint by admitting that Sebastian's story frightens him too. But unlike the children or their mother, he is much too intrigued to opt out of the conversation. Deke is the one character in this scene who doesn't seem to have any fixed convictions about the bird attacks. He drifts this way and that with the shifting tides of debate.

Mrs. Bundy logically concludes the seagulls who attacked Sebastian's boats were only after the fish. She is challenged from behind by Melanie, who asks, "What were the crows after at the school?" Mrs. Bundy throws the question back in Melanie's face. Melanie boldly asserts the birds were trying to kill the children. A conclusion Mrs. Bundy again disputes with science. Sebastian, wavering in his initial opinion about birds deliberately attacking people, now seems inclined to agree with the ornithologist.

Newly arrived in the restaurant, and having a drink at the bar, a traveling salesman butts into the discussion with his own strong opinion. An opinion that neither challenges nor supports any of the views presented so far, but merely vents his own disposition of the moment. Offering no specific complaint about birds, he advocates wiping them out with guns. Perhaps he's experienced a long day on the road, with poor sales. Or maybe he's got trouble at home (did *his* wife change the TV channel while he was watching a ball game?). One gets the impression this silly man would have something mean-spirited to say no matter what topic of conversation he encountered in the restaurant.

Taking the salesman much too seriously, Mrs. Bundy points out the folly of attempting to eradicate an animal with such an enormous worldwide population. Her argument plays right into the hands of the drunkard, who had disappeared from camera view and from the debate for awhile but now returns with his original declaration. "It's the end of the world," he trumpets enthusiastically. For whatever personal reason, he seems as eager to see humankind destroyed by birds as the salesman is to see birds eradicated by humankind. Perhaps put off by the absurd opinions of the drunk and the traveling salesman, Captain Scholes tacks closer to an alliance with the rational but overconfident ornithologist. He now believes the attack described by Melanie was exaggerated in terms of numbers. She insists there were many birds and of varied species. Mrs. Bundy cuts her off again, insisting the idea of different species flocking together is absurd. And that if such a thing ever happened, mankind would not stand a chance. Public debate, following an unpredictable course, can produces strange bedfellows. Mrs. Bundy and the drunken religious fanatic have reached the same conclusion — sort of.

The restaurant's cook emerges from the kitchen to ask what all the fuss is about. Mrs. Bundy and Sebastian joke about a "bird war," mocking the very idea by describing it in terms they believe to be wildly inflated. The woman with two frightened children is not so amused. She defends Melanie's account of the attack on the school, not because she possesses any supporting evidence, but because she fears another attack and is concerned about her kids. Desiring to leave Bodega Bay for San Francisco as soon as possible, she inquires how to get to the freeway. The traveling salesman offers to show her the way, but only after he finishes his drink. Her priorities are not his.

Mitch's arrival with the Sheriff adds to what is by now a cacophony of differing perspectives at the Tides. And it quickly becomes evident that the restaurant is not the only site where opinions are in contention. Mitch and the Sheriff disagree about what happened at the Fawcett farm, from which they have just come. Mitch insists Dan Fawcett was killed by birds. The Sheriff, backed up by other law enforcement officials, claims Dan was killed by a burglar, and that the dead birds found in his bedroom got in later. The frightened mother, still waiting for the salesman to lead her out of danger, challenges the Sheriff by asking if the police were at the school today. Following up, Melanie informs Mitch and the Sheriff about the most recent bird attack.

The drunken religious zealot jumps into the conversation with yet another pronouncement of doom. The salesman signals amused contempt for him to the others, but then mentions another massed bird incident in another town a year ago. Caught up in his new topic, he again ignores the mother's plea to leave. Mrs. Bundy recalls the same incident in some detail, but dismisses it as trivial. "They were all gone the next morning, just as though nothing had happened. Poor things." Her sympathy lies with the birds, not the townspeople. But her tone of voice grudgingly acknowledges the mysterious nature of the incident. She doesn't have the answer to *everything*.

Public debate winds down as participants drop away. The salesman departs with the worried mother and her children, flippantly wishing those remaining good luck figuring it all out. The drunkard repeats his never-changing chant of doom, but is now largely ignored. Sebastian jokes about the whole matter as he gets up to leave. Mitch tries to enlist his help to prepare Bodega Bay for another attack. Mrs. Bundy contemptuously dismisses his concern. Mitch takes Sebastian aside, away from her dissenting voice, to persuade him otherwise, with little success. Melanie follows them, but is in turn distracted by bird calls coming from outside the restaurant. She goes to the window and sees a seagull swoop down and strike a man pumping gas into his car at a service station across the street. The debate inside the Tides ends, overtaken by events outside. "Look," Melanie calls out to the others. Direct, compelling evidence trumps endless debate based on *recollections* of evidence plus various motives that may or may not distort those memories.

The public debate inside the restaurant is a deceptively lighthearted exhibition of human conflict and folly on a communal level. Arguments are made, as often as not, based on emotional needs and prejudices. Little effort is made by anyone to see outside his or her own narrow vantage point. And the debate itself lurches this way and that, sometimes depending on the most trivial factors. The fact that birds have attacked in previous scenes does not invalidate *everything* said by Mrs. Bundy. And it certainly does not validate the drunkard's claim of divine punishment or the traveling salesman's hatred of birds in general. Of all the characters in this scene, Melanie and Mitch seem the most sensible, wanting to prepare for the possible resumption of bird attacks such as they've already experienced. But the bird attack that concludes this scene is a *communal* upheaval, like war, plague or anything else that produces mass hysteria.

Mitch, long accustomed to playing family protector to Lydia and Cathy, is the first to rush to the aid of the stricken man across the street. He paternally orders Melanie to stay inside the restaurant, which she does, for a time. The drunkard doesn't try to help anyone, serving no humane function in what he pronounced to be the end of the world. The woman with the two children returns to the shelter of the Tides, in a panic. Melanie and others gathered in the restaurant watch from a window as gas from the unattended hose flows downhill, across the street and into a parking lot, near a man standing outside his car, lighting a cigarette. Melanie is the first to spot danger, as she was when the sparrows attacked the Brenner family in their living room. She alerts the others observers. They open the window and simultaneously shout their separate warnings to the smoker. The result is an incoherent chaos of sound. Worse than the debate that preceded it. But this time with serious consequences. The man with the cigarette pauses, distracted by clustered shouts of warning he cannot make out. The match in his hand burns his fingers. Reflexively, he throws it to the ground, igniting gasoline, which blows up his car and kills him. The onlookers who tried but failed to save him, and whose confused efforts to do so probably sealed his doom, watch his flaming death in horror.

Worse yet, Melanie watches helplessly as flames rush back up the trail of fuel to its point of origin. Mitch and a few other men drag to safety the first victim of the attack just before an explosion engulfs the gasoline pump and the entire service station. This is the chaos of war, and there is very little control exercised within it.

Reinforcing the war analogy, Hitchcock gives us an overhead shot of the town from high in the sky. At such a distance the fire and the concerns of the people scrambling like ants to escape from or fight it seem almost trivial. Then into that shot fly squawking seagulls. Hoards of them, descending on the town like warplanes. The fire raging below contributes a dull roar resembling that of jet engines, rendering the analogy even stronger. So in addition to being mysterious aberrations of Nature and metaphorical representations of individual human tension and aggression, the attacking birds now echo the Cold War threat of open warfare. *The Birds* was released only a year after the Cuban Missile Crisis frightened much of the world with the prospect of obliteration.

When Melanie exits the restaurant, presumably to help Mitch, the horror she previously witnessed from comparative safety now engulfs her, driving her into the shelter of another, smaller enclosure. A pay phone booth. There she again witnesses the unfolding disaster, but from a more exposed position. An overhead camera shot shows her spinning inside the claustrophobic confines of the glass booth, trying to escape terrors visible on all sides. From her vulnerable vantage point we see an out-of-control automobile plow through a Stop sign (another breakdown of normal social order) and head straight for her/us, before veering away at the last moment, its driver flailing at gulls attacking him inside the vehicle. He slams into other cars parked nearby, then flees on foot.

Melanie tries to flee her inadequate shelter but is driven back by attacking birds. The tiny phone booth is better than no protection at all, but not much. Entrapment is a common theme in *The Birds*. Melanie is trapped now in the booth, and later in an upstairs bedroom at the Brenner home. She is, or was, also trapped in a pattern of self-destructive, overly-defensive behavior by her feelings of abandonment as a child. Annie is trapped in Bodega Bay because of her lingering feelings for Mitch, who is, at least on weekends, trapped in the same place because of his mother's dependence on him.

Another overhead shot of Melanie as she whirls in the terror of confinement. Sirens blare as firemen try to extinguish the fire while being harassed by birds. An abandoned fire hose sprays water in all directions, dousing the phone booth and briefly obscuring our and Melanie's view. A large wagon pulled by a team of panicked horses overturns, dumping its cargo on the street. A pedestrian lurches by, his bloody head covered by pecking birds. Again Melanie tries to abandon the booth, and again she is driven back inside in order to avoid the bloody pedestrian's fate.

We see Mitch approaching from a distance as a bird crashes suicidally into the booth, shattering the glass on one side. Melanie turns her face away to avoid the onslaught, but is immediately confronted by a second attack from a different direction. Her flimsy sanctuary crumbles around her. Curiously, Melanie's red-painted fingernails, looking like bird talons, appear prominently during this attack, forging a visual link between victim and assailants. No human character in *The Birds* physically tries to kill another person. But the *emotional* violence inflicted by people against other people in the film, wittingly or not, is echoed by the increasingly vicious and large scale bird attacks.

Mitch rescues Melanie from her breeched fortress and returns with her to the comparative safety of the Tides Restaurant. Her hair is disheveled, reflecting another degree of lost control over her life. To the fading sound of birds attacking outside, Mitch and Melanie walk hand in hand through the seemingly deserted cafe. After so recently being the site of much activity and conversation, the stillness now permeating the Tides seems eerily abnormal. A further erosion of the social fabric. In a windowless hallway at the back of the restaurant they encounter a group of patrons and employees cowering in fear. Including an obviously shaken, now speechless Mrs. Bundy, whose overconfident, scientific rhetoric could not shield her from the shocking reality of the violence perpetrated by her feathered friends.

As the bird attack subsides, humankind takes up the slack in aggression. And from a most unexpected source. The mother of the two frightened children, the same woman who previously defended Melanie's claim of a bird attack on the school against Mrs. Bundy's skepticism, now turns on Melanie, angrily demanding to know why the birds attacked. "They say when you got here the whole thing started." "They" implies the participation of others in this group in the formulation of a new theory to explain the mysterious bird attacks. And the selection of a scapegoat to take the blame for them. Based solely on the coincidence of bird attacks beginning at the same time Melanie arrived in Bodega Bay, the increasingly hysterical woman accuses Melanie of being the cause. Manny Balestrero, in *The Wrong Man* (1957), knows how Melanie feels when he is falsely accused of a crime and experiences firsthand the inclination of so many strangers to presume his guilt. So does Roger Thornhill in *North by Northwest*.

A subjective camera, sharing Melanie's point of view, puts us in the position of the accused as her/our accuser moves closer and closer, demanding to know "Who are you? *What* are you? Where did you come from?" The questions are rhetorical. Melanie's accuser supplies her own answers. "I think you're the cause of all this. I think you're evil. Evil!" This in no interrogation. It's an inquisition, with precedents older than the Spanish Inquisition and newer than Hitler's and Stalin's notorious show trials. Ironically, the person who accuses outsider Melanie of being the cause of evil in Bodega Bay is herself an outsider. In slightly different circumstances, *she* could have been made the scapegoat. An extreme close-up of the frightened woman making her hysterical accusation is reminiscent of the final close-up of Norman Bates in *Psycho*. One is a visual representation of full frontal madness, the other of full frontal hysteria. But once again, *The Birds* is not *Psycho*. Melanie disarms her accuser with a mere slap of the face. The woman breaks down crying, her paranoid spell broken, for the time being. Melanie too recoils from the ugliness of what she has just witnessed, and of which she was the victim. She leans back on Mitch, whom she now trusts, for support. The nasty tension of communal paranoia at the end of this scene is broken when Deke returns to his restaurant and breathlessly announces the end of the latest bird attack. Mitch and Melanie leave to fetch Cathy from Annie's house, while the small mob that once crowded fearfully into the windowless corridor for safety now flocks back to the window to see the birds depart.

Running up the street past the school and towards Annie's house, Mitch and Melanie spot crows ominously perched on the school roof, telephone lines, playground equipment, *everywhere*. "The crows again!" Melanie exclaims. Mitch cautions her to be quiet. Subjective and reactive traveling shots depict the action as Melanie and Mitch slow to a walk, trying not to provoke the birds into another attack.

Annie's house too is outlined with crows. From Mitch's vantage point, slightly ahead of Melanie's, we and the camera peer through the open gate and see Annie's dead body sprawled at the bottom of the front steps, her bloodied legs obscenely splayed. Obscene in the sense of implied violence. There is something horribly vulnerable about the way Hitchcock positions Annie's body, as there was with portions of Marion's body after her murder in *Psycho*. If, as some critics contend, Hitchcock was misogynistic, he nevertheless pictures the demise of some of his heroines in a shocking manner that, in my estimation, encourages pity for them. If Annie Hayworth was intended to be a throwaway character, why make her violent death seem such a brutal

An impossible image. Mitch Brenner (Rod Taylor), Annie Hayworth (Suzanne Pleshette), Melanie Daniels (Tippi Hedren) and Cathy Brenner (Veronica Cartwright) flee attacking birds in this misleading publicity still from *The Birds*. Despite her growing friendship with Melanie, Annie's life is sacrificed in order to clear the way for Melanie to join the Brenner family.

violation and loss? Commenting on some of the filmmakers who were influenced by Hitchcock's groundbreaking *Psycho*, David Thomson contends some of them "forgot or were incapable of any balancing need for poetry, for compassion for those characters shot to pieces" (Thomson, p. 140).

Shielding Melanie from the terrible sight of Annie's corpse, Mitch characteristically tells her to stay behind while he rushes to the body, as he did when the birds attacked outside the Tides. But Melanie would not be Melanie if she shrank from a challenge, or from satisfying her need to know. Just as she ignored Mitch's instructions at the restaurant, she now rushes to the fence, sees Annie, and screams in horror. And, perhaps more importantly, in anguish, at the loss of a new friend. At the very least, a potential friend. Mitch uses his hand to hide Annie's face, which has presumably suffered the same fate as Dan Fawcett's.

Recovering quickly from shock, Melanie re-focuses her own and Mitch's attention on the original object of their mission. Cathy. Mitch spots the distraught girl through the living room window. Taking her out of the house, he blocks her view of Annie's body with his own, as he did Annie's bloody face from Melanie, then removes her from the porch by way of the side steps. Placing Annie in Melanie's care (again they play surrogate parents to the girl in Lydia's absence), Mitch angrily picks up a rock from Annie's yard to throw at the killer crows gathered on Annie's roof. It is a perfectly understandable, emotional reaction to the loss of his dear friend. But it is also an action that could provoke another attack and endanger Cathy. And this from a man who only moments earlier cautioned Melanie not to speak too loudly lest she provoke the same. Recognizing his folly, Melanie now stops *him*. He reluctantly drops the rock, then gently touches the face of the young girl whose safety is supposed to be his top priority in this scene. Reason trumps impulse, which was not the case with the woman who all but accused Melanie of being a witch in the previous scene. Nor was it the case when Melanie so flagrantly entered the Brenner home without permission in order to satisfy her need to better the prank Mitch pulled on her back at the pet shop.

Weeping for Annie even as she usurps Annie's former roles as Mitch's lover, Cathy's protector and even Lydia's confidante, Melanie urges Mitch not to leave Annie's body where it lies, displaying compassion for a rival with whom she had become reluctant friends. Hitchcock himself suggested a darker motive for this show of compassion. Does she tell Mitch to move Annie's body into the house and out of sight because she wants to bury his memory of her (Auiler, p. 413)? Possibly. But as played by Tippi Hedren, the action seems more sympathetic than underhanded.

Mitch returns to Annie's body, placing his suit jacket over her mutilated face and torso, and gently carries her inside the house. As he does so, we see her bare legs akimbo, one shoe off, a fly already feasting on her blood (the latter probably a lucky coincidence). It is one of Hitchcock's most memorable and heartbreaking images of human fragility.

Mitch and Melanie escort Cathy to Melanie's car, still parked outside the school. But first Mitch returns Melanie's purse, which she had dropped. Like Lydia's china cups, that purse is to some extent a token of order and security in Melanie's life. The camera tracks the trio to the car, glancing at both humans and birds as they warily eye each other. Mitch urges his crying sister to keep quiet so as not to provoke the crows. Another example of suppressing a natural instinct in order to avoid danger. Mitch raises the roof on the convertible. Cathy sits between the adults as Mitch drives them away from the school. In a very convincing portrayal of a child's distress by Veronica Cartwright, Cathy sobs uncontrollably as she recounts how Annie saved her life and sacrificed her own after they stepped outside the house to see what the explosion (at the gas station) was about and were viciously set upon by birds. "They covered her!" after Annie shoved Cathy back inside the house. It's a terrifying account of an incident we were never shown. A tribute to both the courage of Annie Hayworth and the horror of her death. In *Topaz*, the character Juanita de Cordoba similarly sacrifices her life to save a loved one — her purple dress, symbolic of her blood, spilling onto and spreading out on a chessboard-like floor, equivalent to Annie's distorted and bloodied body.

Melanie, Mitch and Cathy are all shocked and saddened by Annie's death. Yet that death makes possible Melanie's full integration into the Brenner family. She and Annie cannot both be Mitch's lover and Cathy's surrogate mother, the latter role clearly played by Annie at school and at Cathy's birthday party. Comparing Annie to the character Mr. Memory in *The Thirty-Nine Steps* (1935), Hitchcock commented that both are doomed by their sense of duty (Truffaut, 98). But Annie's violent death is also a subconscious fulfillment of Melanie's and Mitch's desire to be with each other. Interestingly, in the original script Annie survived until near the end of the film, when she, not Melanie, became the victim of the last bird attack, in the Brenner attic. By substituting Melanie for Annie in that final scene, Hitchcock complicates Melanie's hard fought acceptance into the Brenner household. Annie's death alone does not make that acceptance a smooth process.

Annie left her home in San Francisco and spent three years desperately hanging on to an unsatisfactory but apparently preferable (to nothing) semblance of a romantic relationship with Mitch. What is the emotional cost to Annie of her displacement by Melanie? Of the destruction of her day-to-day ties with the Brenner family? Annie's death metaphorically signifies not only her defeat in a contest with Melanie, but the self-sacrificing manner in which she helped Melanie establish a beachhead against Lydia. What option could have remained to Annie but her sad departure from Bodega Bay. Suicide? Only if Annie were incapable of facing a future without Mitch. And she seems too strong a personality for that. Though impressions can be deceiving. In any case, Annie's death by violent bird attack is a dramatic measure of the severe emotional change in her life triggered by Melanie Daniels' arrival in Bodega Bay.

Later, at the Brenner farm, Melanie assists Mitch in barricading the outside of the house against the another anticipated bird attack. He stands on a ladder while she hands him scraps of lumber to nail over vulnerable windows. For all practical purposes, they perform as partners. In *Rear Window*, L. B. Jeffries and Lisa Fremont, lovers troubled by different lifestyles and expectations, grow emotionally much closer when they collaborate to solve the disappearance of a neighbor lady. On the other hand, Manny and Rose Balestrero, in *The Wrong Man*, are driven further and further apart by the stress of his arrest for a burglary he did not commit. Similar situations do not guarantee identical outcomes. There are too many other factors involved.

Mitch and Melanie glance back towards Bodega Bay. A partly dispersed cloud of smoke hangs over the town. Multitudes of birds float on and circle above the bay, yielding an impression of looming menace. Mitch comments that except for "a little smoke," Bodega Bay looks deceptively normal. His comment could just as easily apply to the film's story of human emotions and relationships in flux. Disruptions seem to come in sporadic bursts. He notes a similar pattern to the behavior of birds. They attack, disperse, then mass again before another attack.

Melanie is unable to contact her father in San Francisco because the telephones are dead. A reduction of the technological infrastructure that binds society together. But electrical power remains functional, for the time being. In these final, climactic scenes from *The Birds*, disintegration of that infrastructure occurs in stages. From inside the house, Lydia calls to Mitch (notably *not* to Melanie) that she is getting some news on the radio. Mitch and Melanie enter the house, where they and Lydia listen to a newscast from San Francisco about a bird attack on the Bodega Bay School (information Melanie earlier gave to her father over the phone), plus sketchy details of another attack. Then on to international news, including a story about United States' relations with Europe and other parts of the world. Hints of the Cold War that underpins but does not dominate *The Birds*. Mitch is annoyed at the newscast's lack of urgency regarding the bird attacks on Bodega Bay, just as he was earlier with the Sheriff's. Viewed from an experiential and emotional distance, the bird threat *does* seem exaggerated, even fanciful. Knowing better, as a painful result of experience, Mitch puts another log in the fireplace, banking the fire to guard against another intrusion of birds down the chimney.

Lydia's delicate emotional state of mind comes to the surface as she fires a series of questions at Mitch about their precarious situation. Possessing no answers herself, she demands impossible assurances from her son and protector, upon whom she depends almost entirely, and whose loyalty to her, as *she* defines it, has recently come into question. He grows annoyed with her demands as she grows angry with his inadequate responses. Moving closer to confront him, she reacts to his "I don't know" with an accusatory "You don't know! You don't know! When *will* you know?! When we're all dead?!" Losing all self control, Lydia concludes her tirade by yelling, "If only your father were here!" The ultimate insult to a son who has sacrificed so much to fill his father's shoes. Lydia, frightened by recent bird attacks and still deeply resentful of Mitch's growing commitment to Melanie, lashes out with the most hurtful weapon at her command. The sainted memory of her late husband, Mitch's father. In *The Wrong Man*, Rose hits Manny with a hairbrush during a similarly stressful encounter, then guiltily admits she is sick. Her comment, "They come at me from all sides," could easily be a line of dialog from *The Birds*.

Deeply upset by the discord between her two primary caregivers, Cathy intercedes her body between Mitch and Lydia, crying out for them to stop. Lydia, realizing how unfair and hurtful she is being to both of her children, reasserts control over her fears, apologizing to Mitch and hugging Cathy while

Mitch places his hands gently on her shoulders. Though damaged, they remain a family unit. But visible behind them, far across the room, is one of the causes of their recent discord. Melanie turns her back on the painful spectacle, knowing she has inadvertently contributed to it. For the moment she is alone again, isolated from the Brenner family. We've just witnessed another attack and dispersal episode, but in human rather than avian terms.

Mitch asks Lydia to make everyone some coffee, giving his mother something to do to feel useful and keep her troubled mind occupied. Cathy accompanies her to the kitchen, allowing Mitch to re-connect with Melanie, whom he will *not* give up, the way he did Annie, in order to appease his mother. He and Melanie return outside to fetch more wood for the fireplace. Melanie, observant as usual (she was the first character in the movie to note unusual behavior among the birds), wonders where a flock of birds flying overhead is going. Mitch speculates it might be Santa Rosa, further inland. The war expands. The scene concludes with a close-up of Melanie's worried, inquisitive expression.

A short time later. Silence pervades the Brenner living room as the camera pans over four characters awaiting their fate after preparing the best they can for the next attack. Could this also be a portrait of an American family awaiting nuclear doomsday so dreaded at times during the Cold War? Lydia sits by herself in a chair against the wall, beneath the painting of her late husband. For her, it is the most comforting location in the room. Melanie sits on the couch, with her arms protectively around Cathy, once again performing Lydia's maternal role. Mitch, following *his* usual pattern of behavior, patrols the room, testing the strength of their defenses. The family is reduced to its own resources. There is no evidence of institutional assistance, except for electrical power.

Cathy asks Mitch (*not* her mother) if she can bring the lovebirds from the kitchen into the living room. Lydia vociferously objects. Cathy pleads, "But Mom, they're in a cage." Lydia rebuts, "They're birds, aren't they!," as though that fact alone were sufficient reason for disliking them. Perhaps it's an understandable objection, under the circumstances. But Lydia has another reason for disliking the lovebirds. As a gift from Melanie to Mitch by way of Cathy, they symbolize the threatened destruction of Lydia's emotional fortress as surely as the gathering birds do her physical house. And in her delicate state of mind, Lydia has about as much tolerance for such a threat as the homicidal husband did for his wife's disruption of the game he was watching on television. Mitch accedes to his mother's weakness. Melanie's lovebirds remain in the kitchen.

Mitch continues his security patrol in that same kitchen, where he glances at the beautiful, docile and confined lovebirds before returning to the living room and taking a seat on the piano bench. From the camera angle Hitchcock gives us as he does so, we see Frank's portrait looming over Mitch, who shoulders the burden of his father's strong legacy and Lydia's over-dependence on it.

Cathy once again breaks the oppressive silence by asking Mitch (again, *not* Lydia, who has largely yielded her parental authority to her son) why the birds are attacking people. He has no answer, just as he didn't for Lydia's more forceful, desperate questions about what might happen next and what they should do about it. The silence resumes. Lydia, trying to maintain some semblance of normality in her world, gets up from her chair, with her sweater wrapped protectively around her shoulders (what an image of fragility!), and meticulously gathers up her china cups from the coffee table. Placing them carefully on a serving tray, she returns the cups to the kitchen, where they are kept when not in use. Concerned, the other characters watch her as she goes through these motions. Completing her self-reassuring task, Lydia returns from the kitchen and resumes her seat. Silence continues.

Close shots of all four characters show them looking up anxiously at the ceiling, anticipating the next attack. Their expressions of worry are similar, yet each gazes up in a somewhat different direction. They share an experience of dread, yet they remain distinct individuals, as their reactions to the attack, when it comes, will demonstrate.

Mounting tension hits eleven-year-old Cathy the hardest. Breathing heavily, she announces, "I'm sick, Melanie." Not "Mother," but "Melanie," who takes Cathy into the bathroom while Lydia remains a helpless, inactive observer in her chair under her husband's portrait. Frozen in place. When she hears the sound of her daughter throwing up, Lydia finally glances in the direction of the bathroom, as though reminded of her neglected duty. But she still cannot rouse herself to go to Cathy. Moments later Melanie returns to the living room with Cathy, holding a wet wash cloth to the child's forehead, and sits back down on the couch. Then we get a shot of all three adults returning to their separate, private contemplations of doom. Cathy, with eyes closed, hangs on tightly to Melanie.

Finally the expected attack comes, emerging out of the oppressive silence. A few, innocent sounding bird calls rise to a terrifying crescendo of screeching, wing-beating mayhem, followed by wave after wave of cacophonous variations. Brilliantly, from a dramatic point of view, and wisely, from a special effects point of view, Hitchcock never lets us see this attack from outside the house. Only the overwhelming *sound* of attack, plus a few isolated breeches of the house's defenses, convey to us the violence of this event. As a result, we the audience share viscerally in the victims' claustrophobic sense of terror. Of being trapped inside a cage. Like the lovebirds. Like all of the pet shop animals. Hitchcock compared this scene to a family's experience of the blitz during World War Two (Durgnat, p. 348).

Everybody stands up. The first casualty of the attack is Melanie. In this moment of crisis, Cathy abandons her and instinctively flees to her real mother for protection. Melanie is left alone, again. With Cathy in tow, Lydia races from one corner of the living room to another in a vain search for emotional and physical shelter. The sonic assault comes from all sides. Melanie retreats to a corner of the couch and curls up on it.

The house's defenses are breeched. Bird screams escalate to an hysterical pitch as a seagull bursts through a window with a loose shutter. Mitch battles to keep the invaders out. It's hand-to-beak combat as he reaches out through the broken glass to close the shutter while birds peck viciously at him. Meanwhile, a cutaway shot shows us action on an untended front. Bird beaks poke ever larger holes through the front door. Hitchcock's editing keeps us informed of separate actions occurring simultaneously. In a tight, overhead shot we see Melanie, feeling hemmed in on all sides, twisting and turning and pressing herself against a wall, crushing a lampshade in the process. Hitchcock told Francois Truffaut he kept his camera back "to show the nothingness from which she's shrinking" (Truffaut, p. 263). *Almost* as though what she feared was a nightmare of her own creation. A phantom. Like Norman Bates reacting to the memory of his mother. But the bird attack is real, as Mitch experiences moments later.

A close-up of Mitch's face grimacing with strain is followed by a close-up of his bloody hand clutching at the shutter knob while trying to swat away aggressive birds. Deafening bird shrieks pulsate louder and softer, lower and higher in pitch. He finally pulls the shutter closed. To secure it, he grabs a lamp off a nearby table, violently yanks it free of an electrical socket and tries to rip out its cord to use as a rope for tying down the damaged shutter. Another common household object, like Lydia's and Dan Fawcett's china cups and the lampshade Melanie crushed, destroyed in the heat of the moment. It might seem trivial to note the destruction of such commonplace items, but they are parts of an everyday sense of domestic order that is important to these characters and to this movie. Unfortunately, Mitch needs both of his hands to rip the cord out of the lamp. He briefly lets go of the shutter. A gull takes advantage of that moment of inattention to punch through again.

Melanie, mastering her fear, starts to leave her protective wall near the fireplace to go to Mitch's aid until, with a great whooshing sound very expressive of his desperation and counterpointing the continuing sound of birds attacking, Mitch succeeds in closing the shutter again and tying it down with his makeshift rope. Meanwhile, Lydia and Cathy abandon one corner of the room in favor of yet another. None of them prove adequate. Observed by the camera from overhead (a bird's eye view, if they could get inside), Mitch goes to their rescue, re-locating them to a chair. But when he tries to leave them to attend to Melanie, Lydia clings desperately to his arm. Mitch has to free himself by force. It's a small but telling moment in a hectic scene.

Unlike Lydia, Melanie's primary concern at this moment is not her own safety but Mitch's injured hand. She grabs a cloth to wrap around it. But Mitch, looking annoyed, pushes her away in order to get a bandage *for himself*. So accustomed is he to taking care of the needs of others, specifically those of Lydia and Cathy, that he finds it difficult to accept the tender care of even the woman he has come to love. In the heat of battle, this is a passing yet not insignificant impression that hints at potential problems in their future relations, assuming they survive the present scene.

After dressing his own wounds, Mitch finally notices the assault on the front door, through which bird beaks are punching and chopping ever larger holes. Rushing to that door, Mitch presses against it with his hands and full body weight. A pointless tactic. Then he improvises a better one, maneuvering a large, wood-backed mirror in front of the failing door. He quickly retrieves a hammer and nails from an adjoining room and secures the surrogate door over the breach. Melanie observes him from the hallway.

Crisis piles on top of crisis as Melanie and Mitch return to the living room. The pervasive bird screeches are punctuated by an even louder shriek. The lights go out. Some birds have sacrificed themselves in a suicidal attack on the electric power lines. Another failure of the social infrastructure that binds people together and affords them some level of security and comfort. The living room is now lit only by the fireplace, which throws up fitful illumination against the prominently shown ceiling. The overall tension of the scene ratchets up a notch or two as a result. Mitch fetches a flashlight from another room. With that modest substitution for electric light he and Melanie spot yet another threat: more holes being punched through yet another door. Mitch immediately leaves to fetch yet another surrogate barrier to reinforce the failing one. But before he can do so, the sounds of attack begin to fade. The birds are leaving, as mysteriously as they came. Mitch and Melanie stop in their tracks.

Through a series of low angle shots, showing a firelit ceiling looming portentously over the heads of Mitch, then Melanie, then Lydia, and finally over all three characters, Hitchcock creates a powerful, apocalyptic impression of a family under siege, from without and from within. War on both macro and micro levels. Placement of the three characters at the conclusion of this remarkable shot generates a great sense of depth. Mitch, Melanie and Lydia share an intense experience of mixed dread, anticipation and relief. At the same time they seem separated from each other by great distances. They are both a family unit and very distinct individuals.

At the start of the final scene in *The Birds*, a burning log crumbles in the fireplace. The fire is slowly ebbing. Potentially another breech in the house's defenses. In the aftermath of the massive bird attack, the Brenner family succumbs to exhaustion. Repeating the pan shot review of the characters from the beginning of the previous scene, Hitchcock shows us Lydia sitting slumped and asleep on the piano bench and once again beneath Frank's reassuring portrait, Melanie sitting up awake and alert on one end of the couch, Cathy lying asleep under a blanket at the other end, and Mitch sitting in a chair, asleep, with his head propped up on his bandaged, bloody hand.

Melanie alone keeps watch over the family, alert to the slightest sound emerging from the silent house. She and we hear a light, indistinct fluttering, as of bird wings. She calls out to Mitch, softly. He doesn't respond. Choosing not to wake him, Melanie retrieves the flashlight and, assuming Mitch's role as family guardian, investigates the suspicious sound herself. In another very effective use of dead silence as a dramatic device, Hitchcock takes us on patrol with Melanie through the darkened house. First the kitchen. Cathy's lovebirds are not the source of the disturbance. Melanie then shines her singular light on the stairs leading up to the second floor. The effect is creepy. Think back to Arbogast and then Lyla Crane ascending the stairs of the Bates house in *Psycho*, unaware of what they'll encounter at the top. Tracking and subjective traveling shots accompany Melanie up the staircase. Occasional, vague yet menacing fluttering sounds draw her upward.

Melanie locates the mysterious sounds coming from behind a door at the top of the stairs. Slowly, hesitantly, she turns the knob, opens the door and peeks inside. Spotting a large hole torn in the roof, she enters the attic room and illuminates it with her flashlight. A canopied bed at the far end of the room is covered with seagulls and crows. So much for Mrs. Bundy's theory that birds of different species never flock together. The light Melanie intrudes into this dark place triggers an immediate and vicious mass attack on her. Reflexively backing away from danger, Melanie collides with the door and inadvertently bumps it shut behind her.

Is it a coincidence that the climactic attack on Melanie Daniels occurs while Mitch, Lydia and Cathy Brenner are asleep downstairs? Who knows what kind of uninhibited violence, triggered by lurking fears or resentment or jealousy or even self-hatred, they might inflict on her in their dreams. Even Cathy. If Mrs. Bates consisted of the worst elements of Norman's mind, periodically surging to the surface and fully unleashed in *Psycho*, this attack on Melanie might be, in part, a subconsciously fantasized attack by three characters who would ordinarily never yield to such impulses. Lydia's lingering fear of abandonment by Mitch in favor of Melanie. Mitch's inclination to judge irresponsible independence harshly, especially in light of his own sacrifice of such independence. Cathy's inclination to pick up on and echo Mitch's and Lydia's judgmental views. Even Melanie's own inclination to self-destruction. All of these things and probably more lurk behind the bird attack in this scene. And the startling absence of bird screeches during this attack, so unlike previous bird attacks and the shower scene in *Psycho*, lends it a strange, eerie, extremely intimate quality. As though it really could be taking place in a dream. A nightmare.

If aurally very different from the murder of Marion Crane, the final attack on Melanie is certainly reminiscent of the infamous shower scene in visual terms. Hitchcock films it in rapid cuts from multiple angles. Birds with their beaks wide open fly directly at the subjective camera. Birds slash Melanie's face, legs and hands, inflicting bloody wounds, as she reaches for the knob to open the door and flee. All to the constant beating of wings. The lack of bird screeching allows us to hear Melanie's muffled cries of distress. And more importantly, her almost reflexive plea to Mitch to get Cathy and Lydia out of harm's way. She is either unable to open the door and escape, or she refuses to expose the Brenner family to danger and thereby sacrifices herself. If the latter, she has become what Annie Hayworth was. Gradually, painfully, Melanie succumbs to relentless attack and collapses to the floor.

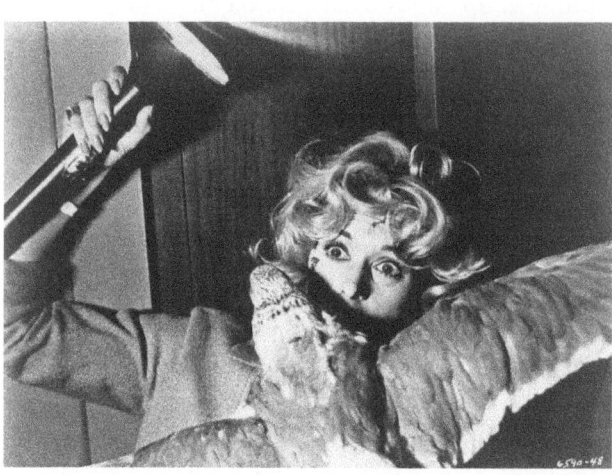

Melanie Daniels (Tippi Hedren) suffers the climactic bird attack alone, upstairs in the Brenner home, while the Brenners are asleep downstairs. By not opening the door to flee, she prevents the birds from invading the rest of the house, sacrificing herself for the Brenner family, in *The Birds*.

Mitch, awake now, calls out to Melanie from the other side of the closed door. He tries but cannot open the door because Melanie's unconscious body blocks it. Perhaps symbolic of her determination to sacrifice herself for the Brenners. A sacrifice Mitch refuses to accept. He forces open the door. The singularity of his one visible eye as he does so conveys his fierce determination to save the woman he loves. Finally he succeeds in opening the door just enough to grab hold of Melanie's arm, while birds attack his already injured hand, and drag her out. Surprisingly, Lydia is visible above and behind her crouching son, slapping at the birds trying to escape the room, forcing them back inside. Suppressing her own worst impulses?

Mitch drags Melanie's unconscious, torn, bloody body into the hallway and closes the door. He carries her downstairs as Lydia leads the way with an oil lamp, calling out "Poor thing! Poor thing!" in a fairly convincing display of sympathy. Mitch instructs her to fetch bandages and antiseptic while he carries Melanie into the living room. Lydia is now more active in defending against attack and coping with the consequences than in any previous scene. But would she have attempted to rescue Melanie if Mitch had not initiated it? Was she merely trying to keep the attacking birds from breaking out into her *own* sanctuary?

Ever in charge, Mitch lays Melanie on the couch and tells Cathy to fetch some brandy. As Mitch pours a glass for her, Melanie awakens and picks up where she left off before losing consciousness. Reacting from instinct, she flails defensively with her hands and arms, striking out at Mitch and, through the subjective camera, at *us*. For a moment, she fulfills Norman's pessimistic yet vivid description of the human condition in *Psycho*. "We scratch and claw, but only at the air, only at each other — and for all of it we never budge an inch." But contrary to Norman's gloomy outlook, in *The Birds* we *do* budge an inch. Maybe more. Mitch restrains and reassures Melanie, "It's alright. It's alright." Cathy, a child upset by the sight of an adult protector reduced to such a state of helplessness, averts her eyes.

Melanie lapses into a passive state of shock. Her torn dress, disheveled hair and the spatters of red blood on her face betray her complete loss of control over her own situation. Mitch pours a little brandy into her mouth, but Melanie, her eyes unblinking, doesn't respond. Lydia returns with medical supplies. Cathy, recovering from her distress, retrieves a lamp at Mitch's request. Lydia gently cleans Melanie's facial cuts with a wet cloth. One of the few times we've seen her in the role of protector and healer.

Distressed at Melanie's unresponsiveness, Mitch insists she must be taken to a hospital. Lydia objects out of fear. "I don't know what's outside there." In more ways than one. Lydia fears both the birds and, on another level, the unknown, changing world that awaits her if Mitch and Melanie stay together. Even as she bandages Melanie's wounded forehead, she works mildly against Melanie's future happiness and that of her own son. But Mitch will not be dissuaded this time. When he reaches the front door, Lydia's voice interrupts him again, but this time merely to request that he try to access the news on the car radio. Her role as the main obstacle between Mitch and Melanie is slowly diminishing.

Reasoning that Melanie's car would be faster than Lydia's truck, Mitch cautiously exits the house and heads for the garage. Our first image from outside the house since the earlier attack on the entire family is of the exterior of the front door, pitted and scarred from bird beaks and talons. Bird crap stains the front porch. Crows and seagulls are perched everywhere, as far as the eye can see, from the floor and railings of the porch, to the roof, to telephone poles and wires stretching away from the farmstead, to the distant bay. These images generate an eerie mood, like the calm both after and before a storm. Whatever physical and emotional forces have been mysteriously stirred up by or since Melanie's arrival in Bodega Bay are still in play.

The potential for violence lurking beneath the ominous calm is evident when one of the crows pecks viciously at Mitch's bandaged hand as he leans against the porch railing. Other birds occasionally strike at his feet and legs as he slowly makes his way to the garage. Inside the garage he discovers, to his happy surprise, a small haven of security, thanks to some wire mesh (another "cage") that prevented the birds from penetrating a broken window in the roof. Moving to the larger door, he starts to open it, decides otherwise, then proceeds to Melanie's car where, obeying his mother's request, he turns on the radio. He and we learn from a newscast that although Bodega Bay appears to be the center of the bird attacks, there have been a few on other communities as well. Authorities have announced they may call in the military to deal with the situation. Another war analogy.

Mitch prudently silences the radio before opening the garage door. Not wanting to provoke another attack, he drives Melanie's car ever so slowly out of the garage and up to the sidewalk leading to the porch. As he returns to the house, birds again peck irritably at his feet and legs. Tension remains high. Inside, Lydia protectively holds onto a staring, passive Melanie, who now sits up on the couch. Lydia asks Mitch what he heard on the radio. He tells her only, "It's alright," just as he told Melanie a few minutes earlier. Ever the protector, he does not share with her any alarming details about attacks on other communities.

A backtracking camera leads Melanie, Mitch and Lydia to the front door. Melanie is bracketed and supported by mother and son. Mitch opens the door. Light from outside illuminates the faces of all three characters, suggesting an emergence from darkness. Or, in the case of the attic upstairs, from a kind of subconscious nightmare. But if the characters' journey out of the house is a healthy development, a reverse angle shot depicts a wider world still fraught with danger. Melanie's fragile little speedster is surrounded in all directions by hovering birds. Ordinary, commonplace birds, just like the film's ordinary, non-psychotic human characters. Ordinary birds that have been re-defined as predators. Which, of course, they were all along.

Mitch and Lydia carefully lead Melanie out of the house. A few bird calls are heard. Signaling the start of another attack? No. They subside. Fear of another attack rouses Melanie out of her passivity. Darting her eyes in all directions, she protests and resists efforts to make her leave the dubious shelter of the house, even if it's for her own good. Mitch reassures her again, and together with Lydia pulls her outside and to her car. Big close-ups of all three characters are juxtaposed with shots of birds. Melanie's emergence from the Brenner house, and from the extremely defensive state of mind to which the final bird attack drove her, stands in sharp contrast to Norman's failure to free himself from the Bates house, to which he emotionally retreated for similar reasons, in *Psycho*. Or in Stanley Kubrick's *The Shining*, Jack Torrance's inability to free himself from the Overlook Hotel on which he had become dangerously dependent. Or in John Carpenter's *Halloween*, Michael Myers' fixation on events that took place years earlier at the house where he grew up.

From overhead (another bird's eye vantage point) we watch Mitch, Melanie and Lydia approach the car. Melanie glances needfully at the other two. Lydia gets into the car's back seat first, then she and Mitch help Melanie inside. Cathy, all but forgotten by the camera and the other characters during this tense interaction among the three adults, calls out to Mitch from the house. Still mindful of the looming bird threat, he first hushes and then goes to retrieve her. Cathy wants to bring the lovebirds with her. "They haven't harmed anyone." Mitch consents. And there is no hysterical objection this time from Lydia. Carrying the cloth-draped bird cage in one hand, he leads Cathy to the car with the other. If birds are linked to violent emotions, impulses and fantasies in the film's human characters, perhaps the lovebirds represent more generous passions. Passions sometimes confined by their opposites. The film's uneasy ending balances ambiguously between two contrary interpretations, as Robin Wood astutely points out. Are Cathy's lovebirds "a touching gesture of continuing faith, despite all, in the goodness of nature and the possibility of order, or an absurd clinging to a sentimental view of life, a refusal still to face reality?" (Wood, p. 172).

Likewise the action inside the car. Lydia gently cradles Melanie, who occupies a lower, dependent position within the camera frame. In close-up we see Melanie's hand tighten its grip on Lydia's arm as she looks up at the older woman. Lydia rests her cheek comfortingly on Melanie's forehead. Melanie's eyes close. She feels secure now. A silent bargain has apparently been struck between former enemies. The fear of abandonment that crippled both women has been soothed away by a new arrangement. Lydia has overcome her extreme dependence on Mitch by becoming a surrogate mother to Melanie. Or is it just "a new manifestation of maternal possessiveness?" (Wood, 172). And even if we give Lydia the benefit of the doubt, what is the cost of this new dynamic to Melanie? Only her reduction from willful independence to abject dependency makes her acceptable to Lydia. What does the future hold for their relationship? Hitchcock told François Truffaut, "It all goes to show that with a little effort even the word 'love' can be made to sound ominous" (Truffaut, 288).

All four characters are shown in a tight, cramped shot inside the car. Melanie's eyes open again when Mitch enters. Mitch starts the car and slowly

**An uneasy truce between humans and birds at the end of *The Birds*.** Melanie (Tippi Hedren), badly injured, has finally earned acceptance into the Brenner family, but at a terrible price. Cathy (Veronica Cartwright), Lydia (Jessica Tandy) and Mitch (Rod Taylor) crowd into Melanie's car with its helpless owner as they flee the Brenner farm, the lingering birds and their own troubled pasts.

drives away. In a frontal shot of its departure, birds are visible in all directions. We also see Lydia's abandoned truck parked in the garage. How appropriate that the Brenners leave their farm, perhaps forever, in the vehicle that brought revolutionary change to their lives. Lydia's pick-up, which during the Fawcett farm scene became an emblem of her fears, is left behind. Along with the framed portrait of Lydia's dead husband.

The screeching sound of birds rises on the soundtrack as we watch Melanie's crowded car pull out of the farmyard, returning to San Francisco from where it came. Our final vantage point is from the open doorway of the abandoned Brenner house. Tension remains, in the natural world and in the hearts and minds of the human characters we've come to know a little better. The future is uncertain. Will Melanie fully recover? Will she and Mitch marry? Will Lydia live with them (a prospect dealt with more humorously at the end of *To Catch a Thief*)? Streaks of sunlight breaking through the clouds hint of hope, but the birds have not dispersed. There is no swell of happy music over a lengthy run out of end credits to cheer us on our way. Only a disturbing cacophony of birds ... birds ... and more birds, as four fragile human beings slink away in the distance.

Hitchcock considered ending the movie with a shot of the Golden Gate Bridge covered with birds as Melanie's car returns to San Francisco. Such an image might have left us with a striking impression of apocalyptic doom suitable for the Cold War era. But the ending he chose instead combines a dose of societal apocalypse with the more intimate impression of a tentative détente between Melanie Daniels and the Brenner family. Without benefit of knife, gun, poison or bomb, all of the major characters in *The Birds* proved capable of inflicting serious damage on each other and on themselves. In a wider world that itself was fraught with danger. With the exception of Annie Hayworth, all of the major characters in *The Birds* survive. And even her death might be interpreted as more figurative than literal. But none of them survived unscathed. Nor with an assurance of lasting peace.

# 3

# Carpenter's *Halloween*
## *Fear Itself*

Little Lindsey Wallace sits on a couch in the darkened living room of her parents' house, watching *The Thing from Another World* on television. She complains to her babysitter, "I'm scared." The babysitter inquires, "Then why are you sitting here with all the lights out?" A logical question. To which Lindsey replies, "I don't know," and continues watching the scary movie, fascinated by its evocation of menace and fear somewhat safely contained within the confines of a glowing box.

John Carpenter's 1978 *Halloween* is a trend-setting, iconic horror film that continues to haunt audiences in spite of the fact that most of us know precisely when, where and how the murderous attacks of Michael Myers occur within its ninety-one minute running time. And those attacks have long since been superseded in frequency, violence and gore by later movies. For me, one of the keys to *Halloween*'s staying power is the surprisingly subtle, sometimes disturbing way in which Carpenter and his team *play* with the dynamics of terror. Nearly every character in the film enjoys frightening others. Some of them enjoy *being* scared as well, up to a point. Only one of them enjoys and indulges in perpetrating the unrestrained terror of extreme violence. *Halloween*'s spectrum of fear runs the gamut from harmless fun, playing with the *illusion* of danger, to cruel bullying, to lethal violence triggered by motives so obscure they render that violence even more terrifying.

The counterpoint of playful fear and grim terror begins with *Halloween*'s opening credits. A carved, candle-lit pumpkin occupies the left side of the screen as credits roll by on the right. The pumpkin wears a smile. Not a fanged scowl or a frozen scream. Just a goofy, gap-toothed smile. Emblematic of Halloween as a fun holiday filled with mildly spooky, pretend fears, the fun of dressing up in colorful costumes and the prospect of getting free candy. By contrast, the core musical theme of *Halloween*, composed and performed by Carpenter himself, evokes a sense of grim, relentless, almost mechanical terror. Nothing playful at all, at least on the face of it.

## 3. Carpenter's *Halloween*

Music is a powerful dramatic tool capable of greatly enhancing emotional response. Unless played at a sufficiently high volume to inflict actual pain on tender eardrums, music can only evoke a *sense* of terror. Except for perhaps rare cases in which a listener is predisposed by some traumatic experience to react to a specific piece of music in a particular way, music does not transmit terror itself. That's why it is usually enjoyable rather than unpleasant to hear the music of *Halloween*, *Psycho* and *Jaws*, to name just a few of the great horror film scores. The main musical themes of those movies strongly suggest but do not embody menace. To experience a whiff of danger yet remain aloof and immune from it is in some sense to feel triumphant over it.

*Halloween*'s opening credits themselves evoke the dichotomy of fear. Each word appears first in blood red, shifts to a bright and sunny yellow, then returns to red before disappearing. And as the credits roll by, the camera ever so slowly closes in on the pumpkin, eliminating its smile and eventually giving us a close-up of its nose and one eye. The nose has a curious cut extending down from its lower right. A slip of the knife that carved it? Or a deliberate, wounding slash? Whichever, the cut slightly mars our initial impression of a happy, smiling face. As do scars and nicks that become noticeable on the right side of the pumpkin as we get closer to it. As for the now singular eye, the pulsing glow of candlelight emanating from its cavernous interior infuses it with a kind of hysteria, especially when isolated from the smiling mouth beneath it. Panic? The famous subjective camera shot that immediately follows *Halloween*'s opening credits has been preceded by a similar shot in which we, the audience, stalk and scare the smile off a pumpkin's face.

Then the pumpkin disappears. The fitful light of animation from within it is obliterated. The left side of the screen turns black as night, while the credits continue to appear and disappear in their red/yellow/red sequence. There is little now to offset the sense of fateful gloom supplied by Carpenter's relentless, metronomic music. Until that music diminishes in volume and is partly displaced by the sound of children reciting a poem about Halloween: black cats, goblins, witches, ghosts and fear. The recitation ends with the kids calling out boisterously, "Trick or Treat!" It's all in good fun now. The children were only pretending to be scared. Though the phrase "Trick or Treat" itself contains the counterpart of bad and good fear that Carpenter plays with during the course of the movie. Perhaps "Trick or Treat!" is *his* wickedly playful nod to his audience, which in 1978 was in for a more intense brush with fear than it expected.

The grim music ceases. The new setting is Haddonfield, Illinois circa 1963. Small town, middle-class America. A simpler, safer, more innocent time. Really? It was also the year of John Kennedy's assassination, followed quickly by the murder of his alleged assassin. Only a year earlier the world teetered on the brink of nuclear war during the Cuban Missile Crisis. And only two years before that, Alfred Hitchcock's *Psycho* changed the face of terror in movies. Perhaps there never were simpler, safer, more innocent times. We just like to remember them that way.

A subjective camera, its movement rendered silky-smooth and convincingly intimate by panaglide technology, silently approaches the well-lit front of a modest, middle-class house. The Myers house. Background music has fled the scene. We hear only the soft, natural sounds of a night in Midwest America. No howling wolves. Just crickets chirping. The coo of a mourning dove — an odd symbolic blend of peace and death. The camera, we and the character whose point of view we share could be a costumed child approaching the house to "trick or treat" for candy. Until we stop short upon seeing a teenage couple kissing just inside the doorway, more exposed to the outside world than they realize through a veiled curtain. We glide to the right, shadowing the teenagers as they move from the entryway into the living room and out of our view. Passing a brightly lit pumpkin sitting on the front porch railing, and similar to the one in the opening credits, we surreptitiously slide around the side of the house and peek through another thinly veiled window to spy on the young couple making out on a couch. We are no longer just innocent trick-or-treaters in pursuit of candy. We are now Peeping Toms.

Inside, the boyfriend picks up a child's clown mask lying on the couch. A mask probably belonging to his girlfriend's younger brother, Michael, who is "around somewhere." In fact, as we soon discover, Michael is the character whose point of view we now share. The boyfriend places the mask over his face and kisses the girl. He uses the mask to induce a playfully mild scare in her, enhancing their sexual foreplay. At his suggestion they transfer the action to her bedroom upstairs, which is a less exposed setting.

The camera, after a moment's hesitation, returns to the front of the house, its faster pace betraying a keener interest than earlier. The smiling pumpkin, traditional talisman of the lighthearted spirit of the holiday, appears and then disappears as the camera's and our focus of attention shifts up to the illuminated windows of the girl's bedroom upstairs. The lights go off. The windows go dark, triggering a resumption of background music and a darkening of the mood in this opening scene. We sense more trick than treat now in the motive of the character behind the camera. But just how serious a trick is still unclear.

Moving faster now, with stronger purpose, we rush past the quaintly grinning, increasingly anachronistic pumpkin and to the back of the house. With no street lamp to provide illumination, it's darker and spookier back here than in front. Music supplies a monotone pitch of suspense, as single-minded as the camera's movement and the unseen character's mysterious mission.

We invade the house through a back door carelessly left unlocked and wide open. As we enter the kitchen, descending piano strokes join the electronic whine of suspense, adding a hint of impending doom to our violation of domestic privacy. A light is switched on, illuminating a plain kitchen in a very ordinary, middle-class home. We see the costumed arm and small hand of a child open a drawer and pull out a large knife (son of Norman Bates' chosen weapon in *Psycho*). An ordinary *kitchen* knife. Not some exotic weapon of war or other sadistic invention. In *Halloween*, as in *Psycho* and even *The Birds*, danger arises from *within* the family structure. From uncomfortably close to home.

Details about the character we accompany are sketchy and a bit out of focus. But the costume seems to be that of a clown, linking it with the clown mask borrowed by the boyfriend. Is this Michael, the teenage girl's younger brother, returning home to play a Halloween prank on his big sister and her boyfriend? At any rate, it's not a vampire, a zombie, a werewolf or marauding extra-terrestrial. It's not even an escaped criminal, yet.

We, the camera and the unseen but now dangerously armed intruder to whom we are visually tethered penetrate further into the house, passing through a pleasant dining room bathed in nocturnal light and into the living room previously glimpsed from outside. It's so *quiet* in here. Because *we* are not part of the Myers family, our intrusion into their home feels wrong, potentially dangerous to ourselves, yet also wickedly exciting. Is this how Charles Manson and his cult of followers felt when they "creepy crawled" through the homes of unsuspecting Los Angeleans late at night, before becoming killers (Sanders, p. 163)? We glance briefly at the couch where the teenage couple made out minutes earlier. Why does the character we accompany care about what happened on that couch? One of many questions raised but not definitively answered in *Halloween*.

From the shadowy living room, we peer up the staircase in the brightly lit entryway. The boyfriend descends those stairs, pulling on his shirt after a brief sexual interlude with the girl upstairs. Talk about a "quickie!" The barely audible sound of his parting conversation with her accentuates the illicit quality of our vantage point. In retrospect, it also evokes how emotionally remote the intruder is from *their* concerns and perspectives. If the boyfriend's postcoital indifference to his girlfriend (evident in both his tone of voice and his body language) seems callow, it is about to be overshadowed by the violent hostility we are nervously beginning to suspect lurks within the intruder we accompany. An intruder who is now *alone* in the house with the unsuspecting girl upstairs.

We creep silently up the stairs, from the bright light of the entryway into a dark hallway on the second floor. How can *we* as a surrogate for the intruder, the character with the power of surprise on his side, be afraid of the dark? Hopefully because we experience this menacing ascent with some empathy for the victim we're approaching, in spite of our proximity to the intruder's physical point of view.

A clock chimes. It's a very domestic, comforting sound. The sound of "home." But under present circumstances, it's difficult not to think in less soothing terms. To paraphrase John Donne, "Ask not for whom the bell tolls. It tolls for thee." From ahead somewhere, unseen but close, we hear the girl humming contentedly to herself. We glance down to see the clown mask lying on the floor. A clown-costumed arm and hand reach down, pick up the mask and place it over the camera lens — our and the intruder's eyes. The same mask the boyfriend playfully used to enhance his foreplay with the girl is now employed by the intruder for a different purpose. But *how* different? Does the intruder intend to play a scary Halloween prank on the girl? Is that to be the climax of this disturbing scene? We enter a bedroom. Michael's? Through the restricted eye holes of the mask we see the girl's discarded clothes lying on the floor. An undisturbed bed. A glimpse of a dart board hanging on the wall: a relatively harmless, enjoyable game that also involves stabbing. Will the knife be used to play a joke that, in the end, will be as much fun for the victim as for the perpetrator? Or will it be used for something far more sinister? Again, the interplay of playful fear and real terror. We enter the girl's bedroom. Nearly nude, she sits with her back to us, suspecting nothing as she brushes her hair back into place after having had sex with her boyfriend. Sex, and the clown mask that mildly enhanced its pleasure, being comparatively equivalent to the harmless fun of the smiling pumpkin sitting on the porch railing downstairs.

We glance at the girl's crumpled, unmade bed where sex has just occurred. That glance suggests the intruder whose vantage point we share has a much darker preoccupation with the girl than just pulling a prank on her. The boyfriend's clowning around, and the smiling pumpkin downstairs, now seem far behind us as we approach the vulnerable girl from behind.

If there is still a remote chance we are in the middle of an elaborate Halloween prank, that chance disappears the moment the girl turns around to face him/us, inquisitively calls out the name of her brother, and is abruptly, savagely stabbed to death. For those of us *not* inclined to fantasize about committing murder, it's a very disturbing event. Through the eyes of a killer, we leave the dead girl's bedroom, walk down the stairs and exit the house through the front door. The relatively unhurried pace of our departure suggests a chilling lack of agitation (fear for one's own fate or revulsion at what we've just done) on the part of the killer. Outside the house, a car pulls up and two adults emerge. Parents of the Myers children. The father reaches towards us and removes our clown mask. A reverse angle shot, the first non-subjective shot of the film, gives us our first objective view of Michael Myers. An innocent looking young boy, wearing a colorful, non-frightening clown costume, but holding a large, bloodied kitchen knife in his right hand. The weapon he used to brutally murder his older sister. The contrast between appearance (clown costume, angelic face) and deed (implied by the bloody knife) is shocking. Michael's mother tucks her hands defensively in her coat pocket. She and Michael's father seem puzzled, not yet comprehending what's happened inside their home. Michael himself seems dazed, unaware of his crime.

All three characters appear frozen in time while the camera, as though in revulsion, pulls up and away, incorporating them, the well-lit and visually inviting façade of their house and a tire swing hanging from a tree limb in the front yard, into an overall still-life portrait of a middle-class American family, home and neighborhood. Destroyed from within by an act of depravity. Carpenter's background music features big, descending chords that complement the bloody knife but counterpoint everything else in this tableaux.

Fifteen years minus a day after the murder of Judith Myers, psychiatrist Sam Loomis and a nurse travel by state-owned automobile to the Illinois State Mental Hospital in Smiths Grove to pick up patient Michael Myers and take him to his parole hearing. The name "Sam Loomis" is Carpenter's nod to a character in Hitchcock's *Psycho*. Though the two characters play very different roles in their respective films. *Psycho*'s Sam Loomis is clueless about the menace lurking near his hometown of Fairvale, California, until the fearless curiosity of his girlfriend's sister forces him to confront it. The other Sam Loomis is the only character in *Halloween* who isn't clueless about the threat of Michael Myers. Both characters, however, end up saving a life through acts of courage.

It's a dark, stormy night, complete with rain, thunder and lightning. A horror film cliché perhaps. Nevertheless, such atmospheric conditions are conducive to the promotion of fear. They offer a taste of the chaos Nature is capable of throwing at us. But inside the vehicle, moodily illuminated by dashboard lights, we and the characters seem relatively insulated from the elements raging outside. Like Marion Crane driving through a rain storm in *Psycho*. The illusion of security.

Discussing their mission, the nurse is uneasy at the prospect of encountering the "jibberish" of their patient. Loomis reassures her, "You haven't anything to worry about. He hasn't spoken a word in fifteen years." But only a moment later he *warns* her about the same patient. "Don't underestimate it." The previously uneasy nurse then *defends* Michael by admonishing the Doctor for referring to their patient by the inhuman "it." Both characters exhibit a slight tug-of-war between their fears and their rationality.

The rain-obscured, fitfully illuminated sight of mental patients, dressed only in hospital gowns, wandering aimlessly on the grounds outside the hospital triggers immediate concern in Loomis and the nurse. It's an abnormal sight implying a breakdown of institutional routine. Abnormality enhanced by off-kilter fence posts lining the grounds, like the leaning graveyard crosses in *Frankenstein* (1931). The patients themselves do nothing frightening. The mere fact of their being outside, unsupervised and improperly dressed for the weather, is enough to upset our sense of order. The thunderstorm, and the resumption of *Halloween*'s main musical theme, intensify our feeling that something is very wrong.

We catch our first, fleeting glimpse of adult Michael Myers as he leaps onto the back of the state vehicle and climbs onto its roof. We can see that he's dressed in an ordinary hospital gown, like his fellow patients. In neither 1963 nor 1978 does Michael start out as a monster costumed in a typically frightening manner. And he never exhibits the intimidating bulk of his namesake in the recent re-make of *Halloween*, or that of another psychotic killer, Jason Voorhis from the *Friday the 13th* movie series. It is the *juxtaposition* of normality and abnormality, of the ordinary and the terrifying, that gives *Halloween* much of its dramatic potency. And in that respect, it's similar to Alfred Hitchcock's two excursions into horror.

Earlier in this scene, the nurse expressed compassion for Michael Myers. By the end of it, this compassionate woman slumps in a ditch beside the road, drenched by rain, gasping for breath and composure, badly frightened by the man whose humanity she tried to restore with a word. The illusion of security and safety she experienced inside the car while driving through a raging thunderstorm is shattered in an instant by an escaped murderer in a not-so-frightening hospital gown.

Night becomes day. Thunder, lightning and rain disappear. Halloween morning in Haddonfield, Illinois is bright, tranquil and pleasant. Especially on a quiet street in a residential neighborhood. Yet Carpenter's music injects a passive menace into this scene. The prowling camera, picking up where it began in 1963, approaches another middle-class family dwelling. Teenager Laurie Strode emerges from a side door in that house and walks past the camera. She is dressed in modest clothing, rather old-fashioned for a 1978 high school student. Print dress, white stockings, matronly sweater. She does not, at first glance, remind us of Judith Myers. And there's no boyfriend in sight.

Laurie carries a hefty load of schoolbooks in her arms. She's the studious type. Her father emerges from the house and reminds Laurie to leave the keys to the old Myers house under the mat by the front door. A sign on the door of his car informs us that he operates "Strode Realty." Standard job. Typical, nondescript exchange of dialog between father and daughter as they leave home and go about their daily routines. School for her. Job for him. Except that we hear their conversation at low volume, as from a distance, so that Carpenter's quietly ominous background score dominates our overall impression of the scene.

As a consequence of that musical domination, the ordinarily beautiful

## 3. Carpenter's *Halloween* 153

features of a small town neighborhood become vaguely threatening. Large, leafy tree branches loom ominously over the comparatively small figure of Laurie Strode, who is shown from a distance. Yet her own mood acknowledges none of that menace. Her step is lively, unconcerned, oblivious of any lurking danger. Part of the beauty of this scene is the way Carpenter so vividly, yet without exaggeration, captures a routine moment of small town serenity, then counterpoints and alters it slightly by the intrusion of grim music. Anyone who grew up in such a town (like me) can recognize and appreciate what this scene visually conveys. Laurie Strode is just a young woman walking to school on a pleasant autumn morning through her peaceful, safe neighborhood, performing an errand for her Dad along the way. But that unforgettable *music*, which never lightens in mood whenever it intrudes on the imagery, makes us nervously aware of how alone and potentially vulnerable she is. For a while there is no one else visible in this quiet neighborhood. Just Laurie and a no-longer-innocent tracking camera. A camera previously linked to stalking and murder.

A younger boy named Tommy Doyle runs towards Laurie along an adjoining sidewalk. He approaches from a perpendicular angle, emphasizing the three-dimensional reality of this attractive residential area. He too carries books and is on his way to school. Similar routines meet and join forces. Laurie is Tommy's babysitter, and it is immediately evident that he likes her in that role. As they cross a street with no traffic, Tommy eagerly inquires if they can carve a jack-o-lantern, watch monster movies on TV and make popcorn later that Halloween evening, when she comes over to baby sit. Monster movies are obviously regarded as enjoyable, not unpleasantly terrifying, by both characters. Just as many of us consider watching *Halloween* a pleasant experience. Otherwise we wouldn't keep watching it. The violent events it depicts are unreal. The unease and fear we might experience watching it are once removed from anything that could justify real terror. Unless, of course, our previous experience includes an overwhelming experience of *real* terror, in which case horror films like *Halloween* might not be to our taste.

As they cross a street Tommy and Laurie pass the word "STOP" printed on the pavement at the intersection. A law enforcement edict to drivers, it is one visible measure of the social order that helps make life relatively safe for the citizens of Haddonfield. But Michael Myers, to whom the concept of "stop" has no meaning, is no longer bound by society's rules and regulations. In retrospect "STOP" is, like the background music, a warning to Laurie and Tommy to proceed no closer to the old Myers house, where exposure to Michael's view will ensnare them in his psychotic fantasies. But they know nothing of his escape from custody. In fact Michael's original crime has become the stuff of local legend, perpetuating his fame but reducing his emotional legacy closer to the level of entertainment than true terror.

We view Laurie and Tommy from a distance, making them appear small beneath enormous tree branches, as they discuss the errand Laurie performs for her father. Tommy's incessant questions make Laurie the patient, adult dispenser of information. A role she plays very well, most of the time. The boy who looks forward to watching monster movies seriously warns Laurie not to approach the old Myers place, which he refers to as "the spook house." Still a child, he is more susceptible to the emotional power of local myths than is Laurie, who ignores his fears and walks up to the front door of the dilapidated, deserted structure.

From inside the house, through a dirty, screened and sharply broken window in the front door, we watch Laurie fearlessly approach while Tommy nervously hangs back on the sidewalk. As Laurie returns to the boy after dropping off the key her father gave her, Michael Myers surprisingly enters the camera frame from an area of darkness at right foreground. Visible only to *us*, as a silhouette of the back of his head, and a patch of disheveled hair to suggest the unruly mind beneath it, Michael forms the third part of a striking portrait in depth. Tommy at a distance and Laurie between them make up the other two parts. From left to right are represented childish superstition, adult rationality, and a mysterious figure of menace who seems to validate Tommy's point of view.

Tommy acquired his fear of the Myers house from a schoolmate named Lonnie Lamb, a dubious source of information that Laurie contemptuously dismisses. "Lonnie Lamb probably won't get out of the sixth grade." In most situations, her contempt would be justified. Most irrational childhood fears prove unwarranted. And when the camera leaves Michael and the Myers house to rejoin Laurie and Tommy on the sidewalk outside, we too can almost doubt the reality of the danger she disregards. Comforted for the time being, Tommy departs for his own school while Laurie saunters down the sidewalk towards hers. She casually sings a song to herself, the lyrics of which celebrate being alone with the man of her dreams. Not difficult to guess what's on *her* mind, and it certainly isn't the legend of the Myers house and its now mythical monster.

Vividly reminding us the monster is real and has returned, Michael enters the film frame at screen right, extreme foreground. Dressed in dark workman's coveralls, only his left collar, shoulder and arm are visible. We hear his prominent, eerily calm breathing as he gazes down the sidewalk at an unsuspecting, diminutive, slow-moving and unprotected Laurie Strode. No other person, no potential source of warning or rescue for the heroine, is visible in this shot. Far in the distance, directly ahead of Laurie, vehicles pass by along a street running perpendicular to her sidewalk. Ironic tokens of daily routine in a small, seemingly safe community.

Dappled sunlight through leafy tree branches adds to the dangerously false tranquility of this setting. If Laurie Strode naively ponders spending time alone with the man of her lonely dreams, what does Michael Myers fantasize about as he watches her? Especially if her romantic desire links her in his mind to his dead sister, Judith. If Michael were inclined to reveal his private thoughts in song, which he is not, what lyrics would *he* sing at this moment? The very obscurity of his perceptions and motivations renders him a more frightening character than if we knew exactly what is on his mind.

Sam Loomis and the hospital director exit the Illinois State Mental facility and head for Sam's car in the parking lot. They argue about the level of danger posed by escaped patient Michael Myers. The Director insists he warned law enforcement officials about that danger. Yet a moment later he *dismisses* Loomis's concern that Michael will inevitably return to Haddonfield to cause havoc. He points out that Michael cannot drive a car. Loomis, the rational, highly educated adult who has somehow come to share young Tommy Doyle's irrational fear of Michael Myers, contemptuously points out that Michael "was doing very well last night" when he drove away in a stolen vehicle. The remainder of the film proves Loomis's fears justified. But in the peaceful sunlight of the hospital parking lot, long after the electrically and emotionally charged atmosphere of the previous night, it's not difficult to appreciate the Director's less alarming view of things.

In a quiet back corner of a small town high school classroom, we and the camera silently close in on the figure of Laurie Strode, seated in a desk as far away from the front of the class as she can get. Laurie is not pathologically shy, but she is more withdrawn and less inclined to take risks than are most of her classmates, as we shall see. Our approach to her is vaguely intrusive, if not quite an act of stalking. By never showing us the entire classroom nor all of its occupants, including the teacher giving a lecture, Carpenter not only saves the expense of hiring more extras, he generates a powerful sense of intimacy with his heroine. We move closer and closer to her private space as she verges on a very troubling encounter.

As we glide towards Laurie, we hear the flat, uninspired and uninspiring voice of the off-screen teacher lecturing on the theme of Fate in the reading assignment she gave her students. None of those students appear engaged by her discussion. One suppresses a yawn. Some take notes. Or are they writing about personal interests having nothing to do with the assignment? Laurie too appears distracted, with the eraser end of her pencil pressed against her lips. She casually glances out the classroom window, partly obscured by Venetian blinds. Carpenter's ominous background music returns as she catches sight of her *own* fate. Not a massive truck with a menacing grill, but a family-friendly station wagon parked across the street. And standing beside it a curiously white-faced man (we know it's Michael Myers, Laurie does not), staring fixedly and patiently in Laurie's direction. Otherwise the view outside the window is perfectly innocuous. Even inviting. Houses, lawn, trees, shrubs and sunshine. Just a single odd ingredient, and even that kept at a discrete distance, mar Laurie's sense of tranquil, if slightly bored, complacency. How much less effective this scene would be if Michael's face appeared in full close-up, right outside the window.

In close-up, Laurie appears utterly alone, isolated from the security of her fellow students and even the instructor's droning but familiar voice. She looks away from the window, glancing around the room to see if anyone else has noticed the mysterious stranger outside. Does she feel guilty about her own nervousness? Ashamed of succumbing, like Tommy before her, to irrational fears?

Laurie glances out the window again. From her vantage point we get a slightly closer view, reflecting her keener attention this time, of Michael staring back at her. Suddenly the tedious routine of a classroom lecture seems like a haven of security compared to the world outside. Creepy music is in tune with Laurie's reluctant fear. Contradicting that music in tone, though not in content, is the disembodied voice of the teacher, who pulls Laurie back into the comforting realm of classroom routine by asking her a question about the assigned reading.

Laurie is mildly startled by the teacher's question. Was she, like other students appear to be, not paying attention? Has she even read the assignment? No and yes. Only momentarily and mildly disturbed by the stranger watching her from across the street, Laurie effortlessly answers the question posed to her. By coincidence, the question and answer have to do with defining Fate as a force of Nature rather than a religious concept. The teacher elaborates on Laurie's answer, defining Fate as "immovable, like a mountain. It stands where man passes away. Fate never changes." Her tone of voice is dispassionate. This is a purely academic discussion, not an experience or even a dramatic representation of Fate. Laurie's voice too is emotionally detached from the topic.

But then she glances once more out the window, into that world of experience outside the relative safety of her sometimes boring classroom. The stranger is gone, along with his vehicle. Laurie appears mildly troubled. Trepidation about who the stranger is, and why he was staring in her direction? Or shame about her own fears? The point is, despite the larger thematic connection between the classroom discussion about Fate as a literary concept and Fate as a literal reality, the droning voice of the teacher and Laurie's glib answer to the teacher's question suggest that neither of them applies the concept of Fate to their own lives outside the classroom. By the end of this Halloween night, Laurie will no longer feel so emotionally removed from the topic of her academic assignment.

The classroom scene in *Halloween* provides an interesting variation on

### 3. Carpenter's *Halloween* 157

the psychiatrist scene at the end of *Psycho*. Like the teacher in Carpenter's movie, the psychiatrist who profiles Norman Bates for the benefit of *his* gathered audience is comfortably detached from the painfully gruesome realities of Norman's actions. Though not bored, like *Halloween*'s teacher, he is emotionally caught up in his own concerns: the thrill of solving a case, the pleasure of having his views accepted as gospel, but not so much the victim's grieving sister and lover or the District Attorney's impending legal case against Norman. The image of Michael Myers staring at *us* from outside the classroom window is roughly equivalent to Norman's shockingly intimate and frightening stare into the camera and directly at us in *Psycho*'s second to last shot. Like Hitchcock, Carpenter cleverly juxtaposes madness/terror as a remote, entertaining commodity with madness/terror as a frighteningly intimate encounter. Insofar as a work of art can push an audience close to the latter.

An even more disturbing little dissection of fear occurs at the Haddonfield Elementary School. The camera, our necessary point of view, glides smoothly to the right, observing school children dressed in various Halloween costumes, none of them very terrifying, leaving school grounds as the final bell rings. A chain-link fence stands between the camera and the schoolyard. Representing both confinement and security for the children? Guess it depends on who is gazing in through that fence, at them. At any rate, the costumed children seem very pleased to escape their school day routine for the comparative freedom and excitement of Halloween night. They scatter in all directions, exhibiting no fear whatsoever of the wider world outside the fence.

Moving past the fence to an opening that provides a less restricted view of the yard inside, we observe kids in several groups, each oblivious of the others. Some race towards and past the camera, ignoring it. Presumably the camera is, as it usually is in movies, disembodied. A boy and a girl, both in non-frightening costumes, linger in the schoolyard. The boy has his hands in his pockets. Is this a slightly nervous after-school rendezvous between potential boyfriend and girlfriend? Neither pays much attention to anyone or anything else. They are absorbed in each other.

Equally oblivious to anyone outside their little group are Tommy Doyle and three other boys approaching us along a sidewalk. Tommy carries a large pumpkin. The other boys, all of them bigger than Tommy, taunt him verbally. "He's gonna get you! He's gonna get you! The boogeyman is coming!" The pumpkin represents Tommy's preferred idea of what Halloween is about. A kinder, gentler Halloween. With monster movies, sure. But movie monsters on TV are confined to a box, and are therefore an acceptable risk. Though sometimes they can be unleashed by an overactive imagination. Tommy's three living tormentors cannot be so easily evaded. They taunt him with the threat of an ill-defined but nevertheless potent threat of terror *unconfined*. And they exhibit no fear of that threat themselves, probably thinking they're too old to be afraid of mythical boogeymen.

Tommy pleads to be left alone, but the other boys are relentless. They crowd him, surrounding him with taunts of "The boogeyman!" Tommy tries to break free. One of the boys trips him. He falls to the sidewalk, crushing the pumpkin beneath him. And with it, possibly, his innocent vision of Halloween. The other boys laugh and run away. Are they satisfied with their accomplishment? Or afraid of punishment by nearby school authorities? We all have our boogeymen, in one form or another.

One of the fleeing little bullies runs towards the camera and straight into the arms of ... Michael Myers! The character whose vantage point we and the camera have shared since the start of the scene, without realizing it until now. Michael grabs the boy by his shoulders. The boy stares up, terrified, into the off-screen face of the *real* boogeyman, then flees for his life. The boy who terrorized Tommy gets terrorized himself. Aside from the satisfaction of seeing a bully get his comeuppance, this encounter beautifully and succinctly illustrates both the fickleness of fear and the difference between fear once removed and fear for real. Only a few yards and a few seconds separates the exploitation of fear for the sake of cruel pleasure and the experience of fear itself. Unlike the boy who meets a local legend up close and personal, his co-conspirators get off scot-free this time, not even noticing Michael as they flee.

Fear exists in multiple forms in this brief but unsettling scene. The *fun* fear of traditional Halloween (costumes, candy, carving pumpkins, watching monster movies), as Tommy prefers. The cruel but still relatively restrained fear of frightening others (the boys who taunt Tommy about the boogeyman), which touches darkly on human motives in even the most "normal" of us. And the *real* fear of *real* danger. Michael could be, potentially, a kidnapper, a child molester or a killer, lurking outside the schoolyard in search of victims. But Michael Myers, the character, is a source of terror deliberately left vaguely defined in order to render him increasingly a mythical embodiment of a broad range of menace. He is a deranged child/sibling, an undecipherable and incurable madman, a stalker, a child molester, an unstoppable killer, and in the end a deathless embodiment of the worst in human nature itself, which unlike the individual monster lives on and on.

Curiously, Michael releases the boy he grabs. Why? Does he have a capacity for mercy? More likely he simply has no interest in this particular child. He turns his attention instead to Tommy, who leaves his smashed pumpkin behind and walks dejectedly across the now deserted schoolyard. The camera, Michael and we glide to the left, shadowing the small, lonely, dejected and very vulnerable-looking boy, watching him through the fence. Is Michael stalking Tommy, waiting for an opportunity to close on him? What a cruel fate if Tommy's tormentor were released by Michael only to have Michael prove the tormentor's taunt a reality for Tommy. Did the chance encounter in front of the Myers house irrevocably mark Tommy as a primary target of Michael's homicidal fantasies? Is it now a matter of Fate?

Or is there something even darker going on in the latter half of this scene? *Halloween*'s main musical theme accompanies Michael and Tommy on their little stroll away from school. But instead of moving into position to intercept the boy, Michael gets into his stolen car, which now ironically bears an official "Seal of the State of Illinois" and the designation "For Official Use Only" on its door (the State too can be exploited by malevolent forces), and slowly parallels Tommy as the boy passes out of the fenced-in schoolyard and onto an open sidewalk. We and the camera observe from the fenced-in back seat of Michael's vehicle — once removed from Michael himself, yet still close to sharing his vantage point — as we close on Tommy. With no obstructions now, we and Michael pull up alongside the self-absorbed child, who is preoccupied with his own troubles and oblivious to our presence. After a few suspenseful moments, the threatening music fades out and we, Michael and the car cruise on by, increasing speed and leaving Tommy in peace, for now. What a strange encounter it has been.

By shadowing the boy but never attacking him, Michael becomes in some ways a *reflection* of Tommy, and of Tommy's troubled thoughts and feelings. What combination of hurt, humiliation and desire for revenge brews in Tommy's mind as he leaves behind his destroyed pumpkin and his innocent view of Halloween? There is no indication in *Halloween* that Tommy will, as a result of being bullied by classmates within what *should* be the safe confines of school, become another Michael Myers. But for a few moments Carpenter juxtaposes the two characters in such a way as to hint at the violent thoughts that, under emotional stress, can arise in all of us from time to time. Overtones of Columbine? Think of Marion Crane smiling with satisfaction to herself as she imagines the anger and frustration of the jerk whose money she stole. Or Lydia Brenner, after the shock of discovering her dead and mutilated neighbor, barreling her pickup into her own farmyard, briefly aiming it at her son and his new love interest before changing direction and slamming to a stop. Though he seems a potential threat to anyone who crosses his path, Michael Myers never attacks a pre-adolescent child in *Halloween*. Perhaps he identifies with them. A case of arrested development?

At a rural crossroads many miles from Haddonfield, Sam Loomis parks his car along the side of the road and uses a public phone booth to warn law enforcement officials that Michael Myers is headed back to his hometown. By way of counterpoint, Sam's warning is issued against an attractive, peaceful backdrop. It's a bright day. Even Sam's car is painted a sunny yellow. But complementing Sam's warning to the police is a clanging railroad crossing nearby, warning of an approaching train.

As Sam leaves the phone booth, he notices an abandoned red pickup, with its passenger door left open, parked behind some bushes off the road. Something looks odd about it. From a position close to the phone booth, we watch Sam head for the vehicle to investigate. As his figure recedes on the right side of the screen, a fast-moving train approaches us on the left. Emerging from behind the same row of bushes that conceals the pickup from the road, the train hurtles past us: an unstoppable, mechanical beast much more intimidating viewed close up than at a comfortable distance. The natural Doppler effect of a sound source approaching and receding adds to that impression. The train serves nicely as a metaphor for Michael Myers, who has relentlessly forced his way back to Haddonfield in the unstoppable pursuit of some obscure goal.

Loomis finds what appear to be discarded pieces of Michael's hospital gown hanging from the bushes and the pickup door. His suspicion is confirmed when he spots on the ground near the vehicle the same red matchbook he noticed in the station wagon he and a nurse occupied the previous night. The vehicle Michael stole from them. Michael's background music returns, echoing the psychiatrist's fears as he hurries off to resume his journey to Haddonfield. But the camera stays behind, sliding slowly to the right to reveal, in foreground, a more alarming piece of evidence overlooked by Sam. The bloodied body of the pickup driver, lying half-concealed in a patch of tall grass. As the scene ends Carpenter's eerie music renders even the usually peaceful sound of crickets disturbing. *Now* this otherwise tranquil rural setting seems a place of isolation and danger. Certainly the driver of the pickup found it so.

Teenagers depart Haddonfield High School at the end of the school day. The oppressive music is gone, for the moment. The bright day and pleasant small town atmosphere face nothing to contradict our impression of them. Laurie Strode and her friend Lynda leave behind the chain-link fence that, as it did at the elementary school, defines the relatively safe confines of school grounds. Laurie carries books and a binder, and is plainly dressed. Lynda, dressed more stylishly, carries only a purse crowded with grooming implements. As she walks she applies fresh lipstick while checking her make-up in a pocket mirror. She is completely absorbed in the conventional routines of being a popular, attractive high school girl. Learning new cheers for the cheerleader squad, attending the football game, getting her hair done, going to the dance, and so forth. She complains of having no time to attend to all of these activities. Laurie gently mocks her, "I don't think you have enough things to do." But that mockery masks envy. Laurie is a bit of a loner, an outsider, though not necessarily by choice. She *wants* to fit in.

Lynda's preoccupations may seem shallow to many of us, but Carpenter, co-screenwriter Debra Hill and actress P. J. Soles never present her as contemptibly so. How many of *our* preoccupations in the middle of an ordinary day would seem likewise? And Laurie's unspoken desire to be more like Lynda cannot be dismissed either. Lynda takes Laurie's mockery in good humor. "Totally!" she chimes in. Whatever divides these two characters in terms of social status, outlook and intelligence, they really are friends who can freely joke with, complain about and share with each other.

Walking home together, Laurie complains rather sheepishly that she, unlike her friend, has nothing to do. Lynda, boldly lighting up a cigarette now that she is safely off school grounds ("safety" being a fluctuating notion in this movie), expresses no sympathy for her. But this is routine teenage girl talk (teenage boy talk, of which there is much less in *Halloween*, is not much different). Disagreement within secure limits. The pumpkin without the knife. No serious arguments ending their friendship. The beauty of this scene and their dialog is how ordinary and everyday they are. Even mundane, from a certain point of view. Yet the actors, Carpenter and Hill portray this slice of small town, middle American teenage routine with understated affection. Not without implied criticism of its blindness to potential dangers from the outside world. But with a fondness for its easygoing complacency and an awareness of its fragility.

The residential neighborhood through which Laurie and Lynda walk home is beautifully tree-shaded and peaceful. In the absence of contrary background music, it's a kind of paradise. Nothing fancy. Yet precisely and deliberately presented by Carpenter as a nice place in which to live and grow up.

Annie, another teen from the same neighborhood, catches up with her two friends, complaining that they didn't wait for her at school. They plead not guilty, reducing the matter to a joke at Annie's expense. Not surprisingly, the joke involves boys and sex. Carpenter's backtracking camera makes us, the audience, feel like a fourth member of this intimate group of friends. We stroll along leisurely with them as they discuss their day at school and their interlocking plans for Halloween night. *We* know the matters they think are so important at this moment are grimly overshadowed by what has invaded their small town. What we suspect is about to intrude on their personal lives. But that knowledge makes their relatively carefree, unsuspecting outlook seem more endangered and precious. Only Laurie, intermittently, has the slightest idea that something threatens their peaceful little world.

An atypical exclamation of "Shit!" from Laurie, who forgot her Chemistry textbook at school, causes the trio, the camera and us to halt. It's a bit of a shock to hear the normally restrained, even repressed heroine use such language. She is genuinely concerned about the consequences of missing a night of studying. Lynda trivializes that concern, bragging that she *always* forgets her schoolbooks and *never* worries about the consequences. But in the midst of this mini-debate about whether or not to take homework seriously, Laurie spots something more troubling up the street. Michael's station wagon approaches the girls. The same vehicle Laurie spotted outside her classroom window earlier. The Chemistry book is forgotten as the car slows down so the driver can get a better look at the girls. Neither we nor they can see him clearly. But the return of *Halloween*'s main theme music echoes Laurie's growing fear of the mysterious stranger who seems to be following her.

Following Laurie's lead, Annie and Lynda finally notice him too. Lynda, her perceptions blinkered by her usual preoccupations, assumes the driver is a cute boy from school. She even assigns a name to him. "I don't think so," Laurie quietly disagrees, as if to herself. She suspects someone or something more sinister, but is not yet willing to share her unconventional suspicions with her very conventional pals.

The station wagon speeds up after it passes the girls. Annie, whom we later learn is the daughter of the town's Sheriff, shouts at the driver, "Hey, jerk! Speed kills!" Daddy would be so proud. Annie probably accepts Lynda's identification of the driver as just a boy from school. The vehicle, now a distance away, screeches to a halt in the middle of the street, and remains there. No back talk from the driver. Nor does he get out of the vehicle to confront his critic. The girls, standing close to one another, perhaps instinctively *huddled* together, are puzzled by the stranger's behavior. It's not the typical reaction of a teenage boy showing off for teenage girls. In a quieter, more cautious, intimidated tone of voice Annie remarks, "God, can't you take a joke?" She speaks the line softly, obviously not intending to be heard by the unseen driver. For only a moment, Annie is conscious of at least the *potential* for danger, and modifies her behavior accordingly.

The station wagon resumes its course, rounds a corner and disappears. Laurie, sensing the driver's hostility if not yet his true intent, reprimands Annie for reprimanding him. "Some day you're going to get us all into deep trouble." A typical complaint of the risk-averse about the risk-taker. But then the background music fades away, the mood of apprehension dissipates, and the three friends resume their walk home, conversing nonchalantly about boyfriends and babysitting plans. The camera again backtracks with them for a ways, restoring us as a fourth member of the group. Until it stops and pivots to a reverse angle. We now watch the girls walk away from us, still talking contentedly, even if that contentment includes occasional complaints and jokes at each other's expense. But they get smaller and smaller as they recede. Their now diminutive figures appear vulnerable, overarched by a looming tree limb above them as uneasy music creeps back onto the soundtrack.

Carpenter, via his camera and soundtrack, keeps shifting his audience back and forth, closer to then further away from the emotional outlook of the girls. By doing so, he encourages both identification *with* them and increasing anxiety *for* them. Unless, of course, the viewer himself is inclined to be

## 3. Carpenter's *Halloween*

Annie (Nancy Loomis), Lynda (P. J. Soles) and Laurie (Jamie Lee Curtis) are three small town teenagers who sometimes bicker, tease and disagree yet remain true friends, in *Halloween*. Their routine walk home from school includes a close encounter with a force of destruction that will, later that night, end the young lives of Annie and Lynda and shatter Laurie's.

a predator. In which case camera positions subjectively aligned with Michael Myers' point of view, or with what *could* be Michael's point of view if he were in the scene at this point, makes stalkers of us all. But I think Carpenter expects more compassion from his audience.

A new camera angle further down the street. This time we track the girls, but from a greater distance. The disturbing music continues, again making us acutely aware of their vulnerability. But once more the music fades out, the camera rejoins the group, and so do we. Lynda departs for her family's house, leaving only two girls left. A reduction of safety in numbers? Because we know more about the lurking danger than do the characters, that thought occurs to us.

Almost immediately after Lynda leaves, Laurie spots her mysterious stalker, Michael in dark coveralls and a white mask, up ahead, standing half on the sidewalk and half on someone's lawn, partially concealed by a neatly trimmed hedge. He's too far away from us, as we share Laurie vantage point, to make out much detail. But he's creepy enough, standing motionless and staring fixedly in our/Laurie's direction. As he did outside the classroom. Michael is the one unsettling element in this otherwise neatly-ordered and comfortably familiar neighborhood. Trees, houses, lawns, hedges — nothing else is out of place in this picture. Just Michael.

The background music resumes, now fully in tune with Laurie's fear. In a tight frontal shot, we see her gazing intently ahead at the stranger blocking her path. Annie, predictably not yet aware of him, searches for something in her purse. Returning to Laurie's vantage point, we see Michael, closer now, step calmly behind the hedge and disappear. The camera moves into an intimate close-up of the two young women as Laurie warns Annie about the odd stranger behind the hedge. She claims it's the same guy Annie yelled at earlier.

Now that Annie has finally been made aware of the stalker's presence, she walks fearlessly towards the hedge, boldly determined to challenge him. We observe her from what we assume is very close to his point of view. But when Annie reaches the hedge, he is not there. Did Laurie imagine him? Did we see a projection of her fantasy stalker? Annie doesn't believe her. So she transforms Laurie's stalker into a joke — a somewhat cruel means of ridiculing her friend's lack of social ease with the opposite sex. Laurie's stalker wants to ask her out on a date, Annie claims. Not as mean as what Tommy's tormentors did to him back in the schoolyard, but nevertheless a taunt of someone perceived by Annie as weaker, more vulnerable than herself. And just as one of the boys who taunted Tommy had a brief encounter with the real boogeyman, Annie has a fateful date with the man of Laurie's nightmares. The reckless ease with which she dismisses Laurie's fears will return to haunt her.

When Annie reaches the hedge, finds no one lurking there, and turns back to face Laurie, we observe her from behind. And even though we know Michael has left the immediate area, memories of the film's extraordinary first shot, in which we subjectively accompanied Michael as he stalked and killed his sister, linger in the mind, making us uncomfortably aware of Annie's vulnerability. According to J. P. Telotte, from her remarkable article "Through a Pumpkin's Eye: The Reflective Nature of Horror," Carpenter builds up a sense of guilt anxiety in his audience by allowing us to observe Michael's potential victims from near his vantage point (Telotte, p. 143). And in this particular shot, he haunts our point of view even when he is not there. Because we know he *could* be.

Laurie approaches the hedge tentatively, with none of Annie's bravado. Seeing no stalker crouching in wait for her, she insists he was there. "Poor Laurie. Scared another one away," teases Annie. She berates Laurie for her shyness, though perhaps with better intentions (of improving her friend's social life) than those of Tommy's tormentors.

Only one yard beyond the hedge, Annie departs for her own house. Michael cannot be far away, despite the disarming serenity of this neighborhood. Laurie continues on alone. Michael's music fades from the soundtrack, displaced by the chirping of birds and a pleasant light breeze. As she walks towards her own home, Laurie looks back in the direction of the hedge, still worried about her mysterious stalker. Though keeping Laurie in sight, the camera mostly shares her point of view when she unexpectedly walks straight into Annie's father, the town's Sheriff, returning home from work. Thinking it might be her stalker, just as we momentarily fear it might be Michael Myers, Laurie screams. Seeing who it really is, she quickly apologizes, embarrassed by her display of fear. Sheriff Brackett, with a big smile on his face, remarks, "It's Halloween. I guess everyone's entitled to a good scare." Clearly he enjoyed being on the *giving* end of that mild fright. "Yes, sir," Laurie respectfully concedes, though perhaps disingenuously. The Sheriff heads for his house, as oblivious of the real danger stalking his neighborhood and his community as is his daughter. He smokes a pipe, which adds to the complacency of his appearance by lending him a rather professorial air of emotional detachment.

Entering her own yard further on down the sidewalk, Laurie glances behind her one last time to make sure she isn't being followed. The only other person in sight is an anonymous neighbor raking leaves in *his* safe, secure front yard. Approaching the front steps of her house, Laurie hears sounds of possible distress from an unseen source nearby. It's amazing how many places there are to hide in a small town neighborhood. Concerned, she stops to investigate. But it turns out to be only a group of costumed children, with adult supervision, getting a head start on trick or treating next door. One of them wears an angel costume. No Frankenstein Monster or Count Dracula in this group. Laurie smiles and chides herself, "Well, kiddo, I thought you outgrew superstition." Relieved, she lightheartedly mounts the front steps and enters her house. The mysterious stalker is banished from her thoughts, for the moment.

What an interesting game of cat and mouse Carpenter has played with us during Laurie's otherwise routine trek home from school. Treating us along the way to brief, inconclusive encounters with a terror *we* know exists but of which the characters in this scene are largely ignorant. Only one of them is observant and insecure enough to have been mildly alarmed. David Ansen, in a *Newsweek* review of the film's original release back in 1978, pointed out, "It's the waiting that's crucial. Carpenter understands that the apprehension of horror is more unnerving than the actual event" (Ansen, p. 116). Plus it allows Laurie and us to feel the *gradual* intrusion of disorder and violence into her otherwise orderly, routine, though never entirely trouble-free world.

Laurie walks into her bedroom on the second floor of her home. It's an appealing, airy room, painted a cheerful pale yellow, with white curtains over the windows. Her bedspread too is white and yellow, mixed with a few other soft colors. The windows are open. Curtains flutter in the refreshing crossbreeze. There is no indication Laurie's parents are at home (we never see her mother), suggesting the windows were left open all day while the house was unoccupied. Small town, Midwestern trust in one's fellow man. The absence of Carpenter's always unsettling music adds to our feeling of comfort and security, which we share with Laurie.

Among the objects visible in Laurie's room are a Raggedy Ann doll sitting on top of a dresser and a James Ensor poster on the wall. An interesting blend of childhood make-believe and adult sophistication. Laurie is a bright young woman. But perhaps she, like the rest of us, can never fully escape our childish vulnerability to fear, whether rational or irrational. On the floor in the corner are a tennis racket and a stuffed, red, heart-shaped pillow. If the latter is a token of Laurie's unfulfilled yearning for love, the former, representing athletic endeavor, may be one way in which she copes with her frustration.

Laurie drops her school books on the bed, goes to the window and casually looks out into the backyard. Home Sweet Home? Not this time. Standing amidst fluttering clothes and sheets (like her bedroom, another gentle mix of white and yellow) drying on the clothesline next door is the masked stranger she saw twice earlier. Standing perfectly still, he stares directly at her, and at us, thanks to a briefly subjective camera. Again Carpenter juxtaposes the alien and menacing with the familiar and comforting. The fluttering sheets and shirts counterpoint and accentuate Michael's *lack* of movement, which eerily conveys his unrelenting if as yet mysterious sense of purpose. His for the moment complete focus of attention on Laurie Strode. With Michael's fateful reappearance in her life, his fateful music returns.

Another point-of-view shot from Laurie's perspective reveals Michael now gone. The backyard view is cleansed of menace, but Laurie's fear, along with the music that seems to simultaneously echo and fuel it, lingers. She slams the window shut and retreats back inside her bedroom. The camera cuts to a more distant view from behind and to the side of her as she cowers. It's not a predatory view linked to Michael, but it certainly makes us more aware of Laurie's vulnerability. The room no longer seems comforting or safe, even though none of its physical contents has changed.

Edging to the right, the camera brings into view Laurie's telephone, allowing us to anticipate its rather shocking intrusion into this already tense situation. Its loud ring catches Laurie off guard, if only for a moment. She picks it up, but her greeting goes unanswered. And into that silence she understandably infuses the menace of her stalker. Even though, in the pre-cell phone era of the late 1970s, there wasn't sufficient time for the clothesline stalker to reach a telephone. A medium shot of Laurie on the phone surrounds her with

## 3. Carpenter's *Halloween*

the previously pleasant features of her bedroom: bright windows, Ensor print and Raggedy Ann doll. But another object has been added. A black globe on which the continents of the Earth appear in yellow. A perfectly attractive globe, but out of the ordinary. Not what we might expect. And in the context of Michael's disturbing appearance outside, a slightly disquieting element in the camera frame with Laurie as she puzzles over her unresponsive caller.

Laurie slams the phone down, breaking the connection with her unidentified caller, just as she slammed the window shut on her unidentified stalker. The phone rings again. Hesitantly, she answers it. It's Annie, as it was the first time. But the first call was not a practical joke intended to scare Laurie, as we might suspect on Halloween. Annie couldn't reply to Laurie's earlier "Hello" because her mouth was full of food. Not uncommon for a teenager.

"I thought it was an obscene phone call," Laurie complains to her friend, who remains skeptical of Laurie's fears as well as contemptuous of Laurie's lack of sexual experience. "You're losing it," accuses Annie, referring to Laurie's paranoia. "I already lost it," agrees Laurie. "I doubt that," adds Annie, referring now to Laurie's virginity. So it's Annie who establishes a link between Laurie's fear of a male stalker and alleged sexual fear of men. Annie doesn't believe Laurie's stalker is real. She pays no heed to her friend's concern because she has little regard for Laurie's opinion, period. Within the narrowly defined value system of their teenage world, Laurie's inexperience calls into question her views on everything, especially men.

Regardless of their different perspectives, the two young women are friends. They arrange to meet up later that evening. Annie will pick up Laurie in a car she's borrowing from her mother. Annie thinks of herself as the wiser, more adult of the two girls. Dismissing Laurie's fears, passing out advice about boys, and in a later scene even arranging a date for Laurie without Laurie's permission, Annie is overconfident in her own understanding of the world at large.

After the phone call, Laurie lies down on the bed, which seems much too small for her (she remains part child/part adult), and tries to restore her peace of mind. "Calm down. This is ridiculous," she chides herself, echoing Annie's harsh judgment of her childish fear. And her own judgment of little Tommy Doyle's superstitious dread of the old Myers house.

6:30 P.M., Halloween night. We observe Laurie emerge from her house from the same camera angle as when she left for school early the same morning. And with the same brooding background music to make us uneasy. Autumn leaves fall in the light breeze, as they did hours earlier. But this time Laurie is dressed in a pant suit and looks more adult, less childlike. She carries a large pumpkin for Tommy to carve, as she promised him. But the pumpkin is heavy. If it is a token of the lighthearted, treat side of Halloween, of terror well-contained and largely toothless entertainment rather than real danger, it's increasingly burdensome for Laurie to maintain that point of view.

We and the camera follow Laurie as she walks to the corner of her lot and sits on a concrete yard marker to wait for Annie. She is relaxed now, free from the fear she experienced in her room earlier that afternoon. A wonderfully intimate medium close-up of Laurie lets us observe her observing the safe, predictable, circumscribed world of her neighborhood. She half-smiles to herself as she glances down the street at a group of costumed children, again with adult guardians, engaged in the traditional fun of trick-or-treat. She turns her head to look in the opposite direction. Same thing. No dialog can be heard. Carpenter gives us a subtly powerful but *general* impression, from Laurie's somewhat detached perspective, of a typical small town American neighborhood on a typical Halloween early evening. And yet that pleasant impression is countered and darkened by the uneasy music that intrudes on the visuals. Everything is *not* right in this neighborhood. The potential for *real* horror lurks just out of sight, beyond the edge of the camera frame. Somewhere. But this time Laurie is unaware of that potential. After three disturbing if indefinite encounters with it during the day, she has returned to her naïve point of view from our first encounter with her. *Despite* the apparent sophistication of her new clothes. Comfortable old habits die hard.

The camera changes angle, giving us a less intimate profile of Laurie as she continues to watch costumed children pass by. Off screen to our left, we notice before she does a car approaching from far down the street. Is it Michael's station wagon? Is he stalking her again? Carpenter keeps the vehicle slightly out of focus and at long range, rendering it easy for us to imagine it's Michael's, until Laurie turns her head and spots it. Camera focus sharpens. It's Annie, in her mother's red car. No danger. Ironically, the *red* vehicle is much less menacing than the nondescript, almost colorless vehicle we *should* fear. Laurie crosses the street to join her friend, holding tightly to the pumpkin she carries into the approaching Halloween night.

As always, Annie is impatient with her friend. "Hurry up," she tells Laurie. Inside the car an innocuous, cheerful rock and roll song plays on the radio, replacing and contradicting the background music heard moments earlier. Annie hands Laurie a marijuana joint, instructing, "We just have time." Laurie reacts to the cigarette as though it were an alien insect. Despite the increased sophistication of her clothes, Laurie still lacks the experience and social ease of her friend. But her deficiency in that area, combined with her intelligence and perceptiveness, gives Laurie a distinct advantage over Annie when it comes to anticipating and coping with a threat from *outside* their world.

Haddonfield Cemetery. Sam Loomis and the cemetery caretaker arrive in Sam's car. The two men enter the cemetery on foot, in search of the grave of Judith Myers. As they walk the caretaker remarks, "Every town has something like this happen," then segues into a spooky legend from a neighboring town. It's the fifteen year old story of "Old Charlie Bolls" (same timeline as "Young Michael Myers"), who used a hacksaw to ... we'll never know. The caretaker tells his tale with obvious relish, despite the violent and tragic events it presumably entails. Most of us thrill to a tale of terror told well, whether it involves accurate reporting, embellished truth or pure invention. But Sam Loomis is too preoccupied with the real life terror of Michael Myers to be amused by any other myth like it, real or fantasized. By cutting the caretaker's tale short, Carpenter makes us aware of our disappointment and therefore of the strangely convoluted role fear plays in our lives. From a certain angle and distance, terror is fascinating.

Reaching Judith Myers' cemetery plot, the two men notice her gravestone is missing. The caretaker blames it on teenagers. A not unlikely occurrence at Halloween. It's an unpleasant, thoughtless, even criminal act. But neither dangerous nor lethal. Sam, looking up and vaguely away as though searching for something, and in harmony with the revival of sinister music on the soundtrack, blames the act squarely on Michael Myers. "He came home" is such a simple, harmless statement of fact, on its surface. But coming from Michael's psychiatrist, it is laced with foreboding. Michael Myers has not returned to Haddonfield for his high school reunion. "The Night *He* Came Home" was the tag line for *Halloween*'s promotional publicity. And a very *good* one. Because it hinted at much more than it revealed.

Sam's fear of Michael, and of what he knows Michael is capable of doing, is both very real, within the context of the film's story, and very entertaining, insofar as both are just characters in a horror film. Moments earlier he had no interest in or fear of "Old Charlie Bolls." But if we can infer from the caretaker's abbreviated story, Mr. Bolls employed his hacksaw against one or more members of his own family. *Their* fear of him was no doubt acutely real and extreme, even though the myth that grew up around that stark reality has over the years become a source of entertainment for others. Like the reality of "Old Ed Gein" and the cinematic myth of *Psycho*. The latter, like all the best horror films, is entertainment that acknowledges and explores the dynamics of terror, but thankfully never *duplicates* it. Unless some weak-minded fool tries to duplicate the myth in real life. But that's a danger with *any* misapplied public commodity, including many held in the highest esteem by much of the general public.

Laurie and Annie drive through the streets of Haddonfield, apparently just cruising around for fun before heading to their respective babysitting jobs. Otherwise it takes them an inexplicably long time to reach a destination not far from the Myers house that Laurie reached rather quickly on foot from her own home earlier that morning. The previously lighthearted rock and roll song playing on the car radio has been eclipsed by "Don't Fear the Reaper," a Blue Oyster Cult classic from 1976. The *sound* of that song complements the lurking presence of Michael Myers and the momentarily absent background music that keeps him in our minds even when unseen. But the song's *lyrics* suggest the opposite. *Don't* fear Death. And that is Annie's attitude as she and Laurie discuss the stalker Laurie saw in her neighbor's backyard. That neighbor is eighty-seven year old Mr. Riddle. Annie, always contemptuous of her friend's fears, teases Laurie for still being "spooked" by the encounter. Laurie denies it, and at the same time makes a sour face after taking a drag from Annie's illegal cigarette. She hands the joint back to her more experienced companion, who smokes it with casual ease. Annie reduces Laurie's fearsome stalker to harmless old Mr. Riddle. "He can still watch," Laurie weakly protests. "That's probably all he *can* do," retorts Annie, discrediting even the mildest of Laurie's fears.

While the young women discuss Laurie's elderly neighbor, the camera cuts to a rear view through the car's back window. Annie's dismissal of old man Riddle as a serious threat, and the radio song lyrics that back her up, are nullified by the sight of Michael's station wagon pulling in behind Annie's vehicle and following at close range. The safe and secure interior of a car filled with pop music and glib teenage conversation is menaced by an outside presence stalking the girls. Think of the cars that briefly followed and seemed to stalk nervous Marion Crane as she fled Phoenix with stolen money in *Psycho*. And Norman Bates wasn't even *in* those vehicles.

A change in camera position brings Annie into the frame while retaining the rear view image of Michael's trailing vehicle. Her attention on the street ahead, the pot she smokes and her conversation with Laurie, she fails to glance in the rear view mirror to notice a very near and present danger, who is definitely *not* Mr. Riddle. Though Michael Myers is certainly a *riddle* of sorts, with mysterious motives and powers.

Making fun of Laurie for being so selflessly considerate as to bring a pumpkin for Tommy Doyle to carve that evening, Annie describes her companion as a "girl scout." Not a term of respect, in Annie's lexicon. Then she bemoans her own sad fate, babysitting like Laurie while her boyfriend sits at home, grounded for his mild acts of pre–Halloween vandalism. "I might as well be one [a girl scout] myself." But Annie is somewhat cheered by the prospect of frightening the wits out of the child she'll be babysitting, subjecting the girl to "six straight hours of horror movies." Annie herself has presumably outgrown the age when the distinction between real and pretend terror can be confusing to a young, vivid imagination. "Little Lindsey Wallace won't know what hit her," she brags. Her attitude resembles that of Tommy's tormentors in the schoolyard, though not nearly as cruel. And it is contrasted by Laurie's very adult efforts to soothe Tommy's fear of the Myers house. But Annie's apparent invulnerability to terror is visually overshadowed by the continued presence of Michael's station wagon closely following her.

Spotting her father's police car up ahead, parked in front of a hardware store, Annie suddenly knows *real* fear, of a sort. She nervously orders Laurie to get rid of the marijuana. As this new fear escalates, the undetected one (undetected by the girls, that is) eases. Michael parks along the street while Annie drives on to the hardware store. We witness this separation from outside both vehicles. Then, back inside Annie's car, Annie frantically orders Laurie to stop coughing before they reach the Sheriff, whose vehicle we watch, subjectively with the girls, getting closer and closer through the front windshield. Even a loving father can be the boogeyman on occasion.

After she parks alongside her father's car, Annie's ensuing conversation with her Dad, occurring through an open window on Laurie's side, is an almost affectionate salute to the perceived generation gap between parents and their children, circa 1978. Sheriff Brackett blames a burglary at the store on "kids," because of the type of merchandise stolen. "You blame everything on kids," Annie retaliates on behalf of all teenagers. This brief little debate between parent and child is neatly amplified by the loud ring of the store's security alarm, which renders their communication gap amusingly literal (father and daughter experience difficulty hearing each other over the racket). But there are no serious consequences. Annie departs with a cheerful, "Bye, Dad." Her father, though looking a trifle befuddled, like many fathers of teenage girls, fondly watches his daughter drive away. Whatever divides them is trivial. The alarm from the store metaphorically cries out to warn them both, in vain, of a much greater danger closer than either realizes. Sheriff Brackett has no clue that he will never see his daughter alive again.

Sheriff Bracket told the girls the burglar stole a Halloween mask, rope and some candy. Could the burglar have been Michael Myers? Possibly. The Halloween mask casts suspicion in his direction. But judging by the security alarm, the burglary occurred recently. And we saw Michael wearing *his* mask, though from a distance and therefore not clearly, hours earlier. If Michael did *not* commit the burglary, the contrast between the real thief, who probably just wanted the Halloween mask for fun, and Michael, whose idea of fun is chillingly lethal to others, is yet another example of the contradictory faces of fear.

As the Sheriff gazes after his departing daughter's car, San Loomis approaches him from the same direction, bringing news of a disturbance far more serious than a little generation gap disagreement. Brackett does not, however, share Loomis's priorities. He must conclude his investigation of the burglary before listening to a stranger's warning about something or other. While awaiting Brackett's return, Loomis glances warily up and down the street. Passing unnoticed behind him, Michael's stolen state vehicle resumes its pursuit of the girls. Once again, the routine of a pleasant autumn day in Haddonfield, Illinois is barely rippled by the lurking potential for genuine horror.

Twilight. Annie and Laurie wend their way through peaceful residential streets towards their babysitting jobs. Laurie worries out loud, and unnecessarily, that Annie's father knew she had been smoking pot. She sure looked uncomfortable and guilty sandwiched between the father/daughter debate outside the hardware store. But Annie is confident her father suspected nothing, and she seems to read him quite well. This is an example of Annie's perception being keener than Laurie's paranoia. Unfortunately for Annie, that is not always the case.

Another of Laurie's fears pops up when she mentions the upcoming school dance. Annie encourages her to ask someone to go with her. She suggests a boy by name, though from her tone of voice it's half in jest. Probably a young man desperate enough to accept a date with any girl. Laurie has a different guy in mind, obviously setting her sights much higher. Ben Tramer. Again judging by Annie's reaction, Ben must be fairly prominent on the high school social register. She teases Laurie about her repressed desire, yet also generously encourages her friend to ask him out.

However different they may be in temperament, experience and outlook, Laurie and Annie are true friends. Teasing, derision and even little acts of cruelty between them are safely contained within a larger net of loyalty and caring. But when the camera cuts away from the conversational intimacy inside Annie's car, we see Michael's vehicle following them very closely. How can they not see it? Maybe because in many ways they are two typical teenagers (male or female, doesn't matter which), often consumed by the trials, tribulations and concerns within their own little world. When she is alone, and not influenced by the dominant personalities of Annie and Lynda, Laurie is more aware of the outside world, including its fascinations (James Ensor prints) and its dangers (stalkers). Michael's aggressive musical theme has returned. The girls can neither hear nor take warning from it. But we can.

Minutes later. The full darkness of Halloween night has descended on Haddonfield. From Michael's vantage point, inside the station wagon, we watch Annie drop Laurie off in front of Tommy's house. We catch a snippet of their parting, routine conversation, heard as from a great distance. Michael and we turn together to watch Laurie head for the Doyle residence. But instead of pursuing her, we turn back towards Annie's car and watch it pull into the driveway of a house across the street. Background music fades out, replaced by the equally disturbing sound of Michael's steady breathing. *So* steady that we cannot detect any emotional agitation within him suggesting fear on *his* part. His mission, whatever it is, proceeds with a clear conscience. Or no conscience at all.

Parking his car, Michael exits with calm, mechanical smoothness, takes up position behind a tree to observe as Annie exits her car and walks nonchalantly to the brightly lit front door of the Wallace house. Michael's eerie music creeps back onto the soundtrack. Knocking politely at the door, Annie has a brief conversation with Lindsey's parents before entering the house with the child while Mr. and Mrs. Wallace leave home for the evening. Probably for a Halloween tradition of their own. We hear their conversation with Annie from a distance, as we did Annie's with Laurie. From Michael's vantage point, but with ears informed by other, less predatory emotions, the voices of parents and babysitter sound so ordinary, so utterly unaware of the danger just across the street. As do the passing voices of unseen trick-or-treaters on the prowl for candy. These unsuspecting voices come and go. Michael remains, his focus and mysterious purpose as immovable as the Fate of which Laurie's teacher spoke so passionately earlier in the day.

To say Michael *hides* behind a tree in order to spy on Annie is an exaggeration. The tree barely conceals him. He is certainly not invisible. But because none of Haddonfield's residents, with the occasional exception of Laurie Strode and Tommy Doyle, *expects* an invasion of madness and violence into their everyday lives, no one perceives Michael as a threat. He could be just another kid, if a bit old for this sort of thing, dressed up for Halloween. Watching from near Michael's point of view as Annie, Laurie, the Wallace's and various trick-or-treaters go about their ordinary Halloween activities makes us all too aware of their vulnerability. John Carpenter's remorseless music, infusing Michael's presence into nearly every scene at some point or other, hangs over the residents of Haddonfield like an undetected Sword of Damocles.

A full frontal shot of the Myers house, similar to the opening scene in the movie but without the smiling pumpkin or any light emanating from within. Shadows of trees sway back and forth across its façade. Camera focus changes to the foreground as the hood of Sheriff Brockett's police car enters at the bottom of the film frame. The word "SHERIFF" appears prominently on its side panel, counterpointing the definitely *un*lawful nature of the threat suggested by the house. There will be a contest between these forces. Eerie background music reminds us of Michael's presence *somewhere* in this small town. Is he back inside the house? Waiting for us? Waiting for Sam Loomis and Sheriff Brackett, who enter the darkened, dilapidated structure with flashlight in hand? "Haunted" houses are always spookier by flashlight, or candlelight, than with full electrical illumination Unless, of course, you're spending the winter at the Overlook Hotel, where even the most sophisticated illumination cannot protect you from the terrors that lurk within your family and yourself.

A creaking front door, the absence of electrical light, torn wallpaper and worn paint render the old Myers house an alien, uncivilized environment. Far from the home-sweet-home it once appeared to be. A "Strode Real Estate" sign posted in the front yard cannot hide the fact that this is an uninhabited, perhaps uninhabitable place, We observe Loomis and Brackett from the living room, looking towards the entryway, as they arrive. Approximately the same vantage point we shared with young Michael as he stalked his sister fifteen long years ago.

The two intruders spot the still-warm remains of a partially eaten dog on the living room floor. An indication of raw, predatory Nature at work in this unsuspecting small town. Carpenter spares us a shot of the mutilated carcass, relying instead on the reactions of his characters to inform us of its relevance. Sheriff Bracket blames the deed on a skunk. "He got hungry," corrects Loomis, *not* referring to a skunk. "A man wouldn't do that," retorts the Sheriff. "This *isn't* a man." Which begs the question, "Then what *is* he?" Part of what makes Michael Myers (what an inoffensive-sounding name) such an interesting horror film icon is his *lack* of definition. Outwardly, he seems very much a human being, at least initially. But during the course of *Halloween* he seems less and less so. And the human qualities he lacks make him ever more difficult to define, and therefore ever more frightening.

Following the same path as Michael fifteen years earlier, the two men ascend the stairway to the second floor bedroom of the late Judith Myers. Loomis explains to Brackett what happened on that fateful night back in 1963. His intent is to impress upon the Sheriff the great danger Michael poses now, in 1978. In other words, he wants to *scare* the skeptical lawman into taking the danger seriously. But in the midst of his attempt to frighten Brackett for his own good, Loomis himself is frightened by an eave that breaks loose from the roof and smashes the very window through which, the psychiatrist had just pointed out, Michael probably glimpsed his sister before killing her.

Reacting from reflex at a phony threat, like the child in all of us, Loomis pulls a pistol out of his pocket. Recovering from the false alarm, he sheepishly explains to the Sheriff that he has a permit for the gun. "Seems to me you're just plain scared," Bracket surmises. And building on that statement of fact, Loomis tries to engender the same fear in his companion. He vividly describes Michael's lack of human qualities. "No reason. No conscience. No understanding in even the most rudimentary sense of life or death, of good or evil, right or wrong." The face of six year old Michael Myers was "blank, pale, emotionless," with "the devil's eyes." That last observation is a mythological, supernatural analogy, not a clinical analysis. Sam's fear of Michael, proceeding from close proximity to his case, has superseded any professional objectivity. There is a strong whiff of fanaticism about Sam Loomis that harkens back to many crusading wise elders in the horror film genre of the 1930s and 1940s, and continuing on through the likes of Dr. Zaius in *Planet of the Apes* (1967). We sense that under a different set of circumstances Loomis could himself be a danger to others. But in *Halloween* the monster he battles seems worthy of his paranoia.

"I spent eight years trying to reach him." But there was nothing to reach. "And another seven trying to keep him locked up because I realized what was lying behind that boy's eyes was purely and simply evil." Evil being the lack of human qualities (conscience and compassion) we normally take for granted in each other. This little ghost story is delivered in a nice tight shot of the two characters, with Sam's sober face occupying screen left and Sheriff Brackett's police uniform badge, with its illuminated star of authority, prominent at right. Moral judgment and the power of law enforcement juxtaposed. Together, Loomis and Brackett decide what to do. The Sheriff's men are to be quietly vigilant, generating no public alarm, while the psychiatrist waits at the Myers house for Michael's expected return.

The exterior of Tommy Doyle's house is as peaceful and inviting as that of the Myers house is creepy and intimidating. Inside, on a couch in the living room, Laurie reads to Tommy from a book about King Arthur, which *was* the boy's favorite story. No longer. Now he prefers more violent fare. Comic books with such titles as Laser Man, Neutron Man and Tarantula Man, which he keeps hidden under the couch because his mother disapproves of them. "I can understand why," echoes Laurie, sounding very parental and grown-up. A bit old-fashioned. Even stuffy. But if Tommy's tastes in fiction are trending towards the more explicitly violent, his fears are still rooted in childhood. "What's the boogeyman?" he inquires, clearly still troubled by his encounter with older classmates earlier that day. He turns now to an adult-like person, but one still young enough to maybe appreciate his fears and with whom he can share the secret of his forbidden comic books, for a comforting explanation.

Before Laurie can supply that explanation, she is interrupted by a phone call from Annie, across the street. And is quickly distracted by the world of teen romance and dating. For the time being, Tommy and his childish concerns disappear from her radar screen. But for Tommy and the Wallace family dog, a German shepherd named Lester, the boogeyman is *not* forgotten. In the matter of irrational fears, a young boy perhaps has more in common with a dog than with his teenage babysitter.

While Annie, standing in the Wallace kitchen, discusses Ben Tramer with Laurie, Lester wanders in, barking loudly at someone or something unseen outside the house. He senses a menacing presence in *his* territory. Annoyed at Lester's disruption, Annie complains in her exaggerated, teenage way, "I'm about to be ripped apart by the family dog." No, she's being *warned* by the family dog about someone who will rip her apart for real. And at her own peril, she ignores him, calling on Lindsey, in the living room, to remove the disruptive animal. "I'm the only one he hates," adds the irritated babysitter, again playing the teenage martyr. Not true at all. Annie and Lester may not be on the friendliest of terms, but at least he *tolerates* her presence in his territory, babysitting a member of *his* family. The alarm he sounds over some invisible threat should at least trigger her vigilance. It's virtually a horror film cliché that animals are more sensitive to the presence of danger than are humans. Lester's reaction to Michael Myers is the same as that of another dog to the as yet unmanifested lycanthropic menace of Larry Talbot in *The Wolf Man* (1941), or a cat hissing at the cursed but not yet hairy Wilfred Glendon in *The Werewolf of London* (1935).

Just as Annie ignores Lester's warning in the kitchen, Lindsey Wallace, preoccupied with a televised monster movie in the living room, ignores her babysitter's plea for relief from the dog's loud barking. Sitting on a couch in the dark, Lindsey watches *The Thing from Another World* (1951). Meanwhile, the Thing from Haddonfield lurks just outside, watching the house, staring up at a cozily lit window. Positioned near his vantage point, we spy on the house and its unsuspecting inhabitants with him. Yet we comprehend little of what he is thinking or feeling at this moment. The near-subjective camera invests the audience with more fear for what might happen to the occupants of the house than it does empathy with Michael. Back inside the kitchen, Lester heads for the door leading outside, and to a fateful encounter with the lurking stranger, while Annie obliviously returns to her phone conversation with Laurie.

Cutting away from that conversation, we re-locate to the darkened Doyle dining room, into which Tommy casually strolls after being deserted by Laurie. He is bored by his babysitter's talk about dating and boys, which audibly fades into the background. He glances outside the dining room window. Sinister music irrevocably linked to Michael Myers returns to the soundtrack as we see what Tommy sees. A starkly illuminated silhouette of Michael across the street, standing perfectly still, staring fixedly at the Wallace house. Also visible in silhouette, laughing trick-or-treaters pass by between us and Michael, along the sidewalk on our side of the street. They take no notice of the stranger clearly visible across the way. After all, Michael isn't *doing* anything to define himself as a menace. Only in the mind of Tommy Doyle, still haunted by schoolyard threats of a boogeyman coming to get him, does the distant, passive figure of Michael Myers inspire fear. The sight of *any* stranger lurking about the neighborhood would do as well. Tommy does not know the identity of this particular stranger, nor is he aware of Michael's recent escape from a mental hospital or return to Haddonfield. Yet his childish fear of a mythical boogeyman coincidently complements and reinforces *our* more knowledgeable, reasonable fear of Michael.

Dressed in an astronaut costume, with an American flag patch on the shoulder, Tommy Doyle, like most children, allows his imagination free reign, especially on Halloween night. Alarmed at what he sees out the window of his formerly secure home, he runs back to Laurie and announces, "The boogeyman's outside!" Laurie, pausing in her conversation with Annie, responsibly checks out Tommy's story. She looks out the window. The menacing shape across the street is gone. For us, his absence intensifies the sense of danger. Has he slipped inside the Wallace house? But for Laurie his absence simply discredits Tommy's claim. "Go watch TV," she tells him — the all too common adult remedy for pacifying an irksome child. "It's just Tommy," Laurie dismissively informs Annie, who earlier reacted to Laurie's fears of a stalker just as dismissively. Laurie should know better. But for the moment this otherwise model babysitter is too caught up in the Ben Tramer situation to be her usual sensitive and perceptive self.

Returning to the other end of the phone line, we spy on Annie through the window in a French door looking into the Wallace kitchen. The kitchen itself is pleasantly well-lit. In effect, we are a Peeping Tom. Then Michael silently steps into the frame and becomes that Peeping Tom, whose point of view we now partly share. Shades of L.B. Jeffries spying on his neighbors through the windows of his apartment in *Rear Window* (1954). Phone talk about boy troubles now seems outrageously naïve, because of what we know about Michael. But for Annie and Laurie it remains a top priority. So distracted is Annie that she absent-mindedly spills melted popcorn butter on her blouse and jeans. She ends her conversation with Laurie in order to attend to her *new* priority, which unfortunately still acknowledges nothing of the much greater threat nearby.

Annie removes her blouse and jeans. Not wearing a bra, she is now dressed only in panties, and is far more exposed to the outside world than she realizes. The camera, for the moment, embodies that world and enhances our appreciation of her vulnerability. She calls out for Lindsey to bring her a robe. But Lindsey is still too absorbed in her own little world, as the babysitter is in *hers*, to pay the slightest attention to anyone or anything outside the darkened living room and the TV that fitfully illuminates it.

Michael continues to spy on Annie through the French doors. Is he aroused by her exposed body? Does he murderously disapprove of it? He reaches up and deliberately yanks down a hanging flower pot, sending it crashing to the ground, then departs. The camera remains where it was. Annie hears the noise and *finally* glances outside her safe little world. But her alarm is mild and lasts only a moment before she turns back to her soiled clothes. Meanwhile, Michael returns to a previous position, standing outside a different window in the Wallace house. He stares up at it, telling us nothing of what so fascinates him about it. Is he thinking of his sister's bedroom window from fifteen years ago?

The camera shares Michael's point of view until it tilts down and pans to the left to show us Lester, growling and barking, approaching him from behind. Will he be Michael's nemesis the same way Michael was Judith's?

Terror from behind? We return to the kitchen, where Annie again pointlessly complains to an all but deaf Lindsey about the dog's incessant barking. How fatally tragic for Annie that she ignores both Lester's and Laurie's alarms about Michael's intrusion into her life. Just as Laurie ignored Tommy's. She even dismisses, after a moment of concern, Michael's own warning of his presence (the dropped flower pot). When Lester's now distant barking turns to a whimper and then ceases, a relieved Annie jokes, "Guess he found a hot date," revealing more about her own preoccupations than about what is happening to the dog.

Cut back to the action outside. In a shot taken from close to the ground, we see the dog's legs droop as he is held off the ground by Michael, whose own sturdy legs, powerfully bent at the knees, are all we see of him. With no perceptible fear and overwhelming physical strength, Michael Myers mercilessly ends the threat posed by the Wallace family's canine protector. Background music screams out about the killing in a low register, before fading out, like Lester's life. One of only two characters in this scene to appreciate the danger Michael poses to Annie, to Lindsey, to the neighborhood and to the unsuspecting community of Haddonfield, the big German shepherd is savagely silenced.

While true terror prowls outside, *The Thing* continues to entertain our characters inside, distracting them from the menace of Michael Myers, yet for *us* metaphorically embodying the same generic dread. Both monsters, mysterious psychopath and predatory extraterrestrial, are fictional reflections of innumerable terrors from the real world outside movie and television screens. Yet Carpenter manages to make *his* metaphor, Michael, seem more real, less abstract, by providing him with a horror movie analogy *within* the dramatic context of *Halloween*.

Laurie and Tommy sit on the couch in the Doyle living room, focused intently on the televised movie off screen. Laurie twists strands of her hair in her fingers, as she did during her recent conversation with Annie. Is she still nervous about her arranged date with Ben Tramer? Is *The Thing* a pleasantly "scary" distraction from that intimidating prospect?

Tommy, on the other hand, is not quite so distracted. He inquires about the jack-o-lantern they are going to make. "After the movie," Laurie curtly replies, never taking her eyes off the TV screen. Tommy tries again, asking about his comic books, which his babysitter was going to read with him. Laurie puts him off again. Clearly he wants her attention for some underlying reason that she is too preoccupied at the moment to perceive. So he comes directly to the point. "What about the boogeyman?" So *that* is what's bothering him. But Laurie again dismisses his claim for her attention. "There's no such thing." So Tommy reveals more disturbing details about his concern. "Ritchie said he was coming for me tonight." Playing rational adult to the boy's irrational fear, Laurie challenges him. "Do you believe everything Ritchie tells you?" Tommy admits not, but sounds unsure of himself. So Laurie compassionately turns her *full* attention to the boy, ignoring the movie on TV, and explains why he should not let fear get the best of him. Tommy's fear is now almost a pleasant distraction from her own fears about Ben Tramer.

Laurie's explanation of why the mythical boogeyman isn't real and therefore should not be feared is most reasonable. Halloween is a time when people play tricks on each other. "It's all make-believe. I think Ritchie was just trying to scare you." Exactly. Ritchie and Tommy's other two schoolmates had no clue about the return of Michael Myers and the danger he poses when they taunted Tommy in the schoolyard. Perhaps it was Ritchie himself who had the shocking, terrifying yet brief encounter with Michael immediately after scaring Tommy. Poetic justice, though fortunately limited to emotional rather than physical consequences. But Tommy insists he *saw* the boogeyman outside the window of his own home a short time ago. Which he did, though only by making a coincidental link between the silhouette of Michael Myers across the street and his pre-existing fear of the boogeyman allegedly targeting Tommy Doyle on this particular night. He is right and wrong at the same time.

Laurie pushes her reasoning a bit further. "What did he look like?" she inquires. If she pins down the source of Tommy's fear, maybe she can more easily explain it away. But with the typically circular logic of a child's mind, Tommy answers, "Like the boogeyman." In other words, whatever form terror takes for us in a given situation *is* the boogeyman. Or at least *our* boogeyman. Applying too narrow a definition to the concept diminishes its emotional impact. And perhaps for that same reason, John Carpenter keeps us guessing as to the real nature of Michael Myers. His physical appearance as an adult, his skewered view of the world, his peculiar motivations, and the extent of his powers. Because he becomes a monster while still a child, his origin is in all of us. But what he became during those missing fifteen years between the murder of his sister and his escape from a mental hospital is open to speculation.

Laurie tries a different approach. If she cannot get Tommy to clearly identify what frightens him, she will wrap him in a security blanket of adult protection. As his babysitter, she will shield him from any harm on this Halloween night, when the boogeyman is scheduled to "get" him. And she offers this reassurance with serene, even amused confidence, believing the boogeyman to be nothing more than a figment of Tommy's overactive imagination. But visible above the boy's head as she makes her promise is the shadowy, slightly out-of-focus shape of a panther, poised to pounce in her direction. It's just a harmless figurine on a stand in the background. But in the dramatic context of Laurie's overconfident promise, it metaphorically conveys the very real and potent danger posed by the mysterious stranger lurking just across the street. The same stranger Laurie noticed and briefly feared three times earlier today. The same fear her rational, adult mind has since repressed. The same menace Tommy Doyle rightly, if for the wrong reasons, identifies as the mythical boogeyman.

Laurie's promise of protection works, for the time being. Tommy is ready to resume the harmless Halloween tradition of carving a pumpkin into a jack-o-lantern. But returning across the street, *we* are not comforted by the sight of Annie Brackett walking through the darkened back yard of the Wallace house to a shed containing the washing machine in which she intends to clean her soiled clothes. Annie is dressed only in panties, knee socks and an oversized white shirt borrowed from the Wallace's. She appears very childlike and vulnerable in this outfit, the brightness of her shirt contrasting with the darkness surrounding her.

The camera observes Annie from a part of the yard adjacent to a corner of the Wallace house. Is this Michael's vantage point as well? He is not visible, nor does he step into this shot at any point. But we often suspect his presence nearby, even when he's not seen. As Annie nears the shed, the camera rises up slightly to include a tree branch at the top of the frame. The branch, again because we think Michael is near, seems to hang oppressively over the teenager's receding form. That and the return of music to the soundtrack reminds us of the grim fate that possibly awaits Annie at the end of the path.

From inside the shed, lit only by moonlight, we observe Annie pound on the sticking door several times before gaining admittance. Once inside she flips the light switch on. But it doesn't work. She will have to perform her task in relative darkness. Advantage Michael. Retrieving laundry detergent from the back of the shed, she is surprised when the front door shuts, apparently of its own accord, then rebounds open again. From a camera angle not aligned with Annie's point of view, we see the shape of Michael Myers standing just outside the door. Veiled by a curtain over the window, yet well-illuminated by moonlight, he appears both human and vaguely inhuman. Odd. With unkempt hair and no eyes visible within his mask's carved out eye sockets. As creepily ill-defined as Tommy's mythical boogeyman.

Annie calls out a wary "Hello. Who's there?" to whoever fiddled with the door. But she soothes her own fear with comfortably familiar expectations. "Paul, is this one of your cheap tricks?" she demands to know. Paul is her prankster boyfriend, presumably grounded for getting caught at it. The prospect of being the victim of one of her boyfriend's Halloween pranks is not displeasing to Annie. She boldly strides to the doorway and sticks her head out to confirm her suspicions. A first-time viewer of *Halloween*, conditioned by previous horror film experiences, might expect Annie's head to be lopped off at such a moment as this. Instead, nothing happens. Annie pulls

## 3. Carpenter's *Halloween*  181

her head back inside, carelessly leaving the door ajar. From our vantage point behind her, we can see more of the world outside that door than can she. If Michael made another appearance, we would see him before she could. But no one appears.

Bored with her babysitting duties, Annie sounds disappointed at not being the victim of her boyfriend's prank. The same, relatively harmless prank (soaping windows and such) that got him into minor trouble earlier. "No tricks for Annie tonight," she complains to herself, with characteristic double meaning. Annie resumes her chore, stuffing her soiled clothes into the washing machine and adding detergent. Coincidently, the brand of soap she uses is "Tide," which is also the name of an irresistible force of Nature. Analogous to the manmade train that barreled its way towards Haddonfield in an earlier scene. Both could serve as metaphors for the relentless Michael Myers.

Another odd disturbance. The shed's door slams shut, this time remaining closed. Puzzled, Annie tries to open it. But it's stuck. She calls out for Lindsey to come and help her. The camera cuts back to its original position in this scene, near the house. Annie's call for help is barely audible, reminding us how truly isolated she is at this moment of vulnerability. Besides, Lindsey didn't respond to any of her pleas for help from *inside* the house. Why would she pay attention now?

In the Wallace living room Lindsey still watches *The Thing*. She appears simultaneously nervous and engrossed. That fine balance of fear and fun that most of us regard as pleasurable. From this location neither she nor we can hear Annie yelling for help from the shed in the backyard.

As the camera swings from a position near Lindsey's point of view to a more objective position in front of her, we see some shadowy movement behind the couch, out of the girl's line of sight. Is Michael *inside* the house, hiding behind Lindsey? Or was the ominous movement we just saw an uncorrected cinematic mistake. Perhaps a member of the film crew making an unscheduled, accidentally suspicious appearance. Either way, it's creepy.

The telephone rings. Lindsey ignores it, as she did Annie's calls for assistance from the kitchen earlier. Cut back to the yard. From just outside the shed, we watch through the window in the door as Annie pleads for Lindsey to pick up the ringing phone she assumes is Paul trying to call her. What could be worse for a teenage girl than missing a phone call from her boyfriend? Well, for one thing, being closely observed by a homicidal maniac, visible to us though not to Annie through a window behind her, at the *back* of the shed. His head slowly sways from side to side in a peculiar, unsettling manner. What fascinates *him* about *her*?

Annie turns around to face the back of the shed. Obviously Michael is gone, because she doesn't react, And because our vantage point has changed too, we no longer see through the back window. Annie pulls some junk out of the way in hopes of clearing a path of escape through that window. Sticking her head and upper body through the opening, she again appears extremely, unwittingly vulnerable to attack (Michael was in that very spot only moments ago) as she was a short time earlier at the front door. Michael passes up so many opportunities to close in for the kill, rendering his motivations both obscure and unsettling.

Cut back to Lindsey, who finally answers the phone. It is Paul, as Annie anticipated. He asks Lindsey to fetch his girlfriend. Annoyed at the disruption of her horror movie fest, she consents, but unwittingly hangs up the phone as she leaves the room. A typical childish oversight. She goes to the backyard and yells at Annie that Paul called. The only reply is a loud "Owe!" Did Michael finally get her? No, it's an "owe" of slightly pained exasperation, not terror. Lindsey runs to the shed and with some effort opens the door from outside. She helps Annie get unstuck from the back window, where she was ridiculously exposed to attack but once again escaped unharmed and clueless about how close she came to death.

Before leaving the shed, Annie makes Lindsey promise not to tell Paul about her embarrassing incident. As they return through the backyard the phone rings again. They both run towards the house. Lindsey gets to the phone first and immediately blabs to Paul about Annie getting stuck in the window. Her little Halloween prank on her somewhat negligent babysitter? Unlike Laurie with Tommy, Annie has demonstrated no inclination to entertain or comfort Lindsey. On the other hand, Lindsey has thus far demonstrated no great need to be entertained or comforted. We cannot assume that Annie would be so negligent if Lindsey were sick or frightened.

Annie takes the phone while Lindsey returns to the living room and her delightfully scary *Thing from Another World*. But as Annie paces back and forth across the kitchen while verbally sparring with her boyfriend, the Thing from Haddonfield stands just outside the kitchen door that both Annie and Lindsey, in their haste to answer the phone, carelessly left open. The camera moves subjectively with Annie as she paces, yet allows us to see behind and beyond her, because of its position in front of her. Thus we can see Michael in the doorway behind Annie, but only when she passes in front of him. On either side of Michael, we are just as blind as she is. A classic Alfred Hitchcock device, allowing the audience to see more of the danger than can his characters. Each time Michael disappears from the camera frame, we wonder if he is stealthily entering the house, approaching Annie from behind. And when Annie turns and walks towards the doorway where Michael *was* standing, he is no longer there. Where has he gone? Is he inside the house now? In the living room with Lindsey? Poor Annie never knew he was so close.

As with Laurie, Annie's relationship with Paul is comfortably antagonistic. They argue, then seconds later agree. Complaining that her boyfriend thinks only about sex, Annie in the next breath all but invites him to do the deed with her. These two teenagers are relaxed enough with each other to bicker and collaborate in equal measure. Entering the darkened living room, Annie approaches Lindsey with a proposition. And like all of Annie's interactions with the child she was hired to entertain and protect, it's selfishly motivated. She wants Lindsey to leave the TV and go with her to pick up Paul. No deal. So Annie sweetens the offer by arranging for Lindsey to watch the next scary movie with Tommy Doyle across the street. Annie can then retrieve Paul herself, and enjoy some alone time with him by getting rid of the annoying child.

While Annie and Lindsey negotiate their bargain, the TV announcer promotes the next movie presentation in an exaggerated, mock-scary voice. "Lock your doors! Bolt your windows! And turn off the lights! Don't go away, cause here's a scene from..." and so forth. The upcoming movie is *Forbidden Planet*. Eerie music from that film's electronic score adds to the spooky effect. Lindsey is young enough to be affected by it. "I'm scared," she confesses. Annie, too grown-up to be frightened by TV and shadowy living rooms, is not. "Then why do you sit here with the lights off?" "I don't know," admits the child. Yet there she sits anyway. Unfortunately for Annie, the TV announcer's fake warning unwittingly describes her very real peril. The danger is both pretend and real, entertaining and terrifying, amusing and not so amusing.

Outside, crossing the street in her skimpy makeshift outfit with Lindsey, Annie passes by a group of fun-loving trick-or-treaters. The ever-smiling pumpkin stands guard over them all from the Wallace's front porch, as unsuccessfully as it did over Judith Myers fifteen years ago.

As Annie and Lindsey pass the back of a familiar-looking station wagon on their way to the Doyle residence (Annie saw the same vehicle several hours earlier, but it didn't make a sufficient impression on her to ring an alarm bell in her mind now), Michael's dark shape rises up behind them, unnoticed by his next victim. From close to his point of view, we observe a half-clad Annie Bracket and little Lindsey Wallace, looking defenseless, ring the doorbell. It's as if the mere possibility of a Michael Myers didn't exist for them.

As she had hoped, once inside the Doyle house Annie quickly loses Lindsey to Tommy. The two children plop down on the couch to watch the movie. As Annie walks through an area of shadow on her way to the kitchen, we hear the TV announcer in the background say, again in his arch-spooky fashion, "And now, the horrifying conclusion to *The Thing*." He could just as well be announcing the horrifying conclusion to the short life of Annie Brackett, whose personal boogeyman waits for her somewhere outside, in the dark.

In the kitchen, Laurie looks predictably maternal in an apron as she scoops the guts out of the pumpkin she brought for Tommy. She finally gets a verbal shot in at her more popular, socially sophisticated friend. "Oh, fancy," she remarks snidely about Annie's expedient wardrobe. But Annie quickly regains the advantage by refusing Laurie's request that she phone Ben Tramer and cancel the date Annie had arranged between them. And by sticking Laurie with Lindsey while she goes to pick up her boyfriend, who has found a way to sneak out of his parent's house after being grounded. Laurie balks at the added responsibility, so Annie simply blackmails her into submission. If Laurie agrees to babysit Lindsey, Annie *might* agree to phone Ben and cancel the dreaded date. Laurie reluctantly accepts the offer. After Annie departs, Laurie glances at the kids on the couch and makes fun of herself. "The old girl scout comes through again." Like Annie, she doesn't mean it as a compliment.

A case can be made that what happens to Annie next, and to Lynda soon after that, is subconsciously linked to Laurie's deep resentment of their social ease, general irresponsibility and comparatively freewheeling sexuality. On a very abstract level, there *is* a psychological connection between Laurie and Michael. But in the parlance of *Forbidden Planet*, is the mass killer of *Halloween* Laurie's "Id monster"? Carpenter denies us a clear picture of Michael's motivations for killing his sister. It might have something to do with sexual jealousy. Then again, it might involve something entirely different. We just don't know. What we *do* know is that regardless of his motivation, Michael totally lacks the psychological machinery to restrain his violent impulses. His actions seem to lack all self-awareness. Laurie Strode, by contrast, is *acutely* self-aware. Sometimes too much for her own good. If Michael is self-indulgence personified, Laurie inclines more towards self-repression, with the saving grace that she can sometimes laugh at her own excesses. And she is certainly not *pathologically* repressed.

Alone now, Annie literally whistles in the dark while striding unafraid to the Wallace's garage to fetch her car. She sings rhapsodically about a guy named Paul, the boyfriend who occupies her thoughts as completely at this moment as *The Thing* occupies the attention of Lindsey and Tommy back in the Doyle living room. Two visually prominent objects in the otherwise dark garage draw our attention. A pair of upright rakes. Possibly Carpenter's sly reference to the rakes in Sam Loomis's hardware store in *Psycho*. In one particularly memorable shot from that 1960 classic, the rakes ominously bracket the head of Lila Crane, who very nearly becomes the next victim of Norman Bates.

The driver's side door of Annie's car is locked. Mildly annoyed, but still blithely whistling in the gloom, Annie walks through the backyard and around to the front of the house, entering through the front door. Carpenter exposes us to so many opportunities for Michael to "get" her. But delays the seemingly inevitable. We watch her enter the Wallace house from across the street, closer to the Doyle residence, and thus from Michael's last known vantage point.

But he is no longer there. Nor did we see him in the garage, in the backyard or along the side of the Wallace house while Annie nonchalantly strolled through those locations. Knowing that he is *somewhere* nearby makes his invisibility now even more ominous than were his frequent, if discrete, appearances earlier.

Inside the house, Annie retrieves the car keys from her purse (how was she going to start the car without them?), then pauses to look at herself in the mirror while combing her hair. Flashback to Judith Myers, combing *her* hair in front of a mirror when *she* was killed. Still singing about Paul, Annie ignores nearly everything around her. Michael could have attacked her with impunity at any time after she left the Doyle house. But not yet.

So distracted is Annie by her anticipated rendezvous with Paul when she returns to the garage that she forgets to unlock the car door before trying to open it. She doesn't comprehend the grim implications of its being *unlocked* this time. How could anyone have entered the car if it was locked minutes earlier? Possibly Laurie left the *passenger* door unlocked when Annie dropped her off in front of the Doyle's. Or maybe someone already inside the car locked the driver's door before Annie tried to open it the first time. And maybe that someone unlocked the door before her second attempt. Michael plays so many odd games with his victims.

Annie gets into the car and is about to start the engine when, finally, something *other* than Paul grabs her attention. The front windshield is fogged on the inside, as if from respiration *within* the vehicle. She pauses, puzzled, then reaches up to touch the mystery. Abruptly the source of that mystery bolts upright in the back seat and reaches forward to grab Annie by the throat. We watch the painfully prolonged struggle from two distinct camera angles: one from the passenger seat inside the car and the other from just outside the driver's side window. Annie's desperate final gasps now fog that window, while vaguely visible behind her is the semi-human, chillingly impassive, masked face of Michael Myers as he strangles her. A quick slash of his knife across Annie's throat, and it's over.

Whatever her shortcomings as a friend to Laurie and a babysitter to Lindsey, poor Annie Brackett in no way deserves *this* gruesome fate. Nor does Carpenter stage it in a way to suggest she does. In the documentary *Halloween: A Cut Above the Rest*, which accompanied a 2003 release of the film on DVD, the director specifically denies any religious fundamentalist agenda involving punishment of sexually active victims. "To me these kids are just engaged in normal teenage behavior. They get killed cause they're not paying attention." He also says, more provocatively, "The movie's about the revenge of the repressed. Jamie Lee has a connection with the killer because she's repressed too." More on that later. Jeffrey Wells, in *Films in Review*, claimed "each murder is precipitated by either the intention or deed of illicit sex... It's as if the victims are being axed for their eager libidos" (Wells, p. 183). But he makes no distinction between Carpenter's moral intention and the motivation of the movie's killer.

The violence of Michael Myers is a massively violent intrusion of the extraordinary and bizarre into the otherwise ordinary, day-to-day lives and drama of Haddonfield's residents. With an expression of total shock in her dying eyes, Annie sags down in the driver's seat of her mother's car. Some portion of her body presses against the car horn, which screams out loudly for the girl who can no longer scream for herself. Cut to an exterior shot in front of the Doyle house. Annie's surrogate plea for help and cry of alarm goes unheard by Laurie and the rest of Haddonfield.

Inside the Doyle living room, Lindsey and Tommy watch *Forbidden Planet* on TV. For a moment we watch it with them, sharing their interest. It's an excellent movie. Then Tommy stealthily sneaks away from the couch, hides behind a nearby window curtain and calls out in *his* spookiest voice, "Lindsey! Lindsey!" The electronic score of *Forbidden Planet* coincidently serves his effort to scare the girl from across the street. The boy who was earlier taunted into fearing the boogeyman by several schoolmates now enjoys *playing* that boogeyman to someone *he* sees as vulnerable to fear. It may be all in good fun. But if he had succeeded, would Lindsey have thought so? Or would she have been as frightened and upset as he was when forced to play the victim?

We never find out. In the midst of *pretending* to be Lindsey's boogeyman, Tommy glances out the living room window and sees the return of *his* boogeyman, Michael, carrying Annie's limp body into the Wallace house through the front door. The moody *Forbidden Planet* music, moments earlier Tommy's ally in his attempt to frighten Lindsey, now turns against him, magnifying *his* fear of the mysterious stranger across the street.

Instinctively retreating from the threat he sees, as Laurie did from her bedroom window when she saw Michael watching her from the neighbor's backyard, Tommy backs into Lindsey, who stands on the other side of the curtain, looking for him. Both children scream in genuine terror. But Lindsey's fear subsides quickly when she sees it's only Tommy. *His* fear does not. He yells hysterically, almost incoherently, about seeing the boogeyman again, outside the window. Laurie rushes in from the kitchen to see what's wrong.

Holding Lindsey protectively close to her, Laurie dismisses Tommy's boogeyman sighting for the second time. "There's nobody out there." A quick shot of the Wallace house across the street confirms her assertion. But *we* know there *was* someone out there. No longer amused by or tolerant of Tommy's outbursts, and concerned for Lindsey's emotional well-being, Laurie threatens to turn off the television and send Tommy to bed if he doesn't stop, in effect, crying wolf. Again, Laurie plays the rational adult quelling what she assumes to be irrational childish fears. She takes her job as babysitter very seriously. Long banished are her own fears (irrational, according to her now deceased friend, Annie Brackett) of the stalker she glimpsed several times earlier.

Tommy grudgingly gives up his cry of alarm and returns to the couch, complaining, "Nobody believes me." His insight about the boogeyman is, of course, merely coincidental. The product of being taunted at school. Nevertheless, we know his warning has real merit. And Laurie, though admittedly lacking Dr. Loomis's fifteen years of personal acquaintance with Michael Myers, makes a mistake by not connecting Tommy's current fears with her own brief but unsettling encounters.

Rejoining Tommy on the couch, Lindsey soothes his hurt feelings. "*I believe you, Tommy.*" Tormenter and taunted forge an unexpected alliance. Laurie shrugs helplessly and smiles to herself as the logic of children defeats her, as it often does many adults. Perhaps Lindsey's budding attraction to the boy next door (she quickly accepted Annie's offer to dump her at the Doyle house) trumps her appreciation of Laurie's attempt to defend her against Tommy's scare tactics.

Outside the Myers house, Sam Loomis waits for Michael behind a large bush in the front yard. The infamous Lonnie Lamb and Tommy's two other tormentors from school approach the house. But this time *Lonnie* is the victim as his former allies dare him to enter the legendary spook house. He nervously advances to the front porch, then hesitates. Yells of "Chicken!" spur him on. But before Lonnie can enter Haddonfield's infamous den of terror, a gruff voice calls out to him from somewhere unseen. "Hey, Lonnie! Get your ass away from there!" It's Sam. All three boys flee in terror. The myth has come alive! Expectations and deception join forces to produce fear.

A tight shot of Sam Loomis grinning to himself betrays his pleasure. Even though he acted to protect the boys from what he regards as a genuine threat, the psychiatrist obviously enjoys *playing* boogeyman to a group of impressionable kids. No less, despite his nobler intentions, than Lonnie and Ritchie did to Tommy. One can assume that Carpenter, his cast and crew likewise enjoyed subjecting *their* audiences to the terrors of *Halloween*. But oh how illusory that mischievous thrill, rooted in the security of proper containment, can be. Just as one of Tommy's tormentors ran straight into the arms of the boogeyman only seconds after threatening Tommy with the same menace, Dr. Loomis's wicked grin disappears abruptly when a strange hand touches him on the shoulder. And thanks to a carefully chosen camera angle, we share in Sam's return to the victim role in that tricky, ever-shifting and decidedly fickle equation of fear.

Loomis quickly recovers composure when he sees the hand belongs to Sheriff Brackett, instead of Michael Myers returning home at an inopportune (for the psychiatrist) moment. Brackett announces he and his men have found no trace of Michael in Haddonfield. His original skepticism about Sam's warning returns. So Loomis tries to reinforce the Sheriff's waning fears, playing essentially the same game, but on a more sophisticated level, he played moments earlier with the foolishly curious kids.

Adding to what he previously revealed about Michael during their conversation inside the Myers house, Sam now describes the killer's inhuman patience, "waiting for some secret, silent alarm to trigger him off." He sums up, melodramatically, "Death has come to your little town, Sheriff. You can either ignore it, or you can help me to stop it." Some commentators describe Sam Loomis as the film's *camp* ingredient. Maybe. But having confronted so much doubt and complacency from mental health and law enforcement officials in the past, Loomis feels he must increase the voltage of his warning now. Sheriff Brackett's own reluctance to take that warning seriously the first time he heard it is compelling evidence of what Sam is and always has been up against. Their mini-debate now is shot from a low angle, against the looming backdrop of the shadowy Myers house, visually reinforcing the psychiatrist's argument. At least for *us*.

Sheriff Brackett reluctantly agrees to continue the police patrol for the remainder of the night. But as he departs he tries to regain tactical advantage over Loomis by telling him, "And if you *are* right, damn you for letting him go." It's an unfair criticism. No one did more to keep Michael Myers locked up than Sam Loomis. It was the complacency of other officials like *Brackett* that made his crusade so difficult. Besides, like the darker regions of human nature itself, Michael Myers cannot be completely contained at all times. What would Sheriff Brackett think or say if he knew that his daughter has already become the first Haddonfield victim of Michael's return? Would he blame Sam Loomis for his loss and pain? And if he had taken Sam's warning more seriously in the first place, would he have acted to ensure Annie's safety on this Halloween night?

If Annie was unaware of the danger hovering near her until it finally, fatally struck, Lynda and her boyfriend, Bob, are *totally* clueless as they park their 70s decorated van outside the home where Annie died. Beer and sex are pretty much all they have in mind. They suspect nothing of what happened to Annie and is about to happen to them. Not even when they discover the lights out and no one at home inside the Wallace house. They switch on lights in the living room and just as effortlessly rationalize away the mystery of Annie's and Lindsey's absence. Then they get down to the more pressing business of making out on the Wallace's couch.

Propped up on a chair behind the couch is a doll-like figure, probably belonging to Lindsey, which the horny teenagers ignore. An inanimate object, the doll abstractly hints at the notion of them being observed. The camera, which until this point in the scene had kept us completely involved in *their* movements and concerns, now slowly backs away from Lynda and Bob. Tense music returns to the soundtrack, signaling to us but certainly not to them the presence of someone else in the house. Sure enough, as we and the camera withdraw, giving us a broader view of the two preoccupied teenagers and their surroundings, Michael's right shoulder appears on the left side of the camera frame. With creepy calmness, not unlike the doll's, he watches Lynda and Bob, who have no idea Death stands so close to them.

At the Doyle residence Laurie passes *her* time supervising and entertaining Tommy and Lindsey. Emerging from the well-lit kitchen into the dark dining room, Laurie, still looking very parental in her apron, carries a jack-o-lantern. The children flank her. Carved into the pumpkin are the usual mouth, nose and eyes, lit from within by a candle. Nothing too grotesque or menacing, this pumpkin represents Halloween at its mildest. In keeping with that image, babysitter and kids make *fun* spooky sounds as they escort the holiday icon into the dining room with measured, ritualistic steps.

Tommy gleefully threatens Lindsey, "He's gonna get you!," in the same way he was threatened by his schoolmates. It's fun to play the boogeyman after you've been his victim. He's just passing on the fear to someone else. Lindsey defends herself, "No, he's not!" But she sounds uncertain. Laurie, the protective adult, intercedes to dial down the fear factor. "Nobody's scaring anybody. Stop scaring each other." Having already dealt with Tommy's meltdown about the boogeyman a short time ago, she is not about to let his or Lindsey's fear get out of hand again.

After placing the pumpkin on the dining table, Laurie glances out the same window through which Tommy first claimed to have seen the boogeyman. Laurie sees the Wallace house across the street, with no lights on inside. Assuming that Annie and Paul are making out in the dark house, she concludes, "Everybody's having a good time tonight." She speaks this line softly, to herself, with a smirk. Laurie's yearning for a boyfriend of her own was evident to us way back when she walked away from the Myers house singing to herself, "I wish I had you all alone. Just the two of us." Suppressing her jealousy of Annie, she turns back to the children and tries to bury her frustration by involving herself in whatever they want to do next. Lindsey suggests they make more popcorn. Responsible adult Laurie decides it's too late for the children to consume more snack food, and suggests watching the rest of the movie instead. It's not an unreasonable substitution. But coming as it does immediately after her thinly veiled expression of frustration over what she suspects Annie and Paul are doing, and what she herself *wants* to be doing, shooting down Lindsey's popcorn idea might also be Laurie's way of indirectly asserting her power over a situation in which she feels powerless. The same way Tommy compensated for being terrorized by Lonnie and Ritchie by in turn terrorizing Lindsey. Or maybe even the same way Sam Loomis enjoyed terrorizing Lonnie Lamb and two other boys (for their own good, of course) while facing a terror (Michael) over which he has often felt powerless. Of course, none of these examples of emotional compensation, or passing along the fear and frustration, are remotely comparable to Michael's violent outbursts. Nevertheless, they may all, including Michael's, proceed from the same psychological equation.

Laurie and the children return to the living room couch and the movie on TV. Laurie sits between Tommy and Lindsey, with her arms protectively around both. Whatever fears the movie provokes in the children, she will be there to comfort them. And the kids, no doubt, provide Laurie with some comfort as well. Then the phone rings, interrupting this cozy little arrangement. It's Lynda from across the street, calling to ask about Annie. Lying on the Wallace's living room couch, she fondles Bob's hair as he reclines between her legs. They are fully clothed. No sex yet. But the prospect is there.

Laurie speculates that Annie and Paul got sidetracked somewhere, but wants Annie to phone her as soon as she returns, to let her know when to put Lindsey to bed. Ever the "girl scout," or in this case the diligent babysitter, she puts the children's welfare first. Concluding their brief conversation, Laurie tells Lynda to have a good time. "We definitely will," Lynda replies, her voice full of unsubtle innuendo. Laurie understands her friend's meaning, and looks sad as she hangs up the phone. Lynda, by contrast, is not conflicted at all. Expressing no particular concern about the missing Annie, she celebrates with her boyfriend the fact that Lindsey is out of the house for the remainder of the night. The two carefree teenagers desert the couch, switch off the living room lights and head upstairs for some uninterrupted fun. Ominously, in the manner of Judith Myers and her boyfriend fifteen years ago. Lynda is not necessarily *callous* about Annie's welfare. She simply has no reason to suspect foul play. And she is too consumed with Bob to think further about it.

From Laurie's vantage point, again looking out the window at the house across the street, we see the Wallace's living room lights go out (minor technical glitch, because those same lights were not on when they should have been, just prior to Lynda's call, the previous time Laurie glanced out the window). She knows what's going on in that house. Not exactly thrilled at her own Halloween night activities, she returns to her *own* couch, to Tommy and Lindsey and the monster movie on TV.

Discarded beer cans and clothing litter the floor of Mr. and Mrs. Wallace's bedroom as Lynda and Bob writhe in sexual bliss under the bedcovers. What would the homeowners think of the way their place is being used in their absence? If anything, the possibility of getting caught adds a mild scare and therefore a bigger thrill to the sex. And for atmosphere, they've lit the candle inside the grinning jack-o-lantern sitting on the nightstand. It's almost like being watched, which for the moment adds to their pleasure.

The phone rings. Yet another untimely interruption, like Lynda's phone call to Laurie. Bob and Lynda argue briefly about whether or not to answer it. Aside from sex and beer, they don't seem the most compatible couple in the world. The ringing stops. Back to sex, which they both thoroughly enjoy. But as the camera slowly swings around the side of the bed to give us a closer look, distracting *us* almost as much as the couple distract each other, a shadow briefly crosses the candle-lit wall in the background. We assume it's Michael, because we saw him inside the house earlier.

Mutual orgasm. Bob immediately pulls out of Lynda and rolls over on his back next to her. "Fantastic!" she raves. "Totally!" His response is a somewhat disinterested "Yeah." Whether it's 1963 and Judith Myers with her boyfriend or 1978 and Lynda with hers, the story is pretty much the same as far as teen sex goes. At least Bob sticks around afterwards. Judith's boyfriend fled the Myers house like a shot. Putting his glasses back on, Bob accepts a post-coital cigarette from Lynda, but with minimal conversation or enthusiasm. He even expects *her* to fetch him another beer from downstairs. Instead, she orders *him* to get one for her. Anticipating their next round of sex, he agrees, leaving her with instructions not to get dressed in the meantime.

Lynda and Bob, presumably like Annie and Paul, are fairly typical American teenagers. Sometimes thoughtless, irresponsible, self-absorbed and cruel, but not excessively so. They are occasionally so completely caught up in their narrow world of romance, sex, booze, cigarettes and popularity that they "totally" lack awareness of what's going on in the larger world around them. And the danger that world potentially poses to them. But they *do not* deserve the fate that strikes them down, no matter how easy it is for an audience watching *Halloween* to glibly make fun of how clueless they are about the danger of Michael Myers. Such an audience reaction is more a measure of its *own* inability to conjure up a sense of violence and its consequences. Laurie Strode, because she is both very intelligent and a bit of a social misfit, is more aware of the wider world than are her friends. Though her prematurely adult perspective as a babysitter sometimes counteracts that awareness.

The camera lingers on Lynda for a few moments after Bob leaves the bed. She snuggles under the covers and luxuriates in her current situation, totally satisfied with her boyfriend, sex, the anticipated beer, the cigarette she smokes and the comfortable bed she illicitly occupies. Far from celebrating her doom, I think Carpenter and Debra Hill want us to feel sorry for Lynda in her naïve illusion of contentment, security and control.

Meanwhile, down in the dark kitchen, an equally confident Bob raids the Wallace's refrigerator for more beer. Squatters rights, until the Wallace's return. Then one of the French doors leading outside mysteriously opens.

Bob walks over to it and calls out, "Annie?" "Paul?" No reply. Closing the door, he turns next to a closet and opens it, grinning to himself and declaring loudly, "Lynda, you asshole!" He assumes he is the victim of a conventional Halloween prank, as did Annie when she called out Paul's name after the door to the shed opened just as mysteriously. And like Annie, Bob views such pranks as a source of pleasurable fear: fear so circumscribed that it generates fun for the victim as well as the perpetrator.

Again, no one is there. Bob hears breathing from behind yet another door, on the opposite side of the kitchen. In effect signaling "Game over," he opens the door while telling the prankster waiting behind it, "Okay, come on out." Expecting one of his friends to jump out and try to scare him, he considers himself above such fears.

But the prankster is neither Lynda, Annie nor Paul. It's a complete and very non-traditional surprise. Michael charges into the kitchen, grabs Bob around the throat and pins his back against the closet door opposite. The visual shock of Michael's attack is amplified by a fierce, low register outburst of music. Nothing passive about it. Gasping for air, Bob struggles with *both* hands against the *one* outstretched arm of his assailant. But in vain. Another, deeper stab of music accompanies a low angle shot of Michael's head and left shoulder, the one that so easily overpowers his victim. His face, like his entire personality, is obscured in shadow. A reverse shot shows Bob being bodily lifted off the floor by the single hand around his throat. Lower down, his feet dangle helplessly in mid-air. Another shot of Michael ramps up the menace. His right hand is upraised, holding a large knife. Perhaps a knife obtained from this very kitchen, as was the case at the Myers house in 1963. A knife that had been previously employed only for harmless, beneficial tasks.

Blue light streaming in through windows illuminate both the knife and the outline of Michael's face. It's as vivid an image of brutality, in its way, as the silhouette of Norman Bates posing as his own mother after he jerks open the shower curtain to attack Marion Crane in *Psycho*.

Michael impales Bob to the closet door with a single, powerful stab through the torso. Life instantly fades from Bob's face. His once churning, protesting bare feet sag. A more distant shot of the two characters in profile reveals a gruesome contrast. Bob's illuminated body hangs lifeless from the closet door. Michael, in black silhouette, stares up at his latest victim, tilting his head from side to side in an almost dog-like expression of curiosity. What is it about Bob's corpse that fascinates him? We will never know, because we don't see the world through his mind, even when Carpenter's camera lets us see it through his eyes.

Upstairs, Lynda passes the time filing her fingernails. Good grooming is so important to a popular teenager. Then, from her point of view lying in bed, we observe the bedroom door open, with a slight creaky sound appro-

3. Carpenter's *Halloween*

Michael Myers (Nick Castle) disguises himself as a ghost and pretends to be (note the eyeglasses) the playfully spooky boyfriend of his next victim, in *Halloween*. Does he possess a bizarre sense of humor? Or is this his grotesquely failed attempt to stage a normal Halloween prank?

priate to a traditional Halloween haunted house. In the doorway stands someone covered in a sheet, with holes cut out for the eyes, and wearing a pair of glasses. Bob's glasses. Lynda, amused but not impressed (curiously, the same smug attitude with which Bob greeted the "prank" downstairs in the kitchen), assumes Bob is trying to scare her the way he assumed she was trying to scare *him*. She sits up and bares her breasts. "See anything you like?" she asks, accepting Bob's ghost costume as the start of foreplay in their second round of sex.

But the ghost doesn't react as anticipated. It doesn't react *at all*. Even his audible breathing remains calm. It's Michael under that sheet. And whatever motivates his actions, it's not the lure of sex. But why did he don the sheet and glasses to play Bob's ghost? Does Michael possess a perverse sense of humor? Or is it some dimly remembered echo from the distance past, when little Michael Myers dressed up in costumes to go trick-or-treating? Is it his pathetic, half-hearted stab at re-creating a *normal* childhood memory? If so, his inability to *be* normal now is particularly frightening. Or is the ghost outfit simply a bizarre whim, the origins of which we cannot begin to fathom?

Lynda attempts a lame joke to break Bob's silence. When this fails, she gets angry with him. She slips her blouse back on and gets out of bed to phone Laurie and ask if she's heard from Annie and Paul. Deprived of sex and beer ("This is going nowhere," she complains), Lynda finally expresses some concern about her missing friends. Unfortunately, she turns her back on the prankster ghost in order to pick up the telephone. To the revival of his aggressive stalker music, Michael enters the room and advances on his next, unsuspecting victim. Like some predatory animal that instinctively recognizes its advantage when approaching prey from behind.

At the Doyle house Lynda's call catches Laurie on the couch, minus the apron but now occupying her time with the equally maternal knitting. Tommy and Lindsey are gone, presumably sent to bed by their responsible caretaker, and the television is off. "Finally," she says to herself as she gets up to answer the phone. She assumes it's Annie on the other end of the line.

Jumping back and forth between the two houses, we see Michael attacking Lynda, strangling her with her own phone cord (the very symbol of her narrow preoccupations), just as Laurie picks up *her* phone. As Lynda fights for her life, her blouse flies open, exposing her breasts again. They are of no interest to the young man killing her. The guttural sounds of Lynda's death struggle are misinterpreted by Laurie. She assumes it's Annie playing another Halloween phone prank, trying to frighten her, as she mistakenly thought back in her bedroom earlier that afternoon. But unlike the bedroom incident, this one yields no explanation. So Laurie becomes genuinely concerned for her mischievous friend, though she expresses that concern in a peculiar and unwittingly ironic manner. "Annie, are you fooling around again? I'll kill you if this is a joke." The ultimate threat re-deployed as a mere expression of annoyance between friends. We all say it, or something like it, from time to time. But we hardly ever *mean* it. It's like the difference between a murder in a horror movie and a real one.

Picking up the phone at the other end of the line, and now free of the sheet he used, for whatever reason, to play ghost, is a character whose *actions* far outstrip his *words*. In fact, Michael never utters a word throughout the film. Illuminated by pale blue light from either the moon or a streetlamp, Michael's face is a mere rubber mask stripped of just enough features to make him appear a less than fully-formed human being. Psychologically, too, he is missing something. Like the alien pod substitutes in *Invasion of the Body Snatchers* (1956). He listens to Laurie's voice, but doesn't reply to her inquiries. Chance (or was Laurie his primary target all along?) has pointed out his next victim. J. P. Telotte sees Michael's mask as "neither grotesquely distorted nor natural, but more resembling the face of a dead man. It therefore not only functions to cloak his human features, but also effectively divorces him from the world of the living, his victims" (Telotte, p. 142). Michael's mask is a Dorian Grey façade, more revealing of the person behind it than is his actual face.

Sensing something not quite right at the other end of the phone line, Laurie hangs up and looks out the window at the Wallace house again. The lights downstairs go on, then off again. What the hell is happening over there? Laurie tries again to call Annie, but no one answers. She walks upstairs to the second floor, which is half in shadow and half lit. We watch her from behind and above the stairway's upper railing. Could Michael already be inside the Doyle house? As our fear ratchets up, anything seems possible.

Laurie quietly checks on Tommy and Lindsey, asleep in Tommy's room. "Sleep tight, kids." In a nicely composed shot of her face, blue-lit in the extreme foreground, and the kids in the background, Laurie glances in the direction of the Wallace house. Having assured herself that the kids are safely tucked in bed, she is now determined to check up on her mysteriously silent friends next door. The tone of Laurie's babysitter responsibilities turns more serious at this juncture, because we know what awaits her across the street if she acts on her admirable impulse. She is now the parental figure for both the kids and her friends.

Back at the Myers house, the camera prowls around the side of a bush to spy Sam Loomis still waiting, though impatiently now, for the return of Michael. He is frustrated and fidgety. Glancing down the street, he is surprised to see a familiar vehicle. He runs to get a closer look. It's Michael's stolen station wagon. Has Sam been so close to his quarry all night? Peering up and down the street, Loomis wonders where to begin his search. He picks a direction and charges off to battle his personal boogeyman. The resumption of a fragment of Michael's principle theme music (the mechanical rhythm of the upper register, minus the heavy, fateful downbeats) seems to fuel the psychiatrist's effort.

The same music, which I would equate with Bernard Herrmann's main title music for *Psycho*, forms a bridge to the next scene, where we rejoin Laurie Strode at the Doyle house. Lingering in the doorway of the children's bedroom, with her hands tucked passively in her pants pockets, she seems indecisive. Then, like Dr. Loomis, she acts decisively. The aggressive music almost becomes *hers* now. She returns downstairs with a sense of purpose in her stride. From out of her knitting bag she retrieves keys to the front door of the Doyle house. She walks outside, prudently locking the door behind her, for the safety of the children left behind.

Standing outside the Doyle's well-lit front door, Laurie hesitates as she looks at the partly illuminated but visually inert Wallace house across the street, separated from her by a pool of darkness. Bob's van, parked outside, appears equally lifeless. Passively unsettling background music echoes Laurie's first scene in the film. We are about to accompany her on another little walk through the neighborhood, but under very different circumstances. It's night, not day. That always makes a difference in mood. Previously Laurie strolled through the neighborhood, on her way to school, with no fear whatsoever. The uneasiness echoed by the music was *ours* alone. *This* time she too suspects something is wrong. But she cannot define it. Is she the victim of an elaborate Halloween prank perpetrated by her friends? Or is it something more serious? Even if she considers the latter, she has no clue how terribly wrong things really are across the street. But *we* do, as we make the journey with her towards Haddonfield's newest haunted. Michael could appear at any time, anywhere.

In the Hitchcock tradition, Carpenter's camera backtracks with Laurie as well as giving us subjective, forward tracking shots from her point of view. We share in her painfully slow but persistent approach to the Wallace house. Think of Lila Crane approaching the Bates house in *Psycho*, knowing less of the danger that awaits her than do we. For *Halloween*'s audience, the Wallace house by now possesses all of the mythic potency of the old Myers house. The distant barking of a dog (harkening all the way back to James Whale's *Frankenstein*) and a light breeze tousling Laurie's hair are dramatic tokens of an ordinary, peaceful, small town Halloween night. They counterpoint the portentous music and Laurie's slight but growing sense that something is out of whack in this neighborhood. It's *too* quiet, *too* peaceful here. Like the proverbial calm before the storm. Or is that distant, noisy dog a cousin of the dearly departed Lester, barking another unheeded warning about Michael's lurking menace?

Carpenter builds tension slowly but surely as Laurie, somewhere between casually and warily, strolls across the street. The candle-lit pumpkin sitting on the railing of the Wallace's front porch still stands guard over the neighborhood, but is by now a brutally ironic symbol of normalcy. The brooding presence of Michael Myers, whether seen or not, has subsumed that grinning token of Halloween fun. In addition, the pumpkin links the Wallace house circa 1978 to the Myers house circa 1963.

## 3. Carpenter's *Halloween*     197

The closer we and Laurie get to the Wallace house, the more intimidating its passive façade becomes. Curtains cover the front windows. There is no trace of life behind them. Laurie climbs onto the porch and rings the doorbell. If anyone hiding inside the house did not know of her approach, they do now. Getting no response, she calls out the names of Bob and Lynda. Still nothing. She leaves the porch, glances up at the second floor of the house and calls out for Lynda again. And again, nothing.

With her hands nervously tucked into her pockets, Laurie walks round to the side of the house, calling out in ever greater puzzlement to Bob and Annie. We and the camera linger closer to the street, with its bright illumination, as though fearful of following Laurie into the much darker regions at the back of the house. Her ever-smaller figure disappears into that darkness, past numerous windows, not all of them blinded, through which someone inside *could* be watching her.

Cut to inside the kitchen, from where we observe Laurie cautiously approach the open French door. Last time we saw it, that door was closed by Bob. Who opened it again? Is the open door bait in a mousetrap set for Laurie? The hanging plant that Michael once pulled to the ground to frighten Annie has been returned to its original position.

Pausing in the open doorway, whether out of respect for the Wallaces' private property (something Lynda and Bob did not share) or from caution, Laurie again calls out to Annie, Lynda and Bob, in descending order of their importance in her life. Once inside the dark kitchen, she closes the door behind her and moves to open the same door Bob once opened, to his dying regret. Will Michael make an encore appearance from behind it? It's like some horrifying variation on that 1970s game show hit, *Let's Make a Deal*. But before she finds out what's behind Door No.1, Laurie is distracted by a slight noise from deeper inside the house. She's being lured to her doom. Prominently lit within the mostly shadowy kitchen is a box of Quaker Oats cereal, with the ever-smiling Quaker on its front. A quaint reminder of the kitchen's normal, pleasurable function in the daily routine of life. A routine Laurie still presumes is in force, but increasingly suspects is not.

Growing annoyed at what she still thinks is a juvenile prank, Laurie calls out to Annie in the same tone of voice with which Bob once called out to Annie, Paul and Lynda. It's both believable and interesting how similarly these characters act in similar situations. They all have the same conventional expectations, rooted presumably in the same prior experiences. Laurie leaves the kitchen and enters the dining room. She quickly thrusts head around a corner and into the hallway, trying to surprise anyone hiding there who might be trying to surprise *her*. Luckily for Laurie, no one is there.

Laurie walks into the living room, but is again distracted by an indefinite noise coming from elsewhere in the house. "All right you meatheads, joke's over!" she admonishes the concealed source of that noise, using an insult from one of the 70s most popular TV sitcoms, *All in the Family*. And again, no reply. So she complains in a harsher voice, "It's most definitely stopped being funny, so cut it out!" There are limits to pranks and practical jokes, beyond which they cease to be amusing or entertaining. But apparently Laurie's friends don't recognize those limits, because again no one answers. Laurie warns, "You'll be sorry." But the lack of confidence in her voice suggests she lacks the power to enforce that threat.

Pursuing the mystery ever deeper into the house, Laurie slowly climbs the stairs to the second floor. Carpenter films her ascent the same way he filmed her approach to the Wallace house. And similar to Detective Arbogast's ascent to the second floor of the Bate's house in *Psycho*. At the top of the stairs Laurie peers down the dark hallway and sees a sliver of light coming from behind the door to one of the bedrooms. Again, similar to the sliver of light that came from Mrs. Bates' bedroom. Will Michael, like Norman in the guise of his mother, emerge from that sliver of light to slash her? No. Laurie approaches and enters the room. Carpenter delays Michael's attack, cultivating a parallel to Hitchcock's film and then contradicting our expectations.

We observe Laurie's entry into the Wallace bedroom from inside. She gets further than Arbogast did. But if Michael is nowhere to be seen, yet, the sight that greets her is almost as terrifying. The corpse of Annie Brackett lies stretched out, in ritualistic fashion, on the bed. Above her head is propped the stolen gravestone of Judith Myers. The bed itself has been carefully re-made since Lynda and Bob had sex there. Still grinning from the nightstand is the jack-o-lantern, now a grotesque mockery of Halloween normalcy.

If Michael Myers were removed from this equation, the carefully staged scene in the Wallace's bedroom *could* be just a holiday prank perpetrated on Laurie by her friends. And a very good one at that. Just as the parlor conversation between Norman Bates and Marion Crane in *Psycho* had, up to a point, an appearance of normal, friendly intimacy. But Michael *is* part of the equation. Just as Norman's obsessive attachment to the memory of his dead mother was part of the equation in the earlier movie.

Why did Michael go to the trouble of posing Annie in front of Judith's gravestone? A compulsion to revisit and re-enact his earlier crime? A deliberate attempt to terrify his next victim? Or a pathetic and sick attempt to stage a normal Halloween prank by someone who is no longer capable of normalcy?

Whimpering in shock and fear, Laurie instinctively backs away from the spectacle of her best friend's corpse, as she backed away from the sight of Michael the stalker through her bedroom window. But one shock follows on the heels of another, and another. Backing up to an open closet door, Laurie is greeted by the sight of Bob's corpse dangling upside down inside, swinging obscenely to and fro by legs mysteriously anchored to something concealed

### 3. Carpenter's *Halloween*     199

at the top of that closet. His movement grotesquely makes it seem as if he were *participating* in a collective effort to scare Laurie. But of course he's nothing more than Michael's pawn now.

Laurie flees to the protection of a different wall, only to encounter Lynda's body lying twisted inside yet another closet. Like Bob, she has been reduced to a prop in Michael's twisted production. Michael Myers himself has appropriated the role of John Carpenter as director, setting up another of the film's mirrored portraits of fear as staged entertainment and fear as sadistic reality. I can't help thinking of Jim Jones and his creepily staged and frighteningly real "White Nights," in which his Jonestown prisoner/victims experienced true terror in an isolated jungle setting. Coincidently, the Jonestown nightmare reached its hellish climax the same year *Halloween* was filmed and premiered. Ah, the good old days.

Retreating for the third time in quick succession, Laurie backs out of the bedroom and into the hallway, pressing herself against a wall next to an open doorway leading to another bedroom. As our eyes become accustomed to the darkness there, we slowly become aware of a faint outline in that doorway. Laurie, facing in a different direction, cannot see Michael's sub-human visage slowly materialize from the gloom. Unaware of the danger behind her, she moves cautiously towards the stairs, overcoming her momentary paralysis in order to get the hell out of this house of horror. Michael lunges at her with his knife, missing his intended mark but inflicting a wound on her upper arm, which sends her reeling back in panic, over the stairway railing. She plunges to the floor below, injuring her leg.

Pulsating stalker music propels the chase that follows as the relentless monster pursues a faster but hobbled heroine through and out of the haunted house. Laurie discovers the front door locked. Another pre-emptive maneuver by Michael? No escape there. So she flees to the kitchen, retaining the presence of mind to lock the door behind her. But like Laurie, Michael too has taken precautions. Laurie's escape route through the French doors is blocked by an ordinary garden rake wedged against the outside door handle. Another haunting visual remnant from *Psycho*, though employed in a different manner.

The two combatants struggle against each other's barriers, Michael smashing through one with his bare fists while Laurie, taking a cue from her pursuer, does the same to the other, sacrificing her hand to broken glass in order to remove the rake and open the door. She escapes just in time.

Fleeing to the better lit, street side of the house, limping badly and even falling once, Laurie screams for help from anyone who can hear her. But there is no one else around. It's late, the trick-or-treaters and their adult guardians have gone home, and this otherwise normal neighborhood is mostly asleep. Running to the house next door as best she can, Laurie pounds on the front door and pleads for help. A light flickers on inside. Someone peeks through the window blinds to see what the commotion is about. Ironically, Laurie's hysterical cries for help *frighten* the homeowner back into the dubious security of his or her house. Laurie's display of fear *promotes* fear, to her own detriment. She is left alone to fend for herself.

Laurie hobbles across the street to the imagined safety of the Doyle house. We accompany her on this painfully slow return via Carpenter's slightly unstable, handheld camera. Laurie desperately searches for the key to unlock the front door. The same door she prudently locked behind her minutes earlier, for the safety of the sleeping children inside. But she cannot find the key, which probably fell out of her pocket during her tumble over the stair railing.

Michael, whose pursuit is delayed slightly for dramatic purposes, emerges from the shadows at the rear of the Wallace house and crosses the street, aiming straight for Laurie. His pace is unhurried, steady, relentless. He seems more machine than man, locked into his murderous pursuit by whatever twisted vision motivates him. From Laurie's point of view, we now see Michael the same way Tommy did earlier. As the *real* boogeyman. The boogeyman Laurie once so blithely dismissed and explained away, in spite of her previous, disturbing encounters with Michael.

Grabbing a flower pot from the front porch, Laurie hurls it against the side of the house, close to an upstairs window, to get Tommy's attention. Curiously, this action parallels, though to opposite ends, Michael's use of a similar object to get Annie's attention in the Wallace kitchen. One of numerous strange links between heroine and monster in this movie. A sleepy Tommy Doyle appears in the window. Laurie screams for him to let her in. Unaware of the boogeyman's approach, the boy complies in an unhurried manner. It is now *Laurie's* turn to feel the frustration of having her fears not taken seriously by others. She slams her hand and presses her body against the unyielding door, trying to force it open by herself. But she has to wait an agonizingly long time for Tommy to let her in.

Once inside and comparatively safe again, Laurie is remarkably controlled and efficient in response to a crisis. No pointless resentment of Tommy's slow response. She locks the front door behind her and decisively orders Tommy to return to his room upstairs and lock the door. She switches off lights in the living room, making it more difficult for her pursuer to see inside, and tries to phone for help. But the telephone is dead. Another diabolical precaution by Michael? Has this entire night of terror been meticulously planned by him, instead of whim-driven as has sometimes seemed the case?

Seeing the curtain over an open window flapping in the breeze, Laurie realizes the killer has gained access to the house. Whimpering, reduced once more to a childlike paralysis of terror, she hunches down in front of the couch and pleads rhetorically to the hostile, encroaching, outside world, "Please stop! Please!" It's the equivalent of hiding under the covers to keep at bay a monster lurking under the bed or in the closet. But do not fault Laurie for her moments of panic. Had she been written and performed as an unflinching, superhuman heroine, the terror she has to overcome would have seemed much less potent.

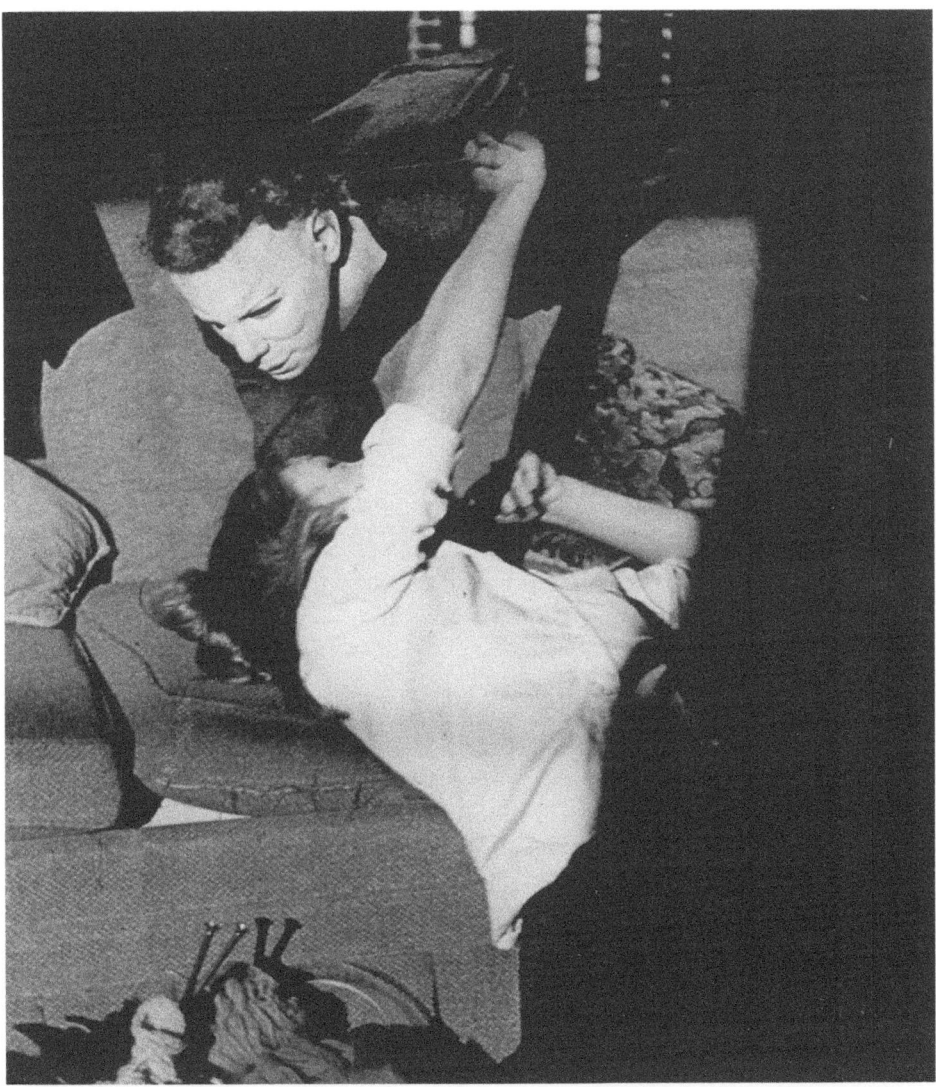

Laurie Strode (Jamie Lee Curtis) fights back, in *Halloween*. This is the second of four times, in quick succession, she is attacked by Michael Myers (Nick Castle), the relentless boogeyman who invades her small town routine like a runaway locomotive, killing Laurie's best friends and destroying her peace of mind.

Laurie is resilient. She regains sufficient self-control to retrieve with her bloodied right hand a knitting needle from her bag. And just in time, as Michael rises up from behind the couch and lashes out at her with his knife. He misses, again. She retaliates, stabbing him in the neck with her needle. Staggering back, he pulls it out, then collapses to the floor. It's the first time we've seen him retreat, or injured. There's no reason to think Laurie hasn't stopped his reign of terror, except the film's prior hints about Fate never changing, and our gut feeling that this is not the end of her ordeal.

A high angle shot of Laurie in her prominent white blouse, collapsing on the couch, occupying a small patch of light surrounded by darkness. She grabs her assailant's knife and cautiously peers over the top of that couch. Michael lies on the floor, motionless and presumably dead. Relieved and exhausted, Laurie collapses. She stares at the knife for a few moments, then drops it in disgust. To her credit, she has *not* caught Michael's fever to kill, despite having her deepest survival instincts tapped.

Elsewhere in the neighborhood, Sam Loomis walks along the street in search of Michael. Sheriff Brackett pulls up alongside in his police car and berates the psychiatrist for not waiting at the Myers house. Explaining that Michael's car is nearby, and therefore so too must be Michael, Loomis reasserts his authority by ordering Brackett to patrol the backs of the houses while Sam continues to investigate the fronts. This is *his* show. As he proceeds down the street, glancing this way and that for his adversary, his hands nervously tucked inside his pockets as Laurie's were when she warily approached the Wallace house, Loomis walks past a tree that has been strewn with toilet paper. Again, the juxtaposition of mildly mischievous Halloween fun and true horror.

Back at the Doyle residence, an emotionally recovered Laurie Strode limps up the stairs to the children's room. We observe her from the same over-the-top-of-the-railing camera angle as we did the last time she climbed these stairs. But *this* time the threat from Michael Myers has subsided. Except for the lingering presence of disturbing background music.

Coaxing Tommy and Lindsey out of their room, Laurie gives them a comforting hug, tells them they are going for a little walk (a soothing version of "get the hell out of here!"), and assures them she killed the boogeyman. But from a camera situated in front of Laurie, *we* see a shadowy movement behind her, at the top of the stairs. Tommy questions Laurie's or anyone's power to exterminate fear. "You can't kill the boogeyman." In most cases, yes you can. But not in *this* movie. And in a larger sense, never *once and for all*.

The children scream. Michael has returned. And so has his aggressive stalker music. In a flash Laurie hustles the kids into one of the bedrooms, tells them to lock their door, and flees to the other bedroom herself, *not* locking the door behind her. In an act of great courage, she deliberately lures the boogeyman away from Tommy and Lindsey and towards herself. She opens doors leading to a balcony outside, making it appear she fled the house, then retreats to a closet. Using a stocking she finds among the clothes there, she "locks" the closet door by tying the doorknobs together. A pathetic defense against so determined and powerful an assailant. But, as it turns out, an obstacle that delays him just long enough for Laurie to fashion a more effective weapon.

Taking his own sweet time, as always, the frazzle-haired boogeyman follows inexorably in Laurie's wake. He is not fooled by the balcony ploy. In our hyper fear of Michael, he seems diabolically aware of his victim's movements and precautions. He approaches the closet door and tries to open it. Laurie cowers as deep in the corner as she can push herself. The whimpering child in her returns. Few of us would react any differently. From inside her brittle shelter, we watch the louvered doors shake violently, barely held together by her flimsy improvised lock. As he did to the Wallace's kitchen door, Michael finally smashes through with his fists. What appears to be Laurie's last line of defense crumbles before her and our eyes. From her crouched position, we watch the door's wooden fragments scatter inward. The breech gets bigger. No longer do we guiltily share the killer's vantage point. We're now trapped along with his intended victim.

Though terrified, Laurie summons the willpower to reach up, grab a wire clothes hanger (like Michael's kitchen knife, another ordinary, domestic object re-deployed as a weapon) and fashion it into a dagger as Michael smashes his way to her. Ironically, his thrashing about switches on the closet light just long enough for Laurie to spot the hanger she incorporates into her self-defense. Incidentally, the swinging light bulb is another flashback to *Psycho*, when Lila Crane's panic sets a hanging cellar light bulb in motion, amplifying the grotesqueness of Mrs. Bates' corpse. But the fitful illumination in *Halloween* helps rather than hinders the heroine.

Michael, leaning in through the shattered closet door, bends down to get at Laurie, who reaches up and stabs him in the eye with her makeshift knife. Michael drops the real one. Laurie quickly retrieves it and thrusts up to stab him again, with his own weapon. Michael falls away from the closet, out of camera range. In a beautiful tight shot we see Laurie, half-hidden under hanging clothes in a corner of the closet, trying to recuperate from yet another terrible shock. And again she succeeds. Pointing the knife out ahead of her, she warily emerges from the closet. Michael's body lies on the floor just outside.

Thinking once again that her ordeal is over, Laurie tosses the knife aside. Yes, I know, audiences yell in frustration at her for doing so. But within the context of the film, neither Laurie nor anyone else, except perhaps Tommy, really believes "You can't kill the boogeyman." Laurie hobbles to the children's hiding place and gives the all clear. When they cautiously emerge, she instructs them to leave the house, go to a neighbor's home and summon the police. Quickly and efficiently quelling Tommy's rising panic, she sends them on their way. Why doesn't she go with them? A flaw in the script? Maybe she knows her badly injured leg would slow them down. A more generous interpretation would be that Laurie senses her proximity would be a greater danger to Tommy and Lindsey because Michael had already bypassed them once in favor of pursuing *her*.

After the children depart, a change in camera angle alerts us to a new danger. Peering behind Laurie from in front of her, as she sits on the floor clinging to the door frame for emotional support, we see Michael's body in the background. Out of focus in ours and removed from Laurie's line of sight, he sits up and slowly, mechanically turns his head in her direction. His stalker music reasserts itself on the soundtrack, telling us all we need to know. *This* monster never dies. In some form or another, he is *always* with us.

From the street outside we watch Tommy and Lindsey flee the Doyle house, screaming. They are observed by Sam Loomis, who senses Michael's presence somewhere behind the front door they leave open. Inside, Laurie's weary face rises into the camera frame. Mimicking her, Michael stands too, rising into the background of the same camera frame. His shape remains out of focus, rendering him in our eyes an even more potent threat because it emphasizes Laurie's careless inattention. We want to scream out for Laurie to turn around. But she doesn't. Michael silently stalks her from behind.

The camera cuts to a more distant shot from elsewhere in the hallway, removing Michael from our line of sight. An emotionally and physically drained Laurie Strode slowly moves away from the doorway. Don't walk! Run!! Michael suddenly appears, lunging out through the doorway and grabbing Laurie by the throat.

Though badly overmatched, Laurie struggles mightily against Michael. She succeeds in pulling off his mask, like an older horror film heroine unmasking the Phantom of the Opera. Perhaps the parallel was deliberate, since it gave Carpenter another opportunity to confound genre expectations. Michael Myers has not become some hideous demonic beast underneath his creepy but still recognizably human façade. Instead, judging from the brief glimpse we are afforded in the hallway gloom, Michael's physical appearance is quite normal. Almost handsome. With some vague flaw about his left eye. Pretty much what we would normally expect after our glimpse of young Michael back in 1963. Whatever psychological malfunction exists within the boogeyman, his outward appearance, sans mask, is deceptively ordinary. Like that of Norman Bates, and the seagulls, sparrows and crows (as opposed to more recognizably predatory hawks, eagles and falcons) in *The Birds*.

Through perseverance, courage and fierce determination, Laurie Strode briefly succeeds in exposing the very human origins of the mysterious boogeyman. When she pulls off his mask, Michael releases her. He quickly pulls the mask back over his face, presumably to restore his terrifying, mythical, superhuman identity and resume his merciless attack. That's when Sam Loomis, arriving in the nick of time, shoots him. The sound of his gunshot is loud and powerful, befitting the duration and intensity of his crusade. Michael staggers back into the room from which he emerged. Laurie, cowering on the floor, covers her ears with her hands and places her fate in the hands of her rescuer. *Halloween*'s wise elder, in the grand tradition of Professor Van Helsing in *Dracula* (1931), Dr. Waldman in *Frankenstein* (1931) and Dr. Muller in *The Mummy* (1932). But maybe like Inspector Krogh in *Son of Frankenstein* (1939) and Maleva in *The Wolf Man* (1941), there is a touch of the dangerous fanatic in Dr. Loomis. Something that, under the wrong circumstances, could itself become a monster.

The psychiatrist advances to the doorway. Inside the bedroom Michael still stands, his dark silhouette looking as powerful as ever. Until five more blasts from Sam's gun send him staggering out through the doors Laurie previously opened, onto the balcony, over the railing and plummeting to the ground. In an overhead shot from that balcony, we look down on Michael sprawled out on the grass. A low stab of music punctuates his "death," as it earlier punctuated the death of Bob.

Loomis, still standing in the bedroom doorway and therefore not yet in a position to see his victim lying on the ground below, impulsively pulls the trigger of his now empty gun one more time. It's a mechanical, fear-driven action, just enough like Michael's automated behavior to be a little creepy.

Aftermath. Silence. Laurie removes her hands from over her ears. She looks up at her protector and inquires plaintively, "What's the boogeyman?" The same question Tommy Doyle once asked her. For the moment, Laurie is reduced by the overwhelming experience of terror to a state of unreasoning, superstitious, childlike paranoia. Dr. Loomis, the wise elder, scientist and reasonable adult, turns to her and confirms her worst fears. "As a matter of fact, it was." The opposite of what she told Tommy. Experiences too extreme to deal with emotionally can permanently alter one's view of the world. Laurie's answer to Tommy's question was intended to soothe away his fears, resulting in an inability to sense and prepare for the approach of real terror. Dr. Loomis *reinforces* Laurie's fear, which may plunge her into a permanent state of paranoia. Is that the better course? And does rampant paranoia have anything to do with the mysterious origins of Michael's own warped view of the world around him? How much of Michael lurks within Sam Loomis, and now Laurie Strode?

Sam's shadow, and the fear that has consumed him for many years, passes over Laurie's face as he walks out to the balcony and peers over the railing.

From *his* vantage point, we see an eerily empty back yard below. Michael is gone. Just the twisted branches of what looks like a dead tree. *Halloween*'s title music, and Michael's principle motif, returns to the soundtrack, trapping us in the same sense of dread that long ago took possession of Sam Loomis and just a moment ago may have done the same to Laurie Strode. In a reaction shot, Sam appears not at all surprised by Michael's disappearance and presumed revival. Laurie, crying, again covers her eyes with her blood-stained hands. See no evil. The old hide-under-the-covers defense? Or a natural, in the long term perhaps even therapeutic denial of deathless, unstoppable evil? Sam looks up and to the side, wondering where the boogeyman has gone.

As though fuelled by *Halloween*'s music, the camera returns us to various locations in the film where Michael has already been and could be again. The Doyle stairway. The Doyle living room. The Wallaces' living room. The stairway leading to the bedroom where Annie, Lynda and Bob lie dead. The exterior of the Doyle house, with its front door dangerously left open. Goodbye to small town trust. And finally, the exterior of the old Myers house. The origin of the legend of Michael Myers. In none of these locations do we see anyone. Yet we *hear* Michael's distinctive breathing, steady and calm once more, growing louder and louder. The boogeyman has slipped away into the darkness, or into myth, as this Halloween night comes to a close. Yet he seems to be *everywhere*, as Carpenter himself once remarked in *Halloween: A Cut Above the Rest*. Such is the terrifying, potentially world view changing impression left in the wake of his violence, especially in the minds of the few who survived encounters with him during his brief but memorable re-emergence from the seemingly safe confines of a fifteen year old local myth.

Carpenter has said of Michael Myers, "This guy is a human, but he's not. He's more than that. He's not exactly supernatural, but maybe he is. Who knows how he got that way?" (*Halloween: A Cut Above the Rest*). He is whatever our fear makes of him. A de-fanged joke. A red herring. A means of frightening others and ourselves, for either cruel or mutual fun. A grim echo of the potential for malevolence we see in ourselves or others. The personification of a myriad of natural forces or chance occurrences that have the potential to hurt or kill us. Michael is "simultaneously ourselves and a monster, terrifying in his total other-ness" (Telotte, p. 148). Or, as Jamie Lee Curtis phrased it in a 2012 Arts and Entertainment television documentary entitled *Inside Story: Halloween*, "The shape is more an idea than a specific person." Speaking more broadly about the film as a whole, "There's something very beautiful about it." Yes. So long as Michael Myers is confined to fiction. So long as he remains just an image on a movie screen.

The repetitive *Halloween* theme rolls on and on as the film's closing credits match it step for step. Will or even *can* Laurie, Tommy and Lindsey fully recover from their horrifying Halloween night? Michael Myers may haunt them for the remainder of their lives, polluting or distorting their sense of normalcy in some way or other. And what of Sheriff Brackett, who has yet to learn that his own daughter was a victim of the threat he never took very seriously?

Way back in 1978, when I was twenty-five, I first saw *Halloween* in a theater in East Grand Forks, Minnesota. I was alone. After the movie, I had to walk down a very dark, deserted alley to get to my car. And I vividly recall thinking to myself how ridiculous I was to be so nervous. It was *only* a movie. But you can bet I checked out the back seat of my car before getting inside. And locked the doors before driving away. Paranoia can be infectious.

After decades of exposure to *Halloween* and its many bloodier and more shock-driven imitators, Carpenter's original no longer has quite the same power to scare me. Seeing it now is more like visiting an old friend than encountering someone new and unfamiliar. But what still fascinates me about the film is its multifaceted portrait of fear itself: what generates it, what amplifies it, how we react to it, how it defines the way we look at the world, and the sheer variety of its presence in our lives.

Like all the best horror films, *Halloween* contains sufficient ambiguity to allow for variations of interpretation. It's a fictional exercise in the dangers of complacency, yet also a convincing dramatization of the corrosive power of fear. It's hardly "realistic," yet vividly depicts real settings and both portrays and arouses real emotions. It's both subjective and objective. It's wickedly playful and deadly serious at the same time, allowing the audience to choose which way to approach it. And very much like *Psycho* and *The Birds*, albeit with a different hand at the creative tiller, it powerfully juxtaposes the ordinary with the extraordinary, the normal with the abnormal.

Marion Crane. Sam Loomis. Caroline. Lowery. Cassidy. The car salesman. The highway patrolman. Arbogast, Sheriff and Mrs. Chambers. And Norman Bates himself, in *Psycho*. They're all linked by a continuum of human thought, feeling, motivation and behavior. The best and the worst of them. The same goes for Melanie Daniels, the Brenner family, Annie Hayworth, the people of Bodega Bay, and in some ways even our not so friendly feathered friends in *The Birds*. And for Laurie Strode, Sam Loomis, Annie, Lynda, Sheriff Brackett, the children and, of course, Michael Myers in *Halloween*. None of these characters is wholly removed from their compatriots. All of them are variations on each other. A fact which doesn't make them equally dangerous or frightening or reprehensible. Quite the opposite.

If Marion and Norman share a sense of frustration, entrapment and a desperate, reckless need to escape, they clearly differ in the matter of degree, and in their abilities to rise above their compulsions. Melanie, the Brenners, Annie and the residents of Bodega Bay all display a capacity for destructive and self-destructive behavior. But despite subconscious or unconscious urges, none of them quite attains the homicidal rage of the aberrant birds who attack them. And though Laurie Strode may share a repressed, sublimated sexuality with Michael Myers, she does not possess his utter lack of self-restraint or conscience. It's the *potential* for the unleashing of the worst in us, and the subsequent, terrifying danger to life, limb, compassion, sanity and happiness that makes these three movies among the most intimate of horror films. And the better for it. Surviving them can, if you're lucky, spark a little more appreciation for the small, unspectacular pleasures in life: a casual walk through a tree-lined neighborhood on a pleasant day, a congenial conversation with a friend, or even a routine afternoon at the same old job. Things can be, and sometimes with very little warning are, much worse.

On the bookplate of my copy of Janet Leigh's *Psycho: Behind the Scenes of the Classic Thriller*, Ms. Leigh inscribed "Happiness!" along with her autograph. In the lingering shadow of that great film and the two others discussed in this book, I can't think of a better wish for people. Who would know better than Marion Crane?

# Selected Bibliography

Ansen, David. "Trick or Treat." *Newsweek* 92, no. 23 (December 4, 1978): pp. 116–117.
Auiler, Dan. *Hitchcock's Notebooks*. New York: Avon, 1999.
Durgnat, Raymond. *A Hard Look at Psycho*. London: British Film Institute, 2002.
*Halloween: A Cut Above the Rest*. Writer Steven Smith. Prometheus Entertainment and Compass International Pictures, 2003.
*Inside Story: Halloween*. Writer/Producer Phil Nobile, Jr. The Biography Channel, 2010.
Leigh, Janet. *Psycho: Behind the Scenes of the Classic Thriller*. New York: Harmony Books, 1995.
*The Making of Psycho*. Writer/Director/Producer Laurent Bouzereau. Universal Home Video, 1997.
Newman, Kim. "Pure Horror." *Sight and Sound* 11, no. 11 (November 2001): p. 66.
Sanders, Ed. *The Family*. New York: Thunder's Mouth Press, 2002.
Sarris, Andrew. "Hitchcock." *Focus on Hitchcock*, ed. Albert J. LeValley. Englewood Cliffs, NJ: Prentice-Hall, 1972. pp. 87–90.
Sullivan, Jack. *Hitchcock's Music*. New Haven: Yale University Press, 2006.
Telotte, J. P. "Through a Pumpkin's Eye: The Reflective Nature of Horror." *Literature Film Quarterly* 10, no. 3 (1982): pp. 139–149.
Thomson, David. *The Moment of Psycho: How Alfred Hitchcock Taught America to Love Murder*. New York: Basic Books, 2009.
Truffaut, François. *Hitchcock*, rev. ed. New York: Simon & Schuster, 1985.
Wells, Jeffrey. "Halloween." *Films in Review* 30, no. 3 (March 1979): pp. 182–183.
Wood, Robin. *Hitchcock's Films Revisited*, rev. ed. New York: Columbia University Press, 2002.

# Index

Numbers in *bold italics* indicate pages with photographs.

*All in the Family* 198
Ansen, David 165
Auiler, Dan 93, 98, 102, 106, 132

Balsam, Martin *54*
Bass, Saul 7
Beethoven, Ludwig van 74
*The Birds* 1–4, 33, 58, 71, 75, 81–130, *131*, 132–139, *140*, 141–143, *144*, 145, 149, 204, 207
Blue Oyster Cult 169, 211, 212
Bogart, Humphrey 52
Brando, Marlon 77
*Bride of Frankenstein* 3

*The Cabinet of Dr. Caligari* (1919 film) 46
Carpenter, John 2, 4, 5, 30, 143, 146, 147, 151, 152, 155, 157, 159–166, 168, 173, 174, 178, 179, 184–187, 191, 192, 196, 198–200, 204, 206, 2077
Cartwright, Veronica *131*, 132, *144*
Castle, Nick *193*, *201*
*Citizen Kane* 70
Cuban Missile Crisis 128, 147
Curtis, Jamie Lee 3, *163*, *201*, 206

Deacon, Richard 89
Debussy, Claude 104
*Dial M for Murder* (1953 film) 105, 213
Donne, John 150
"Don't Fear the Reaper" 169
*Dracula* (1931 film) 205
du Maurier, Daphne 83, 84
Durgnat, Raymond 4, 7, 12, 29, 30, 74, 136

Ensor, James 166, 167, 172

*Family Plot* 83
*Films in Review* 185
*Forbidden Planet* 183, 184, 186

*Foreign Correspondent* 124
*Frankenstein* (1931 film) 3, 45, 152, 196, 205
*Frenzy* 118
*Friday the 13th* 152, 214

Gavin, John 67
Gein, Ed 73, 169
Grant, Cary 8

*Halloween* (1978 film) 2–5, 30, 71, 124, 143, 146–162, *163*, 164–192, *193*, 194–200, *201*, 202–208
*Halloween: A Cut Above the Rest* 185, 206
*Hamlet* (stage play) 109
Hedren, Tippi 12, 89, 93, 108, *131*, 132, *140*, *144*
Herrmann, Bernard 7, 8, 21, 23, 24, 28, 30, 37, 39, 42, 44, 46–49, 56–58, 61, 66, 70, 71, 73, 76, 78, 80, 85, 195
Hill, Debra 160, 161, 191
Hitchcock, Alfred 1, 2, 4, 5, 7, 8, 12, 13, *16*, 17, 19, 23, 25, 27, 30, 33, 42, 43, 45, 51, 53, 55, 57, 62, 64, 69, 71, 73, 74, 76–93, 95–98, 102, 104–106, 108, 115, 117, 122, 124, 128, 130, 132, 133, 136–140, 143, 145, 148, 151, 152, 157, 182, 196, 198
Hitler, Adolf 130
Hunter, Evan 83, 215

*Inside Story: Halloween* 3
*Invasion of the Body Snatchers* (1956 film) 195

*Jaws* (1975 film) 147
Jones, Jim 199

Kennedy, John F. 147
Kubrick, Stanley 143

*The Lady Vanishes* (1938 film) 69, 125

Leigh, Janet 7, 11, **16**, **31**, 43, 45, 208
*Let's Make a Deal* 197
Loomis, Nancy **163**

*The Making of Psycho* 56
Manson, Charles 149, 216
*Marnie* (1964 film) 110
*The Moment of Psycho* 123
*The Mummy* (1932 film) 205

Newman, Kim 4
*North by Northwest* 7, 8, 69, 96, 130
*Notorious* 90, 96, 102, 106

Oakland, Simon 77
O'Casey, Sean 124
*The Old Dark House* (1932 film) 30

Perkins, Anthony 7, **31**, **54**, 67
*Planet of the Apes* (1968 film) 174
Pleshette, Suzanne 93, 108, **131**
Poe, Edgar Allan 40, 58, 217
*Psycho* (1960 film) 1–5, 7–15, **16**, 17–30, **31**, 32–53, **54**, 55–85, 91, 92, 94, 96, 101, 104, 119, 124, 130, 131, 139–141, 143, 147–149, 151, 157, 169, 170, 184, 192, 196, 198, 199, 203, 207
*Psycho: Behind the Scenes of the Classic Thriller* 208

*Rear Window* (1954 film) 9, 30, 40, 43, 85, 96, 133, 177
*Rope* (1948 film) 124

*Saboteur* 82
Sanders, Ed 149
Sarris, Andrew 84, 85, 98
*Shadow of a Doubt* (1943 film) 82, 90, 105

Shakespeare, William 109
*The Shining* (1980 film) 143
Soles, P.J. 160, **163**
*Son of Frankenstein* 205
Stalin, Joseph 130, 218
Stefano, Joseph 27, 43, 56
*Strangers on a Train* (1951 film) 86, 121
Sullivan, Jack 8, 117

Tandy, Jessica **144**
Taylor, Rod **131**, **144**
Telotte, J.P. 164, 195, 206
*The Thing from Another World* (1951 film) 146, 176, 178, 181–184
*The 39 Steps* (1935 film) 69, 133
Thomson, David 14, 15, 79, 123, 131
"Through a Pumpkin's Eye: The Reflective Nature of Horror" 164
*To Catch a Thief* (1955 film) 90, 145
*Topaz* (1969 film) 82, 83, 132
*Tristan und Isolde* (opera) 108
*The Trouble with Harry* (1956 film) 91, 104
Truffaut, François 108, 124, 133, 137, 143, 219

*Vertigo* 2, 7, 11, 75, 96, 108

Wagner, Richard 108
*The War of the Worlds* (novel) 83
Wells, H.G. 83
Wells, Jeffrey 185, 186
*The Werewolf of London* 176
Whale, James 30, 45, 196
*The Wild One* 77
*The Wolf Man* (1941 film) 176, 205
Wood, Robin 8, 10, 17, 79, 84, 98, 118, 143
*The Wrong Man* 19, 130, 133, 134

www.ingramcontent.com/pod-product-compliance
Ingram Content Group UK Ltd.
Pitfield, Milton Keynes, MK11 3LW, UK
UKHW041958140426
5217IPUK00015B/868